GENERAI
PROP. ... ...W

D0892838

Pearson Education

We work with leading authors to develop the strongest educational materials in law, bringing cutting-edge thinking and best learning practice to a global market.

Under a range of well-known imprints, including Longman, we craft high quality print and electronic publications which help readers to understand and apply their content, whether studying or at work.

To find out more about the complete range of our publishing, please visit us on the World Wide Web at: www.pearsoneduc.com

GENERAL PRINCIPLES OF
PROPERTY LAW

Sukhninder Panesar

Longman

An imprint of **Pearson Education**

Harlow, England · London · New York · Reading, Massachusetts · San Francisco
Toronto · Don Mills, Ontario · Sydney · Tokyo · Singapore · Hong Kong · Seoul
Taipei · Cape Town · Madrid · Mexico City · Amsterdam · Munich · Paris · Milan

Pearson Education Limited

Edinburgh Gate
Harlow
Essex CM20 2JE

and Associated Companies throughout the world

Visit us on the World Wide Web at:
www.pearsoneduc.com

First published 2001

© Pearson Education Limited 2001

ISBN 0 582 42332 5

British Library Cataloguing-in-Publication Data
A catalogue record for this book is available from the British Library

10 9 8 7 6 5 4 3 2 1
05 04 03 02 01

Typeset by 30 in 10/13pt Sabon.
Printed in Great Britain by Henry Ling Ltd,
at the Dorset Press, Dorchester, Dorset

CONTENTS

PREFACE

This book has its origins in the growing recognition that an undergraduate study of property law should encompass a much wider discussion than the law of real property. Furthermore, the book begins on the premise that the law of property is a very complex subject and that a number of factors contribute to this complexity. One important factor is the 'compartmentalisation' of the various branches of property law without recourse to an explanation of the basic ideas and principles of property law. It is argued that the law of property, and its various branches, can become a more accessible subject if students are exposed to the idea and nature of property and the very basic principles that govern property relationships.

This introductory book aims to examine some of the fundamental principles of property law. The book begins with an examination of the legal idea of property with the objective of allowing the student to think about property as a right rather than a thing. The purpose of such inquiry is to aid the student in understanding the function of property as the governance or regulation of rights in things, rather than things themselves. At the initial stage of discussion the student's mind is focused into thinking why the law should protect rights in things. The book continues with an examination of how property lawyers classify property, in particular the distinction between real and personal property and legal and equitable property. As well as examining important concepts such as ownership, possession and title, the book examines the methods by which property rights are acquired. Other important themes in the book include, how the idea of property changes with time, the pressures on property lawyers to adopt new categories of property, the increasingly difficult distinction between proprietary and personal rights; and fragmentation of ownership.

There is no doubt that the majority of students find property law an immensely difficult and technical area of the law. For those who teach the subject, it can often be an uphill struggle to make this area of the law interesting. I am of the strong opinion that the law of property can become both an interesting and more accessible area of the law provided that students are allowed to think about the broader concerns of property and property law.

I would like to thank all those people who have encouraged and supported me during the time in which this book was written. I would like to express my sincere thanks to Barry Mitchell for providing me with the initial encouragement and confidence to write this book. I am indebted to him. I would like to thank Pat Bond and Anita Atkinson at Pearson Education for their invaluable support and patience. Finally, and most importantly, I would like to thank my family in England and in Kenya for their patience, encouragement and support.

Sukhninder Panesar

ACKNOWLEDGEMENTS

We are grateful to the following for permission to reproduce copyright material:

Blackwell Publishers Ltd for an abridged extract from 'The law of property and legal theory' by R. Cotterall in *LEGAL THEORY AND COMMON LAW* edited by W. Twinning 1986 and an abridged from *ANARCHY STATE AND UTOPIA* by Nozick; The Butterworths Division of Reed Elservier (UK) Limited for adapted extracts from *ELEMENTS OF LAND LAW* 3/E by Gray; Cambridge University Press for an extract from 'Original Acquisition Justification of Private Property' by A.J. Simmonds in *PROPERTY RIGHTS* edited by Paul E. Frankel, Fred D. Miller Jnr and Jeffrey Paul; ITPS Ltd for abridged extracts from *OWNERSHIP AND OBLIGATION IN COMMERCIAL TRANS-ACTIONS* by Goode published by Sweet & Maxwell, *MEGARRY'S MANUAL OF THE LAW OF REAL PROPERTY* 7/E by Meggary, *CENTRAL ISSUES IN JURISPRUDENCE: JUSTICE LAW AND RIGHTS* by Simmonds published by Sweet & Maxwell and abridged extracts from the article 'Otto Khan Freund, Introduction to K Renner in *THE INSTITUTIONS OF PRIVATE LAW AND THEIR SOCIAL FUNCTIONS* by K. Renner 1949 published by Routledge; MaxMillan publishers for abridged extracts from *A FIRST BOOK OF JURISPRU-DENCE FOR STUDENTS OF THE COMMON LAW* 2/E by Frederick Pollock published by Macmillan, London 1904; Oxford University Press for abridged extracts from *THE RIGHT TO PRIVATE PROPERTY* by Waldron 1988; Thomson Legal & Regulatory Group Asia Pacific Limited for abridged extracts from *PRINCIPLES OF PROPERTY LAW* by Jackson © LBC Information Services, a part of Thomson Legal & Regulatory Group Asia Pacific Limited, http://www.thomson.com.au; The University of Chicago Law Review for an abridged extract from the article 'Possession as the origin of property' by Rose in *THE UNIVER-SITY OF CHICAGO LAW REVIEW* Vol 52 1985; University of Toronto Press Inc for an abridged extract from *PROPERTY: MAINSTREAM AND CRITICAL POSITIONS* by Macpherson and Tulane Law Review Association for an abridged extract from 'Rights of exclusion and immu-nities against divesting' by A.M. Honore orginially published in *TULANE LAW REVIEW* No. 34, 1960.

TABLE OF CASES

TABLE OF STATUTES AND STATUTORY MATERIALS

1

STUDYING
PROPERTY LAW

'Most Students are bored by property law. Although the subject is adorned with magnificent textbooks, their bulk and complexity can be stupefying and even the most intelligent reader may find it difficult to shake free of the detail which encrusts the basic concepts. Those who teach (and examine) the subject have long been familiar with "the Blackacre syndrome." For the pupil in its clutches, the law of property is all about a place called Blackacre – a principal mansion house, girt by a timber estate, and settled on A for life, without impeachment of waste, with remainder over; and the main character is perceived as pacing the library (rich in volumes settled with land) while muttering peevishly "since I've no entail to bar, think I'll extinguish a few manorial incidents."'[1]

The above extract paints an all too familiar picture of a university education in property law. Students find the subject difficult to grasp; often boring, lacking a conceptual framework and wondering at times the contemporary worth of their study. For those who have attempted to make the subject more accessible, they have done so by presenting the law as it is rather than the way it was. Yet, the truth of the matter is not so much the inherent complexities of land law, but rather the manner in which we as teachers of property law teach the subject of property law. One of the fundamental shortcomings in the study of property law in law schools throughout England and Wales is the lack of emphasis on the general principles of property law. It is this shortcoming which plays a central role in hindering the effective understanding of property law. The traditional focus of property law has been on the study of land and trust law.[2]

---

[1] B. Rudden, 'Notes Towards a Grammar of Property', *The Conveyancer* (1980) at p 325.
[2] This has been partly influenced by the legal profession and professional bodies who recognise Land Law and Equity and Trusts as two of the core subjects needed for entry on to professional courses.

Whilst it is not doubted that the study of land and trust law should be an integral part of an undergraduate law course, the potential danger of this traditional approach is its tendency to misrepresent the idea of property and property law.

The underlying assumption appears to be that there is no conceptual framework of rules governing the enjoyment and management of resources in general. Indeed, some writers tell us that 'there is no such thing as the general law of property'.[3] Instead, there has been a fragmentation of the law relating to resources according to the type of resource in question. There is no difficulty in finding textbooks on land law, intellectual property law and the law relating to goods; yet, there is immense difficulty in finding a text on 'the law of property' or anything remotely resembling that. Even where such a text is found, a reader expecting to find a conceptual framework of rules and principles relating to the use, acquisition and transfer of resources in general is soon disillusioned. He may find some attempt to introduce the notion of property and the nature of property law, but will soon discover that his reading is swiftly focused to a particular resource such as land or goods.

The potential problem faced by those who study property law is the lack of a conceptual framework in which to understand their study. Furthermore, unlike other areas of civil law such as contract and tort, the boundaries of property law remain rather vague. For example, one might ask a student of law to explain the concept of property and the function and content of the law of property. There may be very little to say about the concept of property; in so far as the function and content of the law of property, the response is merely piecemeal. The student may point to the fact that the law of property is concerned with the acquisition, use and transfer of land. He may also point to concepts such as equity, trusts and intellectual property, but is unlikely to provide a unifying central theme to both the concept of property and property law. It may be asked why there is this inherent difficulty in addressing issues such as why the legal system recognises property, the nature of property and the function of property law. In searching for possible defences in favour of the student, two principle arguments are identifiable.

In the first place, issues such as the concept of property, how private property regimes come about and the possible justifications thereof, have not necessarily been to the fore in a university education in property law. Instead, such questions have attracted a wealth of literature from political theorists and social scientists.[4] Despite this, it may be asked whether we are doing any justice to our understanding of property rules by leaving such questions to the domains of political, economic and social theory. The assumption

---

[3] Murphy and Roberts, *Understanding Property Law* (2nd edn, 1998) at p 38.
[4] See Chapter 2.

appears to be that political, economic, and social theory can be divorced from any discourse on the system of property rules. Furthermore, an equally important assumption appears to be that the practising lawyer need not concern himself with such problems. His role is to consult legal materials and advise his client on property transactions; his role is facilitated by recourse to piecemeal legal materials such as manuals on real property, personal property and intellectual property.[5] It is submitted that these assumptions need to be seriously challenged. One commentator writes, 'a university education in law should encourage an appreciation of the principal lines of justification for private property regimes and of critiques by leading thinkers. The perspectives offered by the various schools of thought have been and continue to be reflected in case law, they also influence policy makers and legislators.'[6] Furthermore, Cotterrell, questioning how theoretical analysis can aid the understanding of contemporary problems of property law doctrine, explains that such theoretical analysis can help the lawyer's understanding by attempting to explain how such doctrinal problems have arisen and what conditions and causes have contributed to them.[7]

Secondly, in so far as resources are concerned, both the judiciary and academic lawyers have treated one resource as not necessarily more important but fundamentally different in nature so as to deserve a distinct body of rules. Land is said to be different from other resources in that it is permanent, indestructible and to be enjoyed by successive generations. Historically, land had been the most prized resource and as such has attracted the most significant attention – particularly in the 1925 property law legislation, which remains the single most important property law legislation up to the present day. Land law, also referred to as the law of real property, has been flooded with an immense amount of textbook literature. With regard to other resources, often described as movables or goods, the law (described as the law of personal property) has been until recently conceptually underdeveloped. Unlike land law, personal property law was never subject to the doctrine of estates, which had the effect of projecting rights in land upon the plane of time.[8] Instead such resources and rights therein were simply explained by the concepts of possession and ownership – concepts involving considerable complexity, as will be seen later.[9] The outcome of all this has been that the manner in which property law has developed in English law has been very piecemeal; this approach has had the effect of shaping both the textbook tradition and law school curriculum on property law.

---

[5] See J. Harris, 'Private and Non-Private Property: What is the Difference?' (1995) 111 LQR 423.
[6] R.G. Hammond, *Personal Property Law: Commentary and Materials* (1992) at p 37.
[7] R. Cotterrell, 'The Law of Property and Legal Theory' in W. Twinning (ed), *Legal Theory and the Common Law* (1986) at p 92.
[8] See, F. Pollock and F.W. Maitland, *The History of English Law* (2nd edn, 1898), Vol II at p 10.
[9] See Chapter 6.

It is submitted that the above assumptions and the fragmented approach to property law require serious challenge in the twenty-first century. It is not submitted that every single resource to which the legal system attaches importance can be explained by one single text – such a suggestion would indeed be fallacious and no property law commentator could possibly provide a text which explained all the substantive rules relating to both land and other resources. Land will always have specific attributes which will require a distinct commentary; similarly, intangibles such as intellectual property. The matter is neatly explained by Professor Goode: '... land is governed primarily by property law concepts, goods and choses in action by commercial law concepts; land law is concerned essentially with status, commercial law with obligations.'[10] However, is it true to maintain that there is no conceptual framework governing the acquisition and enjoyment of resources in general? It is submitted that it cannot be denied that there is a general body of rules, principles and concepts that apply to all resources; these combine to form the general law of property. Professor Goode, despite his comments above, nevertheless concludes by saying that '... many of the rules of property apply equally well to land and chattels.'[11] Recognition of such a body of concepts, principles and rules illustrates that the law of property is concerned with the relationships between subjects and objects of a legal system.

Where a legal system recognises and allows subjects of the system to control the creation, acquisition and transfer of things which form objects of the subjects' actions, it becomes important for the legal system to devise rules which govern the activities of acquisition, use and transfer. Given that land is merely one of many objects within the legal system, a concentrated study of land law can provide nothing more than a study of a specific branch of property law. Concentration on a specific branch of property law such as land law cannot provide a student with a general understanding of the principles of property law. It seems clear, at least from a methodological perspective, that a sound understanding of the general principles of property is crucial to an effective understanding of more specific branches of property law. The traditional approach to property law amounts to a compartmentalisation of the study of property with little attempt to link the discussion to a common theme. The danger of studying law by compartment is no better explained than by Jackson who writes:

'[T]here has been an increasing tendency to study law by compartment, which has led to a division of the study of law concerned with objects of the system according to the nature of the particular object (e.g. land, goods, copyright or debt) but, while the content of the right may in some cases vary according to

---

[10] R.M. Goode, *Commercial Law* (1982) at pp 51–52.
[11] *Ibid.*

the nature of the object, its function rarely does. The division seems to impart a sense of false distinction which perpetuates itself by an increasing reluctance to enquire whether the distinction between objects and subjects is one of form or substance. It is questionable, therefore, whether we do not do a disservice to any aim of a coherent legal system by emphasis thereon, rather than on the regulation of the acquisition and use of objects no matter what their nature.'[12]

Furthermore, over one hundred years ago, and certainly by the time of the 1925 property law legislation, land may have been the most prized object in the legal system. However, today, with the rise of the modern corporation and emerging forms of investment, there is a growing need to understand property and property law in its contemporary environment. One writer, recently commenting on the changes taking place in property law over the twentieth century, opines that the

'rationalised structures erected at the start of the century are now beginning to breakdown. This is not necessarily because of any inherent weakness in the structures themselves, more because times have changed. Commercial, social and domestic relationships now are of course very different from what they were at the start of the century, but it is not just that they are different – they are very much more diverse. It is this last factor – the increased diversity of commercial, social and domestic relationships – that is prompting a growing awareness of a need to recognise a wider range of property interests than those envisaged at the start of the century.'[13]

The recognition of the shortcomings of the traditional approach to property law has prompted many law schools to rethink their teaching of property law. Emphasis is being placed on property law courses which have, as their aims and objectives, an appreciation of some of the fundamental concepts and principles of property law. The primary objective of this text is to introduce the reader to the general legal principles and concepts associated with property. The work commences with an examination of the legal concept of property – in particular, its meaning, extent and purpose. An important section of the work addresses the justificatory theories advanced for the recognition of proprietary rights. An attempt is made to show that the legal concept of property is influenced by social, political and economic factors. Amongst the issues considered, the following questions are raised: How do property lawyers classify property and why is classification important? What are ownership, possession and title and how can these concepts be illustrated with case studies? How are proprietary interests created and transferred? What is the difference between proprietary rights and personal rights, and is there a clear

---

[12] David C. Jackson, *Principles of Property Law* (1967) at p 2.
[13] A. Clarke, 'Property Law – Re-establishing Diversity' (1997) 50 Current Legal Problems at p 119.

demarcation between these respective rights? How can ownership be fragmented and what are the contemporary reasons for fragmentation of
ownership? Consideration is further given to the manner in which the idea of
property changes with time. The objective of the text is to introduce the
reader to some basic principles of property law, which are not necessarily confined to any specific object or context. The reader is expected to gain an
appreciation of both real property and personal property and also the various
contexts in which property principles operate (such as family and commercial). It is hoped that by explaining the boundaries and content of the
subject-matter of the law of property, the text will further assist the reader's
understanding of this area of law; and, further, that the methodology
employed in this book will make the learning process in property law much
more enjoyable.

2

THE LEGAL CONCEPT
OF PROPERTY

THE LEGAL MEANING OF PROPERTY

If the ordinary person in the street was to be asked to define 'property', it is not difficult to imagine the type of answer one might receive. 'Property', it will be said, 'is something tangible such as my house, my land, my car' and other identifiable objects that come to his memory. The central characteristic of the lay person's definition of property is the emphasis on objects or things as representing property. From a legal perspective, the lay person's response is inaccurate for two reasons. In the first place, the lay definition of property confuses the concept of property with the objects of property and the property relationship. Secondly, the definition attempts to focus on objects of property that are predominantly tangible in nature whilst the truth of the matter is that, in contemporary property law, objects of property are increasingly becoming intangible.[1]

How do property lawyers define property? In law, property lawyers treat the notion of property as one relating to *rights* to or over things. Property is not the thing itself but the right in or over the thing or object in question.[2] We

---

[1] See Cunningham, Stoebuck and Whitman, *The Law of Property* (1984) at p 1.

[2] The misconception of property as things is explored by C.B. Macpherson in 'The Meaning of Property' in C.B. Macpherson (ed), *Property: Mainstream and Critical Positions* (1978) at p 7. The transformation of property from a right to a thing took place during the industrial revolution and the development of the full capitalist market economy. Prior to this, in England during the earlier part of the seventeenth century, property meant nothing more than a right to a revenue rather than the thing itself. Given that land was an important commodity, a person could have only certain rights in land, which at all times vested in the Crown. Furthermore, by law and the manorial custom, these rights were not fully disposable by sale or will. It was as a result of the industrial revolution that land became predominantly more and more 'parceled' and absolute and consequently transferable. It was natural to speak of the land itself as one's property rather than the right in or over the land itself. The blurring of the distinction between things and rights was further encouraged by the state's recognition of the individual's right to transfer and sell his property.

can go further and say that property arises whenever there is a relationship between a subject and object of the legal system. By subjects we mean those individuals having legal entity, such as a person or a corporation, and by objects we mean all those things of value which the legal system has accepted as capable of control. The consequence of finding a property relationship between a subject and an object is that the subject will acquire a *proprietary right* in the object, the nature of which will vary from right to right. In this respect, Noyes provides us with an effective definition of property when he writes,

> '[T]he term property may be defined to be the interest which can be acquired in external objects or things. The things themselves are not, in a true sense, property, but they constitute its foundation and material, and the idea of property springs out of the connection or control, or interest which, according to law, may be acquired in them, or over them.'[3]

Legal systems recognise certain entities as subjects upon whom they confer certain rights and impose certain duties. Such subjects can be individual human beings or artificially created entities such as corporations. In the same manner, legal systems recognise objects that are capable of control by subjects. These objects have no rights and neither do they owe any duties; they simply constitute those material resources in which the subject is capable of acquiring a proprietary right or interest. Such objects or things can be tangible or intangible; for example, objects can range from physical resources such as land, goods and animals to intangible resources such as debts, copyrights and shares.

Noyes' definition can be explored with some examples. A person may purchase a house, but what makes the house his property? Does one say that because he is in possession of the house it becomes his property? Take the following example – I may be in possession of this textbook, but what makes this textbook mine? The answers to these questions become plainly obvious when we differentiate between two concepts – namely, ownership and possession.[4] A legal system that differentiates between physical possession and ownership consequently defines property as a right. What makes the house mine is my right to the house and my right is one of ownership. What makes the textbook mine is not the fact that I have possession thereof, but the fact that by receiving it – either by purchase or gift – I have acquired ownership to it. My property is my ownership. Ownership is merely one example of the types of property right a person may have in an external object.

One object may sustain more than one proprietary right – in other words, more than one person may have rights to the same object in question. In the context of land, a person may have absolute ownership but at the same time

---

[3] C.R. Noyes, *The Institution of Property* (1936) at p 357.
[4] For a detailed examination of these concepts see Chapter 6.

he may have mortgaged the land to a building society or bank. The bank will have a proprietary interest in the land in the form of a mortgage. The owner of the land may have leased his land for a period of time to another, called a tenant. The tenant does not acquire absolute ownership of the land but has a lease granting him certain rights in the land. Finally, the owner may have granted another a right of way over his land such as a right to walk over the owner's land. In land or real property law terms, one would say that the owner has granted an easement to another person enabling him to walk over the owner's land in order to effectively utilise his own land. The holder of an easement has rights over another person's land but again different in nature from absolute ownership, mortgage or a lease. What one can see is that the nature of the proprietery interest is different in each case; in particular, the level of control or connection with the object decreases from absolute owner-ship of land to the mere grant of an easement. Property, in legal terms, therefore means a right to a thing rather than the thing itself. Bentham explains that property is a legally protected 'expectation ... of being able to draw such or such an advantage from the thing in question according to the nature of the case.'[5]

The legal analysis of property as a right in the sense of an enforceable claim to a thing is a good starting point in the discussion of the definition of property; it is, however, a starting point which requires much more elabora-tion. The definition of property as a right to a thing is incomplete for at least three reasons. In the first place, the definition assumes that private property is the norm. Most legal systems distinguish between three broad categories of property – namely, private, common and state property. Although this text is primarily concerned with concepts in private property law, any serious dis-cussion of private property cannot take place without first distinguishing it from alternative property regimes.[6] Secondly, the definition of property as a right fails to explain that property; and, in particular, private property is better explained as constituting a bundle of rights and relations between sub-jects than simply a mere right to a thing. This matter is better understood by reference to the Hohfeldian normative jurisprudence of legal rights and legal relations.[7] Finally, the analysis of property as a right fails to explain that the meaning of the term is not constant but one which is always changing. The idea of property is influenced by political, social and economic factors. The changes are related to the manner in which people wish to see property and their expectation of it. It is also for this reason that the concept of property is

---

[5] J. Bentham, *Principles of the Civil Code* (1830).
[6] R.S. Tawney, 'Property and Creative Work' in Macpherson (ed) *Property: Mainstream and Critical Positions* (1978) at p 136 argues that '[I]t is idle to present a case for or against private property without specifying the particular forms of property to which reference is made ...'
[7] W. Hohfeld, *Fundamental Legal Conceptions* (1923).

controversial. There are arguments in society as to what property ought to be and exactly what purpose it should serve. The changing nature of property is explored in more detail in Chapter 5.

TYPES OF PROPERTY: PRIVATE, COMMON AND STATE

Most Western legal traditions differentiate between three broad categories of property – namely, private, common and state.[8] Sometimes the difference is simply said to be between private and non-private property.[9] What makes these categories branches of a conceptual tree is that they all refer to rights recognised and enforced by the state through law. What distinguishes one from the other depends on the nature of the right and the persons to whom the right is given. At the heart of the matter there is the ever-continuing political debate as to who should control the material resources in so far as the means of production, distribution and exchange. What resources should be vested in private control and what in state control are issues influenced by political economy. Socialist regimes would argue for a balance between state and collective property whilst capitalist would prefer a greater shift to private property.

Private property

The idea of private property revolves around the fact that a resource or material object in question belongs to some individual or individuals.[10] The individual has the power to determine how the object shall be used and by whom. His power to do so is recognised and enforced by the state. The hallmark of a private property regime is that the individual has the right to exclude others from the enjoyment or benefit of the object or thing in question. In correlation to this, others are required to respect his private property and enforcement is made through appropriate trespassory rules. It is often said that examples of private property include 'my car, my house and other objects that belong to me'. Yet, property lawyers analyse property in terms of rights to things as opposed to things themselves. My house belongs to me because I have ownership in it, and, thus, my private property in this case is my ownership of the house.

---

[8] This categorisation is not necessarily clear-cut. Political and legal theorists have often discussed private, common and state property along with communitarian and collective property. It is not altogether clear whether the latter are specific examples of one of the former types or whether they are distinct types of property. The matter is discussed later, but see Waldron, *The Right to Private Property* (1988) at pp 38–43; also J. Harris, 'Private and Non-Private Property: What is the Difference?' (1995) 111 LQR 423.

[9] See Harris, *op cit*.

[10] As to how private property regimes come about and how the process of distribution of resources takes place is a matter both for philosophers concerned with distributive justice and justificatory theories of private property. See Chapter 2; also Dworkin, 'What is Equality?: Equality of Resources' (1981) 10 Philosophy and Public Affairs.

One of the fundamental shortcomings in much discourse on private property is that such discussion is often confined to ownership; that is, the particular right in question is that of ownership. For example, in the context of land, ownership is understood in the sense of a person being vested with a fee simple absolute in possession – that is, a freehold title.[11] As such, the analytical framework of private property is built entirely around the concept of ownership. Private property, however, does not consist merely of ownership but consists of a much broader class of rights such as a lease, a mortgage, an easement, a copyright and so on. It is at this point that one encounters conceptual problems surrounding private property.[12] Do these broader class of rights have the same characteristics as the right of ownership? In order to answer this question one must examine the meaning of the right to exclude others in the context of property law. As noted above, the hallmark of a private property right is the right to exclude others from the enjoyment and interference with a particular resource. This aspect of the right to exclude others requires a little more analysis in order to understand the nature of a private property right.

Property lawyers often distinguish between two types of right – namely a right *in rem* and a right *in personam*. A right *in rem* is a right in respect of a thing, a *res*. The right is said to 'bind the whole world' in that every subject in the legal system must respect the right. For example, ownership of my house must be respected by every person in the sense that all must refrain from trespassing on it. Bell explains that a right, which binds the whole world, has two aspects to it: the right can be both defensive and assertive in nature.[13] As concerns every subject in the legal system who must refrain from interfering with my right without my permission – that is, the aspect of abstention – the right is defensive in nature. A right that binds the whole world can also be assertive in nature. Where someone wrongly takes possession of my land I have the right to a remedy for infringement of my defensive right, but I also have the right to claim my land back. In contrast to a right *in rem*, a right *in personam* is a right between specific individuals – for example, a right of a person to see the performance of a contractual obligation by another. Rights *in personam* only bind specific individuals.

The meaning of the term right *in rem* has been the subject-matter of much discussion and controversy amongst jurists.[14] The idea that such rights bind the whole world and allow the right holder to exclude others is explained by Honoré:

---

[11] See Chapter 4.

[12] See K. Campbell, 'On The General Nature of Property Rights', (1992) 3 Kings College LJ 79.

[13] A.P. Bell, *The Modern Law of Personal Property in England and Ireland* (1989) at pp 6–7.

[14] See, Hohfeld, *Fundamental Legal Conceptions, op cit*. Hohfeld's analysis of rights *in rem* has been the subject-matter of much criticism. Hohfeld avoids the discussion of such rights binding the whole world, instead concentrating on the assertion that such rights are essentially individual rights between a large number of people. This blurs the distinction between rights *in rem* and rights *in personam*. Bell, *ibid*, at p 7, explains that this is misleading: '... one should not lose sight of the wood just because one has discovered that it is made up of trees.' The better analysis of rights *in rem* is provided by T. Honoré in 'Rights of Exclusion and Immunities against Divesting' (1960) 34 Tulane LR 453. See also J.E. Penner, *The Idea of Property In Law* (1997) at pp 23–31.

'[A] first point to notice is that the rights classified as *in rem* are protected by claims to abstentions, not to performances on the part of persons generally ... The protection of these rights against persons generally consists in a general prohibition of interference, not in the general command to perform something, and there appears to be no instance, either in the Anglo-American or continental lists, of a right protected by a claim that persons generally should perform something ... Hence, it seems safe to assert that the class of rights which jurisprudential writers seek to characterize under the heading right *in rem* ... is of rights protected by claims to exclude all persons who have not an exemption resting on a particular title.'[15]

The idea of property, therefore, revolves around the notion of exclusion of others. The right to exclude others arises because the proprietary right in question is said to be a right *in rem*. Ownership allows exclusion of others, likewise those lesser rights such as a lease, mortgage and easement have exclusionary aspects to them. The holders of these rights can prevent interference by others; furthermore, such a right to prevent interference is not restricted to the grantor of the right but also extends to his successors.[16] When one speaks of exclusion of others it is important to bear in mind that the aspect of exclusion must be seen in the context of the particular property right in question. For example, the holder of an ownership right has the right to exclude all others from trespassing on to his land. Wrongful interference amounts to a trespass for which the owner has the right to recover his land as well as the remedy of an injunction and damages. The holder of a proprietary right such as a right of way has the right to stop all others from preventing him using the right of way which has been granted to him. Wrongful interference constitutes the tort of nuisance and the holder of a right of way can seek an injunction and damages to compensate him for any loss suffered. It is thus apparent that the particular property right will determine the cause of action against others in question.

The aspect of 'excludability' is taken by the courts as a central requirement before a resource can be admitted into the category of private property. If it is not feasible for a person to exercise regulatory control over the access of strangers to various benefits inherent in the resource, the resource cannot be an object of private property. The resource will, as discussed below, be confined to common property. In the well-known case of *Victoria Park Racing and Recreation Grounds Co Ltd v Taylor*[17] the High

---

[15] Honoré, *ibid*, at pp 458–459. Penner, *ibid*, more recently explains the idea of exclusion in Chapter 4 of his work.

[16] The idea of a right *in rem* is also explained by S. Bright, 'Of Estates and Interests: A Tale of Ownership and Property Rights' in Bright and Dewar (eds), *Land Law: Themes and Perspectives* (1998) at pp 538–539. Bright argues that when one refers to rights enforceable against the whole world one means that such rights are not enforceable against persons generally but that they are enforceable against the successors in title to the burdened land.

[17] (1937) 58 CLR 479.

Court of Australia was faced with one of the most difficult problems of property law – that is, when will a resource be admitted into the category of private property. The case is principally one on the law of nuisance, although subsidiary arguments were presented in the law of privacy, copyright, unnatural use of land and the recognition of something referred to as a quasi-property interest.[18] The plaintiff owned a racecourse and its main source of revenue was admission fees to the race meetings it conducted on the course. The racecourse was enclosed by a fence so that no one else was allowed into the course without first obtaining a ticket. The defendant, Taylor, owned a cottage opposite the racecourse and built on his land a tower which enabled him to overlook the racecourse – in particular, the boards and semaphores which contained racing information. Taylor arranged with another of the defendants – the Commonwealth Broadcasting Corporation – that they purchase from him a licence to use the tower to broadcast descriptions and results of the races. As a result of this, attendance at the racecourse decreased along with the profits. The plaintiff sued for an injunction on the grounds of nuisance and breach of copyright. The High Court of Australia decided that the facts did not give rise to any wrongdoing on the part of the defendants.

The significance of *Victoria Park Racing* to property lawyers is the fact that the plaintiffs had clearly thought that they had a property interest worthy of protection. The question is, what was the property interest in? The defendants had not physically trespassed on the plaintiff's land. As to whether a person could commit a trespass by merely overlooking someone's land, Latham CJ relied on the nineteenth century common law cases and held that 'any person is entitled to look over the plaintiff's fences and to see what goes on in the plaintiff's land'.[19] Furthermore, there could be no property in a spectacle.[20] If the defendants had not interfered with the plaintiff's land, what did they interfere with? The minority judges clearly believed that the plaintiff had a property interest in its commercial venture – in particular, the valuable information generated thereby, which had now been misappropriated by the defendants. The majority rejected this on a number of different grounds; more importantly, however, on the grounds that the plaintiff did not have any property in its commercial venture and that there was no general cause of action based on unfair competition.[21] Dixon J summarised the position in the following manner:

---

[18] *Ibid* at 482–491.

[19] *Ibid* at 494.

[20] There is no general right to prevent a person from looking at another person's land. Lord Camden CJ made the famous statement in *Entick* v *Carrington* (1765) 19 Howell's State Trials 1029, 1066, that 'the eye cannot by the laws of England be guilty of a trespass'.

[21] (1937) 58 CLR 479; see the judgment of Dixon J at 509f.

'[The courts] have not in British jurisdictions thrown the protection of an injunction around all the intangible elements of value, that is value in exchange, which may flow from the exercise by an individual of his powers or resources whether in the organization of a business or undertaking or in the use of ingenuity, knowledge, skill or labour. This is sufficiently evidenced by the history of the law of copyright and by the fact that the exclusive right to invention, trademarks, design names and reputation are dealt with in English Law as special heads of protected interests and not under a wide generalization.'[22]

The majority judgments in *Victoria Park Racing* all point to one common theme: a resource will only be admitted by the courts into the category of private property on the general principle of exclusion. Where this is not possible then statutory intervention becomes important.[23]

Common property

Common property differs from private property in that the resource in which an individual is given a right is not exclusive to him alone. Society recognises that certain resources cannot in principle – and neither, for that matter, practically – be given to the exclusive use of the individual. Examples of common property include air, common land and public parks.[24] The hallmark of common property, and thus, what makes it different from private property, is that individuals are given the right to use but they have no rights to exclude others from the enjoyment of the resource. Instead, they have the right not to be excluded from

---

[22] *Ibid*.

[23] On the notion of exclusion, see K. Gray, 'Property in Thin Air' (1991) 50 MLR 252. For a defence of the minority judgments in *Victoria Park Racing* and the general recognition of property in intangibles, see D.F. Libling, 'The Concept of Property: Property in Intangibles' (1978) 94 LQR 103. The principle adopted in *Victoria Park Racing* does not represent the position in the United States. In a much earlier and equally well-known case, *International News Service* v *Associated Press* (1918) 248 US 215, the United States Supreme Court recognised a novel quasi-proprietary right in information generally. In the case the defendants had used news material belonging to the plaintiffs in order to reproduce their own news reports. This was beneficial to them since the time difference between the East and West coast of the United States meant that they could publish the same news at the same time as the plaintiffs by simply telegraphing the information to their West Coast offices. Although they had not breached any copyright since there was no direct copying of the words, the Supreme Court held that the plaintiffs had a proprietary interest in their news reports which allowed them to exclude others from enjoyment thereof. Although the plaintiffs in *Victoria Park Racing* relied on the decision in *International News Service*, the majority judgments rejected it on the grounds that there was no property interest in information generally.

[24] There is, however, considerable confusion as to what is specifically included in common property. Macpherson gives the example of a highway or a motorway as a specific example of common property in *Property: Mainstream and Critical Positions, op cit* at p 4. The same example is explained under the heading of 'collective property' by Waldron in *The Right to Private Property, op cit* at p 45. Waldron, however, treats the idea of collective property as meaning state property and his work specifically makes it clear that state property and collective property mean the same thing (at p 40).

the benefit of a particular resource.[25] It is important to understand that, whilst private and common property differ in nature in the sense of exclusion of others and the right not to be excluded respectively, both are examples of individual property rights. That is to say, in both cases the state creates and enforces both private and common property, but the property (that is, the right) belongs to individuals. It is often difficult to accept that common property constitutes individual rights. The main objection seems to be that common property is restricted in terms of use. For example, I may have the right to the use of common land or a public park, but the state or its agents will invariably restrict my use. I have the right to walk in a public park but my visit to the park may restrict me from using a metal detector to dig up objects from the soil. Yet this is no objection in denying common property the status of individual property. Even in the context of private property – for example, the ownership of my car – such a right is restricted. I have the right to drive my car but not at speeds above those stated by law and neither on my neighbour's land.[26]

Common property should be distinguished from communitarian property, which is in substance a special type of private property. The right to a resource may be vested in more than one person at the same time. It is not unusual to hear of joint, group or corporate property. The size of the subjects of communitarian property may vary considerably from case to case. For example, in the context of land, ownership may be vested in more than one person so as to produce co-ownership of the land. Equally, ownership may be given to a much larger group such as a corporation. Corporate property is a good example of communitarian property.[27] Large corporations, the activities of which are managed by directors and executives responsible to shareholders, hold the means of production. A common group of individuals with a common interest constitute a legal person (a corporation), whose activities they control with their shareholding interests. Like any other private owner, the corporation has the power to acquire and alienate its assets. The characteristics of communal property are that individuals within the group have a common interest in the resource; collectively they have the right to exclude outsiders from the resource in question.

A recent example of communitarian property is provided by the decision of the High Court of Australia in *Mabo* v. *State of Queensland (No 2)*.[28] Communitarian property existed and still does exist alongside modern

---

[25] Natural lawyers argue that the initial state of property – that is, before any private or state property regimes – was that all property was common. All resources were given to mankind in common: see J. Locke, *Two Treatises of Government* (1690).

[26] As to the meaning of ownership and the benefits and burdens thereof, see Chapter 6.

[27] The classic work on corporate property is that of Berle and Means, *Modern Corporation and Private Property* (1932) – see Chapter 5.

[28] (1992) 66 ALJR 408, overturning the judgment of Blackman J in *Milirripum* v *Nabalco* (1971) 17 FLR 141 some 21 years earlier, who had held that Aboriginal title to land had not survived British commonwealth settlement of the continent.

private property regimes in relation to land holding in many parts of the
world. The decision is illustrative of the dangers involved in applying modern
private property law models to the communal ownership of land and the
subsequent denial or rights of indigenous people.[29] The case involved an
action by a number of Murray Islanders seeking declaratory remedies in relation to their native title to land on Murray Island, one of a group of three
islands in the Torres Strait Region. The Islands did not form part of the
British Dominions until their annexation to Queensland in 1879; however,
the occupants of the Islands, called the Meriam people, had occupied these
lands well before 1870. The question was whether the Meriam people were
vested with a communal title which burdened the radical title of the Crown
on settlement. The matter fell to be determined by reference to the prevailing
common law around 1879. The High Court ruled that the Meriam people
had a communal native title to land and as such was effective against the
whole world, except for those portions which had been surrendered to the
Crown. The nature of the land holding under this communal title was to be
determined by the customs of the group. As a communal group the Meriam
people had the benefit of trespass rules against the outside world but inter-
nally their system of land holding was to be determined by custom and
mutual understanding.[30]

State property

Whilst private and common property concern individual rights to resources
given and enforced by the state, the idea of state property does not entertain
any question of individual rights. The idea of state property is not always
clear-cut and different writers have attached different meanings to it. At one
level state property can be said to be rights to resources which the state has
created and kept to itself.[31] Thus, examples would include state factories,
state-owned buildings and state enterprises. The state has the right to use

---

[29] For a more detailed analysis of this case see R.D. Lumb, 'Native Title to Land in Australia:
Recent High Court Decisions' (1993) 42 ICLQ at p 84.

[30] The potential problem with the High Court of Australia's ruling in *Mabo v State of
Queensland (No 2)* is that, although the Crown held the radical title to the Murray Islands on
settlement, the native title was not a title created by grant nor was it a common law tenure. In
this respect there are many doctrinal problems within understanding exactly what interest the
Meriam people had in the land. It is confusing to describe the title of the Meriam people as conferring 'ownership' in the strict sense since, and will be seen in Chapters 4 and 6, such a term at
common law (which was clearly applicable in *Mabo*) means an estate in fee simple. The Court
rejected Kent McNeil's argument that the native title of the Meriam People was better analysed
as one of a joint tenancy of a fee simple held of the Crown as soon as the Crown acquired title
to colonial land upon settlement. This would, although not changing the decision, be more effective from a doctrinal point of view: see J. McNeil, *Common Law Aboriginal Title* (1989).

[31] This is the view taken by Macpherson, *Property: Mainstream and Critical Positions, op cit.*

these resources and such a power to do so may be vested in its agencies. In this respect, state property is similar to private property in the sense that the resources in question are the private property of the state. State property is, however, also used to describe a situation where certain material resources are vested in the state and allocated by the state amongst its citizens on the basis of the collective interests of society as a whole.[32] Examples in this respect, include housing, education, transport and health where powers are vested in the state and its agencies.

PROPERTY AS A BUNDLE OF RIGHTS AND RELATIONS: HOHFELDIAN ANALYSIS

At one level of analysis private property is a right in or over external resources which arises as a result of the relation between a subject and a resource. The proprietary right I may have in my motorbike is ownership. It has already been seen that my proprietary right is a right *in rem* in that it binds the whole world. The question arises as to the significance of a person having a proprietary right. Is it sufficient to conclude that property is merely a right arising as a result of the relationship between, say, an owner and a thing? It is submitted that such an analysis is incomplete. This premature account of property fails to explain that the significance of having a proprietary right is not simply that there is a simple right vested in a subject, nor that a simple relation exists between a person and an object. The essence of having property, that is, a proprietary right, lies in the fact that it comprises bundles of mutual relations, rights and obligations between subjects in respect of certain resources or objects. The importance of learning property as a bundle of mutual rights and relations is summed up by Ackerman:

> '[I] think it is fair to say that one of the main points of the first-year Property course is to disabuse entering law students of their primitive lay notions regarding ownership. They learn that only the ignorant think it meaningful to talk about owning things free and clear of further obligation. Instead of defining the relationship between a person and his "things", property law discusses the relationships that arise between people with respect to things. More precisely, the law of property considers that way rights to things may be parcelled out amongst a host of competing resource users. Each resource user is conceived as holding a bundle of rights vis à vis other potential users ...'[33]

---

[32] This is the view taken by Waldron, *The Right to Private Property*, *op cit* at p 40, although he describes this under the heading of collective property but makes the point that what he is discussing is the same as state property in Macpherson's book. See also, A. Clarke, 'Property Law: Re-establishing Diversity' (1997) 50 Current Legal Problems at 124.

[33] B. Ackerman, *Private Property and the Constitution* (1977), at p 26.

It is, therefore, unreal to think of property merely as a right to a thing without further discussion. Jurists who have dealt with the legal notion of rights tell us that rights cannot exist between people and things simply because things cannot have rights and duties, and neither can they be bound by and recognise legal rules.[34] Legal relations exist between persons and not things. If this is the case, how then do we explain property rights? The most effective analytical discussion of rights is provided by the American jurist Hohfeld;[35] despite its faults, it remains the most important in the context of property rights. In order to understand Hohfeld's analysis of rights and the idea of property as a bundle of rights and relations, take the example of A as the owner of a motorbike. The owner of the motorbike has a number of different rights, obligations and relations concerning different people in respect of the ownership of his motorbike. Hohfeld explains that his ownership right consists of a complex aggregate of rights (or claims), privileges, powers and immunities.[36] A has the right to prevent every other person from wrongfully interfering with his motorbike, such as riding it without his permission. The motorbike is his alone and his *claim right* to it is recognised by a duty on others to refrain from interfering with his motorbike. A is under a duty himself to numerous people: he must obtain the appropriate licence from the authorities before he can ride his motorbike; A is under a duty not to ride the motorbike at speeds above those stated by the law; and A must not ride his motorbike on his neigbour's land without permission. A is entitled to paint his motorbike any colour he chooses – we may say that he has a *liberty* to do so. A has the *power* to transfer his motorbike to any one he chooses either on his death or during his lifetime. Finally, A has the right not to have his motorbike taken away from him or his ownership altered in any way; he has an *immunity*.

It is apparent from our analysis of A's ownership of his motorbike that in substance property comprises a bundle of rights, obligations and relations between subjects with respect to the ownership of a thing. Hohfeld pointed out that when lawyers talk about 'right' they use that term to refer to a number of different notions. The notion of 'right' can be reduced to four things: (a) claim rights; (b) privileges (this notion is also taken to mean liberties[37]); (c) powers; and (d) immunities. As such, any legal right – for example, the right of ownership – could be broken down by analysis into a combina-

---

[34] C.R. Noyes, *The Institution of Property* (1936), at p 290.

[35] W.N. Hohfeld, *Fundamental Legal Conceptions* (1923). See also, N.E. Simmonds, *Central Issues in Jurisprudence: Justice, Law and Rights* (1986); also, M.D.A. Freeman, *Lloyd's Introduction to Jurisprudence* (1994) at pp 379–393.

[36] Hohfeld, *Fundamental Legal Conceptions* (1923) at pp 96–97.

[37] See, G. Williams, 'The Concept of Legal Liberty' in Summers (ed), *Essays in Legal Philosophy* (1968) at p 121.

tion of these four notions. Three of these notions have correlatives or what may be described as opposites. Claim rights are correlative to duties: in our example A has a claim right to his motorbike which means that others, such as B, are under a duty not to interfere with A's claim right. Privileges or liberties are not correlative to duties or rights: A may paint his motorbike any colour he chooses; B has no right to demand a particular colour. We have seen that A has a power to transfer his motorbike to another by sale or gift. In Hohfeld's analytical scheme, powers are correlative to liabilities. This means that the legal position of another person is liable to be changed by the exercise of a power: for example, A has the power to leave his motorbike in his will to B, thereby effecting a change in the legal relation of A and his motorbike on his death. Finally, immunities – A has immunity against having his title altered or transferred by the act of another – are said to be correlative to disabilities in that no other persons can change the position of the owner.

The Hohfeldian analytical scheme is important for property lawyers for at least two main reasons. In the first place, it explains that the idea of private property as a right is better understood as constituting in substance a bundle of rights and relations. Secondly, it facilitates an understanding of the way in which ownership in English law can be broken down into smaller rights and interests. Each of the smaller 'segments' or rights are distinct and can exist separately, but when in the hands of one person they constitute full ownership. Thus, for example, whilst it may be useful to know that A is the owner of a motorbike and as such has a number of privileges or liberties in respect of his motorbike, it is possible for A to give B a liberty to use the motorbike without giving any of the other rights and powers which A has. In the context of land, A, the owner of land, can give B the right to use his land in the form of a licence or easement without transferring any other rights or powers to B. Further still, whilst A has the power to alienate his motorbike to C, he can create such a power in B which is not accompanied by any other legal right or rights lesser than full ownership: for example, A can create in B a 'power of sale' or a 'power of appointment'.[38] In the context of land, A can mortgage his land to a mortgagee thereupon creating in the mortgagee a power of sale in the event of default of payment by A. In both the case of a power of appointment and of a power of sale in the context of a mortgage of land, the ability to perform an act – such as to alienate the object to another – arises because the holder of the power has a liberty to do so. This essentially means that the owner of the thing in question has expressly granted the holder of the power such a power.

---

[38] The idea of a power consists of an authority to do certain things, which affect property not belonging to the appointee and also known as a donee of a power. Such powers may be bare powers or fiduciary powers. Powers of appointment are explored in Chapter 7.

THE FUNCTION OF PROPERTY LAW

The organising idea behind property is the relationship between persons or subjects in respect of objects or material resources within the legal system. In this context, what then is the function of property law? Where a legal system allows its subjects to control the use of things such control requires rules to govern the activities of the subject. Thus, property law is concerned with how subjects may acquire rights in objects, what objects may be the subject-matter of property, how such objects are to be used, and finally, how such rights are completely extinguished or transferred from one to another. One of the fundamental concerns of property law revolves around the concept of ownership. It is unreal to think of ownership as an indivisible concept. Ownership consists of a bundle of rights that may be distributed amongst more than one person in respect of the same object. In this respect, the law of property also becomes an inquiry into how, and for what purpose, such smaller rights are created in subjects and which of the several competing proprietary rights in the same thing should have priority.

3

JUSTIFICATIONS FOR PRIVATE PROPERTY

JUSTIFYING PRIVATE PROPERTY

The preceding chapter looked at the idea of property in law. Property was analysed as a right held by an individual in or over external resources; in other words, a right in the sense of an enforceable claim to a resource. The ownership of my land, my dog and my car is only good in so far as there are appropriate trespassory rules protecting my right of ownership. If there are no such rules protecting the infringement of my ownership I have no enforceable claim and consequently no property. However, it is not quite true to say that it is the aspect of enforceability that alone gives birth to property rights and a private property regime. Enforceability is of course important in making property a legal right, but the enforceability itself must arise from a state's belief that there are sound justifications for recognising property as a legal right. In this respect one writer comments,

> 'property is not thought to be a right because it is an enforceable claim: it is an enforceable claim because it is thought to be a human right. This is simply another way of saying that any institution of property requires justificatory theory. The legal right must be grounded in a public belief that it is morally right. Property has always to be justified by something more basic; if it is not so justified, it does not for long remain an enforceable claim. If it is not justified, it does not remain property.'[1]

Whether one agrees with Macpherson on the point of property being a human right, it is clear from his discourse on property that such an institution requires justificatory theories. The basic question can be summarised in

---

[1] C.B. Macpherson, *Property: Mainstream and Critical Positions* (1977) at 11.

the following way: why does the legal system not only recognise my ownership of a thing, but also enforces it through appropriate trespass rules? It is
generally accepted that justificatory theories of private property, certainly in
the western philosophical tradition, divide roughly into two. This is no better
summarised than by Getzler who writes:

> '[t]here is a notion of property as presocial, a natural right expressing the rights
> of persons which are prior to the state and law, this being the view of Hugo
> Grotius, Samual von Pufendorf, John Locke, Immanuel Kant, and George W.F.
> Hegel; and there is a notion of property as social, a positive right created instru-
> mentally by community, state, or law to secure other goals – the theory of
> Thomas Hobbes, David Hume, Adam Smith, Jeremy Bentham, Emile
> Durkenheim, and Max Weber.'[2]

The philosophical analysis of property is an ever-continuing process both with
respect to the broader question of property and the more specific institution of
private property. This is attributable to the fact that the meaning, function
and existence of the institution of property are not constant. The concept of
property changes with time and is influenced by a number of factors, not least
the way in which the dominant classes in society expect the institution of
property to serve. In the same way as the dominant classes of society change,
so does the institution of property.[3] For example, Aristotle, questioning the
proper system of property in an ideal constitution, argues for a regime of private property as the best means of attaining net productivity in the utilisation
of land.[4] Aristotle argues, 'when everyone has his own separate sphere of
interest, there will not be the same ground for quarrels; and the amount of
interest will increase, because each man will feel he is applying himself to
what is his own.'[5] This line of argument has more recently been advanced by
Demsetz who writes that the 'primary function of property rights is that of
guiding incentives to achieve a greater internalization of externalities.'[6]
However, philosophers such as Plato[7] argued for a regime of communal property as opposed to private, and more recently Marx, commenting on the evils
of private property, argues for the abolition of private property and the transfer of the ownership of the means of production to the state.[8]

---

[2] J. Getzler, 'Theories of Property and Economic Development' (1996) XXVI(4) Journal of
Interdisciplinary History at p 641. See also, J. Waldron, *The Right to Private Property* (1988);
S. Munzer, *A Theory of Property* (1990); and more recently, M.J. Radin, *Reinterpreting
Property* (1993).

[3] For a critical review of the recent and continued philosophical analysis see L. Becker, 'Too
Much Property' (1992) XXI Philosophy and Public Affairs, pp 196–206.

[4] Aristotle, *The Politics* (translated by E. Baker, 1946).

[5] *Ibid*, p 49.

[6] H. Demsetz, 'Towards a Theory of Property Rights' (1967) 57 American Economic Review:
Proceedings and Papers at p 348.

[7] Plato, *The Republic* (translated by Desmond Lee, 1974).

[8] K. Marx, *The Communist Manifesto* (Harmondsworth, 1976).

This book is primarily concerned with the institution of private property and it is justificatory theories of private property that are considered here. An appreciation of some of the dominant justifications for private property is an important aspect of a study in property law. The ideas behind these various lines of thought continue to be reflected in both case law and legal policy-making process. Before we examine some of the principal justifications for private property it is important to note that such justificatory theories, and commentary thereupon, usually encapsulate three separate questions. The first is the basic question: 'What principles decide which individuals have ownership rights over what things?'[9] This is different from the second question, which seeks to ask, what are the social or public functions of private ownership? The third question, closely related to the second, simply asks: 'What individual interests are served by the existence of private property as opposed to some other property regime (such as communism)?'[10] Thus, in dealing with justificatory theories for private property, it becomes apparent that theorists either attempt to justify private property by simply looking at the acts of an individual in respect of external resources or they attempt to look at the broader question of the goals achieved by the existence of private property. The latter does not necessarily entertain questions as to how people become owners of things, but merely seeks to provide a plausible explanation for the existence of private property.

OCCUPATION THEORY OF PRIVATE PROPERTY

One of the earliest justifications for private property is contained in what has been called the occupation theory. This theory attempts to answer the relatively simple question of how things become the subject-matter of private ownership. It is taken for granted that things are ours because we have acquired them from another person who has ownership to pass on to us. Such acquisitions can occur through a voluntary transfer such as a gift or a bequest in a will or simply by a purchase for value. Thus, the law prescribes methods by which ownership can be acquired from another – for example, a transfer by deed or mere delivery of the thing in question. The law does not, however, tell us how that chain of ownership began; in other words, why was ownership of the thing recognised in the first place?

Early philosophers such as Hugo Grotius[11] and Pufendorf[12] argued that the earth's resources were given to mankind in common. Likewise, Blackstone wrote: '[T]he earth ... and all things therein, are the general

---

[9] R. Epstein, 'Possession as the Root of Title' (1979) 13 Georgia Law Review 1221.
[10] J. Waldron, *op cit*, at p 1.
[11] Hugo Grotius, *On the Law of War and Peace*, Book 2, Chap 2, 1, 4–5 (Kelsey translation, 1925).
[12] Samuel Pufendorf, *Of the Law of Nature and Nations* (J. Churchill *et al* (eds), 1703).

property of mankind, exclusive of other beings, from the immediate gift of the Creator ... all was in common among them, and that every one took from the public stock to his own use such things as his immediate necessities required'.[13] In this sense of communal property, private property was born through individual taking, which, Blackstone commented, was basically for his or her own need. If individuals will claim the material things of the earth thus effecting demand, such philosophers argued that the resulting scarcity value would naturally require a system of allocation in order to preserve peace and order. Without such a system there would be constant disputes as to what belonged to one person and what to another. The system which gave rise to the institution of private property was first occupation – hence, the occupation theory or justification for private property.

The essence behind the occupation theory is that, given that all material resources are given to mankind in common, such material resources become the private property of individuals through the consent of, or agreement with, the rest of mankind. The division of property takes place by reference to agreements. Such agreements can be express – that is, a clear acceptance by a group of individuals that material resources (for example, land or animals) – will be distributed amongst themselves on a mutual understanding. In the absence of such express agreements, an implied agreement could be found on the simple basis of first occupation. The basic principle emerging here is that the first occupation gives rise to private property; put into the words of the common law, 'possession is the root of title'.[14]

If the occupation theory holds that an implied agreement will be found amongst individuals that a thing has become the private property of another through occupation, when does first occupation take place? Despite the apparent simplicity of the theory, the question of who has taken first possession is much more difficult when applied to factual situations. The central problem relates to the actual point at which it occurred and the amount of labour needed to take first possession. The problem is particularly acute when there are overlapping efforts to take first possession. The seminal case that attempts to answer these questions is *Pierson* v *Post*,[15] a classic wild animal case from the early nineteenth century. The case involved an action of trespass by Post against Pierson on the grounds that Pierson had interfered with Post's property in a wild fox. The facts of the case are relatively simple: Post in possession of certain dogs was hunting on an abandoned beach and,

---

[13] Sir William Blackstone, *Commentaries on the Laws of England* (1765–69), Vol II, para 1.

[14] The concept of possession is discussed at length in Chapter 6. The notion that possession is the root of title is clearly embedded in the common law: see, for example, *Asher* v *Whitlock* (1865) 1 QB 1; *Perry* v *Clissold* [1907] AC 73; Megarry and Wade, *The Law of Real Property* (6th edn (2000), p 89); Pollock and Wright, *Possession in the Common Law* (1888).

[15] 3 Caines R 175 (NY Sup Ct 1805).

having caught sight of a wild fox, he led pursuit for it and had the fox in his gunsight. Before Post had any chance of killing the fox, Pierson intercepted his pursuit and killed the fox and took away the carcass. Pierson's interception took place with the full knowledge that Post was in hot pursuit of the animal. The basis of Post's action was that his pursuit had given him property in the fox that had now been interfered with by Pierson.

The judgments in the case are very interesting and attempt to lay down some general principles on when first occupation or possession occurs. Tompkins J delivered the decision of the majority who held in favour of Pierson. After citing a long list of authorities both English and American, and consulting the opinion of jurists, the majority held that actual capture and control of the thing in question could give rise to first possession. The hot pursuit of Post was insufficient to give him any property in the fox. Furthermore, it mattered not that Post could have killed the fox had it not been for Pierson's interception. For the majority, possession meant a clear act whereby the entire world understands that the pursuer has 'an unequivocal intention of appropriating the animal to his individual use'.[16] Anything short of such an act would be insufficient to give property in the animal. There are sound justifications in this position in that, in the absence of a kill and complete control of the animal, when does the court assign possession? The underlying objective of the majority ruling was to avoid constant disputes and quarrels about when possession takes place. Livingstone J dissented on the grounds that the question of first possession should not be decided by a judge but by a panel of hunters.[17] In his view the matter would have clearly been decided in favour of Post by such hunters; furthermore he thought that the majority ruling had the effect of discouraging fox hunting.

Professor Rose has argued that there appear to be two principles emanating from the decision in *Pierson* v *Post* as to when first occupation takes place.[18] First, notice to the whole world through a clear act, and second, the reward of useful labour.[19] These two principles require discussion because they seem at first instance to be rather contradictory. The former principle suggests that first occupation takes place when there is an act clear to the whole world that control has been taken by the possessor. The second principle, however, suggests that first occupation takes place by mixing one's labour – for example, by hunting the thing in question. The second principle on its own leaves a number of difficulties: first, it leaves a number of questions unanswered in the decision in *Pierson* v *Post*, and second, it fails to

---

[16] *Ibid* at 178.
[17] *Ibid* at 180.
[18] C. Rose, 'Possession as the Origin of Property' (1985) 52 The University of Chicago Law Review 73.
[19] *Ibid* at p 78.

explain the difference, if any, between the occupation theory and the rather different labour theory of property, which is discussed later. If the principle is to reward labour then what about the labour employed by Post in his pursuit of the fox? On this second principle, Post should have been entitled to the fox as his property. Despite these initially apparent contradictions, the two principles work hand in hand. The central principle is that of notice to the whole world through an unequivocal act to appropriate. The question can be put in the following way: who has exercised a better control?[20] Labour is important only in so far as making that communication effective. Thus the facts of *Pierson* v *Post* can be explained by stating that, although Post had employed some labour in hunting the fox, his labour had never reached the important stage of communicating notice to the whole world. Pierson's labour had the effect of making that important notice to the whole world.

The rule emanating from the occupation theory of private property is that objects become the private property of individuals when such individuals have taken occupation of them. Occupation is only effective when there has been a clear act of appropriation and which has been communicated to the whole world. Pursuit and acts which fall short of such an unequivocal act of appropriation are insufficient because of the problem of assigning possession when there are two or more overlapping efforts to take occupation. The principle behind the occupation theory is thus clear enough; however, it may be questioned whether the theory has any contemporary significance in property law. The primary objection to its continued reliance in contemporary property law is that it is based on facts, which are both historical and primitive.[21] The conditions operating at the time of writers such as Grotius and Pufendorf simply do not exist in a complex system of resources which we witness today. Resources are not as commonly held today as they were before; rather, they are increasingly parceled into private property. This process, having its origins in the seventeenth century, was a result of the spread of the full capitalist market economy in western political systems.

It is submitted that, despite the historical and primitive conditions operating in the occupation theory, the theory remains an important one in present day property law. There are several reasons why the theory is important. In the first place, it cannot be denied that the theory provides the most basic justification for private property. It tells us why private ownership came about in the first place. Many theories on private property attempt to justify the insti-

---

[20] This question is employed by the courts in many of the English law cases relating to finding and is also central to the question of whether someone has exercised an appropriate adverse possession of land to thereby extinguish a former legal title. These matters are discussed in Chapters 6 and 8.

[21] The theory has been criticised by some as being a mere description of the origin of property: see, for example, Lowie, 'Incorporeal Property in Primitive Society' (1928) 37 Yale Law Journal 551.

tution of private property, yet they do so not by reference to how such property came about, but rather by looking at the social and economic functions of private ownership. Such theories often fail to explain how the chain of ownership began in the first place, instead taking it for granted that the legal system has a concept of private property. In this respect, Epstein writes:

> '[I]t could be decided that ownership is necessary to create effective incentives for the development and improvement of property or to reduce or eliminate conflicts between private persons. Yet even if these points are true, such broad justifications for ownership do not solve the more particular question of how given bits of property are matched with given individuals'.[22]

Second, the principal line of thought developed in the occupation theory still continues to be reflected in modern property law. It may well seem that the cases such as the capture of wild animals are more academic than real life legal disputes in property law; however, analogous facts do appear in present day property law. One commentator writes, 'these cases are not silly ... people still do find treasure laden vessels, and statesmen do have to consider whether someone's act may support a claim to own the moon, for example, or the mineral nodes at the bottom of the sea'.[23] More importantly, however, the principles operating in the occupation theory are still used by the courts in resolving modern day property law disputes. The rule of notice and communication finds itself applicable in the common law cases governing the finding of abandoned and lost objects and also in the law of adverse possession. It will be seen in Chapters 6 and 8 that the common law treats ownership as a relative concept; where objects are lost or abandoned the law allows the finder to assert a full-blooded ownership right against everyone except the original true owner. In such cases of abandoned and lost objects the law has to prescribe conditions under which the finder can assert an ownership right against others. Where objects have been found in a communal or public area, the principle of first occupation has been applied to assign ownership. Thus in one case, *Parker v British Airways Board*,[24] a passenger who found a gold bracelet in the executive lounge of an airport was allowed to keep the proceeds of sale. His finding had given him an ownership right binding on the airport, which had not made any attempts to control or appropriate lost objects in a public part of the airport. The passenger had, in the context of the occupation theory, made effective notice to the whole world by picking up the bracelet and taking control thereof. The airport authority had made no attempt to control lost property by putting up an effective sign to indicate that such lost objects belonged to the airport.

---

[22] R. Epstein, *op cit*, at p 1221.
[23] C. Rose, *op cit*, at p 75.
[24] [1982] QB 1004.

The degree of effort or labour needed to make the communication to the whole world depends on the nature of the resource in question. In *Pierson* v *Post*[25] the degree of effort needed to take control, and thus make communication to the whole world, was to physically capture the wild fox. However, some resources are incapable of entire physical control; their first occupation is judged by reference to their nature. For example, in *The Tubantia*[26] the plaintiffs had been doing some salvage work on a wreck that had sunk in 1916 in the North Sea. The plaintiffs, having spent some £40,000 on the salvage work, managed to make an artificial hole in the side of the wreck and began the process of recovering the contents of the wreck. In 1923 the defendants appeared at the site of the wreck and began their own efforts to recover the wreck and the cargo. The plaintiffs sought a declaration that they were entitled to the wreck and its cargo and that the defendants had interfered with their possession of the wreck. In applying the very same principles enunciated in the occupation theory, the court went on to hold that the plaintiffs were doing with the wreck what an owner or purchaser would have done; their occupation was sufficient to exclude the defendants from interfering with their wreck.

Similarly, in the law and policy relating to the adverse possession of land, the rule of notice and communication sufficient to give occupation is clearly a central requirement. The principle of adverse possession recognises that long uncontested possession of land by a trespasser confers upon such a person an effective title to the land. Leading land law commentators attribute this process to the self-defining quality of property in land as an empirical fact rather than a question of form based on some abstract theories of ownership. Two such commentators write: '[O]n this view property in land is more about fact than about right; it derives ultimately not from words upon parchment but from the elementary primacy of sustained possession.'[27] At first instance, disputes relating to the adverse possession of land do not concern questions of first occupation of land. However, the cumulative effect of the Limitation Act 1980[28] and long undisturbed possession by the trespasser do not move the facts too far away from the factual

---

[25] 3 Caines R 175 (NY Sup Ct 1805).

[26] [1924] All ER Rep 615.

[27] K. Gray and S.F. Gray, 'The Idea of Property In Land' in Bright and Dewar (eds), *Land Law: Themes and Perspectives* (1998) at p 19. In referring to 'words upon parchment' the authors cite Blackstone who could see 'no foundation in nature or in natural law, why a set of words upon parchment should convey the dominion of land ...' (*Commentaries on the Laws of England* (4 vols, Oxford University Press, 1765–69; rep University of Chicago Press, 1979), ii, 2).

[28] The Limitation Act 1980, s 15(1) lays down a general rule that '[n]o action shall be brought by any person to recover any land after the expiration of twelve years from the date on which the action accrued to him.' The effect of this section is to extinguish the title of the paper owner. The principles relating to adverse possession are discussed in more depth in Chapter 8.

situation of first occupation. In such cases of adverse possession the common law requires the trespasser to have asserted a 'complete and exclusive physical control'[29] over the land in question.

The principle of first occupation has recently been the subject-matter of much discussion in Australia relating to the rights of aboriginal peoples. It was observed in Chapter 2 that the High Court of Australia in *Mabo* v *Queensland (No 2)*[30] was forced to recognise the communal native title of the Meriam people to land on Murray Island. Such communitarian property, a form of private property, was vested in the aboriginal peoples by virtue of tens of thousands of years of occupancy. The radical title of the Crown upon settlement was burdened with this native title and as such these people were not trespassers. First occupation was therefore clearly important in recognising such title to the land. In this respect it is important to note that, although legal systems have modified rules of acquisition through statute, such legal systems are nevertheless forced to recognise the rights of individuals and communities who have been in possession of land long before those modified rules of acquisition.

Finally, the occupation theory is regarded by economists to have a special role to play in the facilitation of trade and the functioning of an effective market.[31] Property plays an integral part in economic affairs, since by definition economics deals with all things that are both desired and scarce. Communication and effective occupation together have the effect of making it clear who is the owner of a thing; such clear titles facilitate trade by introducing certainty in the market place. Every item of property must be owned by somebody, or by some people in the form of collective property. In the absence of ownership value cannot exist; unequivocal property claims not only allow efficient resource utilisation but they also allow property to be traded at its highest value.

LABOUR THEORY: PROPERTY A NATURAL RIGHT

Legal and political philosophers in the seventeenth and eighteenth centuries claimed that the right of individuals to own and dispose of private property was a natural right of the individual. John Locke, for example, in his *Two Treatises of Government*[32] argued that private property rights existed before the state and independently of laws prescribed by the state. Property rights were natural rights of individuals and thus governed by principles of natural

---

[29] *Powell* v *McFarlane* (1977) 38 P & CR 452, *per* Slade J at 470.
[30] (1992) 66 ALJR 408.
[31] See, R. Posner, *Economic Analysis of Law* (2nd edn, 1977) at pp 21–31.
[32] J. Locke, *Two Treatises of Government* (1690), Book II; see 'Of Property' in C.B. Macpherson (ed), *Property: Mainstream and Critical Positions* (1978) at p 17.

justice; governmental interference or reorganisation of these rights was not permissible without the consent of the individual.[33] Such natural rights were vigorously defended by political philosophers and indeed formed the basis of revolutionary arguments. In the French and American Revolutions such natural rights were clearly embedded in the resulting declarations. Article II of the French Declaration of 1791 holds that 'The end of all political associations, is the preservation of the natural and imprescriptable rights of man; and these rights are liberty, property, security, and resistance of oppression.'[34] The Fifth Amendment to the Constitution of the United States of America provides: 'No person ... shall be deprived of life, liberty, or property, without due process of law; nor shall private property be taken for public use without just compensation.'[35]

The idea of natural rights is far from clear. With a history of some two thousand five hundred years, what constitutes natural law and natural rights has provoked and continues to provoke different answers.[36] The traditional line of argument behind natural law is that there are certain rights which are derived from the law of God, nature or reason. There are certain moral principles which depend on the nature of the universe and which are discovered by reason. It is these principles, such as the right to life, liberty and pursuit of happiness, which form natural rights and are protected by natural law. Such laws are not prescribed by state; they exist before the state and are higher laws that all states and legal systems therein are subject to. Although it is commonly accepted that natural law is derived from nature itself and discovered by reason, there have been different lines of thought as to what exactly is meant by nature and reason. If such laws are discovered by reason, then whose reasoning prevails? Such a question is by its very nature subjective, and thus susceptible to many different answers. D'Entrèves has pointed out: 'many of the ambiguities of the concept of natural law must be ascribed to the ambiguity of the concept of nature that underlies this.'[37] Despite this, Freeman points out that 'views as to the content of these principles have sometimes diverged but the essence of natural law may be said to lie in the constant assertion that there are objective moral principles which depend upon the nature of the universe and which can be discovered by reason. These principles constitute natural law.'[38]

---

[33] For a detailed account of Locke's discourse on property see Tully, *A Discourse on Property: John Locke and Adversaries* (1980), and J.P. Day, 'Locke on Property' (1966) 16 Philosophical Quarterly at pp 207–221.

[34] Quoted in A. Ryan, *Property* (1987) at p 61.

[35] S.E. Finer, *Five Constitutions* (1979) at p 106.

[36] For a good overview of natural law thinking, see M.D.A. Freeman, *Lloyds Introduction to Jurisprudence* (6th edn, 1994) at p 79 and R. Tuck, *Natural Rights Theories* (1979). The most forceful recent statement on natural law is provided by Finnis, *Natural Law and Natural Rights* (1980).

[37] *Natural Law* (rev edn) (1970) at p 16.

[38] M.D.A. Freeman, *op cit*, at p 80.

John Locke argued that the right to private property was one of the natural rights of an individual and consequently protected by natural law. The right was natural, not in the sense that every individual was born with the right to property; rather, the right was acquired through conduct that is natural to man. Private property rights were acquired by natural, moral and rational conduct which individuals left to their own devices would perform. As such private property was acquired separately and did not arise through the prescriptive law of the state. Locke maintained that it was God and not sovereign that gave property, and thus private property existed even before sovereign and state. The role of government was to protect the right of property along with other rights such as the right to life and liberty. Indeed, such argument was used to refute the claims of Charles I in England that sovereign could interfere with the property of individuals without their consent for the public good. Like Pufendorf[39] and Grotius,[40] Locke begins his justification for private property on the same premise that resources are given to mankind in common; the original state of property is that it is held in common. The basis of his thesis thereafter can be summarised in three main points. In the first place, every man[41] has a right to his own person: we may describe this as self-ownership. Second, every man has a right to own his own labour. Finally, every man has a right to own that with which he has mixed the labour of his own person. Mixing one's labour with the common resources which God has given to mankind extracts that which was held in common into private ownership, this process taking place as a result of the natural conduct of man and not through the process of law prescribed by the state.

Locke begins his justification for private property on the same premise as the occupation theory – that is, the earth and all the resources within it are given to mankind in general. Locke writes:

> 'God, who hath given the World to Men in common, hath also given them reason to make use of it to the best advantage of Life, and convenience. The Earth, and all that is therein ... belong to Mankind in common, as they are produced by the spontaneous hand of Nature; and no body has originally a private Dominion, exclusive of the rest of Mankind, in any of them, as they are thus in their nature state ...'[42]

God gives the earth and the resources within it to man in common; no individual has an exclusive dominion. In this respect, Locke attempts to show that the state and sovereign have no exclusive rights to resources which allow them to interfere with and control those resources *per se*.

---

[39] *Op cit*: see note 12.

[40] *Op cit*: see note 11.

[41] The use of the word 'man' is deliberately used here reflecting the ideological thinking of the time and the role of man as being far more important in acquiring property rights.

[42] *Two Treatises of Government* (1690), 'Second Treatise of Government', Chap 5, para 26, reprinted in C.B. Macpherson (ed), *op cit*, at p 17.

In this state of common property, Locke attempts to show that private property is born out of two natural principles. The first is that every individual has by nature property in his own person, sometimes referred to as self-ownership. Locke writes, 'every man has Property in his own Person. This no Body has any Right but to himself.'[43] The Lockean idea of ownership in one's self has been the subject-matter of much debate.[44] Waldron writes that, 'a more promising suggestion is that self ownership and the ownership of actions amount for Locke to a right to personal liberty.'[45] To have ownership in one's person is to have ownership in one's actions; such actions belong to him since he has a natural right to perform them without any obstruction. The second principle, and one which flows from the first, is that one of the actions which an individual will perform is to labour on resources which have been given in common. Labour of an individual belongs to the individual alone, consequently, Locke argues that when such labour is mixed with common resources such resources are taken from the common and put into the sphere of private property. Labouring gives the labourer an exclusive private property right to the resource or thing in question. The object in which labour has been expended contains something which the labourer owns and as such any taking of the object or other interference amounts to a violation of the individual's natural right to the object.

Labour is thus the central feature of Locke's justification for private property; however, it does not explain the extent of private property. It is fair to say that labour on resources will give individuals private control of those resources; yet there are some unanswered questions. How much private property can an individual acquire under the Lockean theory? How much labour need one expend before he or she becomes entitled to the thing; and does labour have to reflect the value added to the resource in question? Locke addresses the first question in his theory; the latter is not discussed and as such has been the more critical aspect of his theory. Although labour gives birth to a private property right, Locke does impose restrictions on the amount of such property. In his writings one identifies two limitations on the labour principle, namely, the 'spoilation proviso' and the 'sufficiency limitation'.

First, although labour will give private property, if the labourer does not use resources, then, despite his labour, those resources do not belong to him but become common again. He writes, 'God has given us all things richly ...

---

[43] *Ibid*, para 27, at p 18.

[44] See, for example, J. Tully, *A Discourse on Property: John Locke and his Adversaries* (1980) at p 105, who argues that the term 'person' is a technical term quite distinct from 'body'. Tully argues that such use of the word person more accurately describes personal identity: thus, an individual has ownership in his personal identity. For a critical account of ownership in one's self, see P.J. Day, 'Locke on Property' (1966) 16 Philosophical Quarterly.

[45] Waldron, *op cit*, at p 181.

But how far has he given it us? To enjoy as much as any one can make use of to any advantage in life before it spoils; so much may be by his labour fix a Property in. Whatever is beyond this is more than his share, and belongs to others.'[46] This has often been referred to as the 'spoilation proviso',[47] and has been described by Waldron as 'a generous one, because Locke's concept of use is very broad. It is to any advantage of life and therefore is not confined to consumption or production for consumption, but also includes, for example, aesthetic uses and the use of objects as a commodity in exchange.'[48] Although Locke provides for this spoilation limitation, he does not see that there would by any problems of excessive concentration of private property into certain hands at the expense of others. This is simply because in his thesis he regards right and convenience to go hand in hand. Thus, any labour which is mixed with more than what is needed for one's convenience simply goes back into the common. Locke noted that, 'there could be no reason for quarreling about Title, nor about the largeness of Possession it gave. Right and conveniency went together; for as a Man had a right to all he could employ his Labour upon, so he had no temptation to labour for more than he could make use of.'[49] This proviso works well enough in a social and economic climate where right and need go together; however, as Dunn has pointed out, the role of exchange and money did put a rather different emphasis on the matter.[50] Dunn writes that the introduction of money meant that 'right and conveniency no longer went together. The entire social and economic order of the seventeenth-century England rested upon a human institution about whose moral status Locke felt deeply ambivalent.'[51]

The second limitation on property in Locke's theory is that an individual who does labour must leave behind enough resources of the same quality for others to appropriate. This is necessary because the function of property in Locke's theory is the satisfaction of need. Without such property individuals cannot exist; human needs dictate that there should be private property. This limitation has been described as the 'sufficiency limitation';[52] it seeks to make appropriation illegitimate when there is insufficient left for the needs of

---

[46] J. Locke, 'Second Treatise of Government', para 31, in C.B. Macpherson (ed), *op cit*, at p 19.

[47] See, J.H. Bogart, 'Lockean Provisos and State of Nature Theories', *Ethics*, Vol 95 (1985).

[48] Waldron, *op cit*, at p 207.

[49] J. Locke, 'Second Treatise of Government', para 51, in C.B. Macpherson (ed), *op cit*, at p 27.

[50] J. Dunn, *The Political Thought of John Locke* (1969) at p 40.

[51] *Ibid*. Writers like Dunn have sought to argue that the introduction of money was somewhat at odds with Locke's theory. Waldron, *op cit*, at p 209, however, argues that in respect of Locke's spoilation proviso, it is not rendered ineffective by new conditions in economy. This is simply because the amount of appropriation is determined by labour and not the proviso. Providing there is labour and some element of use and consumption, use having a very wide meaning, the labourer is entitled to everything which does not perish.

[52] C.B. Macpherson, *The Political Theory of Possessive Individualism: Hobbes to Locke* (1962) at p 211.

others. Locke writes, '[F]or this Labour being the unquestionable Property of the Labourer, no Man but he can have a right to what that is one joyned to, at least where there is enough and as good left in common for others.'[53] At first instance, this limitation of the right to appropriate seems rather paradoxical. For example, Thomson writes, 'if the first labour-mixer must literally leave as much and as good for others who come along later, then no one can come to own anything, for there are finitely many things in the world so that everyone taking leaves less for others.'[54] The Lockean justification for private property works well under conditions of plenty, since under conditions of plenty and lack of scarcity this sufficiency limitation will never be violated. The social and economic conditions operating at the time of Locke's writing may well have made it impossible for appropriation to become illegitimate by virtue of the sufficiency limitation. The reason for this is that Locke associates private property rights with convenience, such convenience being the satisfaction of human needs and subsistence. Anything beyond this would be improper – for example, the idea of property and convenience going together is illustrated when he states that there would be enough land in the world for twice its population, 'had not the Invention of Money, and the tacit Agreement of Men to put a value on it, introduced (by Consent) larger Possessions, and a Right to them...'.[55]

The sufficiency limitation works well under conditions of plenty, but under conditions of scarcity all appropriation becomes illegitimate for the reason stated above. Does the Lockean justification for private property, therefore, become redundant? This is a question which has provoked different responses. One response is that in an age of scarcity, unilateral appropriation becomes no longer possible and property must be distributed in a different way, for example through consent. Perhaps the most effective interpretation of the sufficiency limitation is that provided by Waldron.[56] Waldron explains that the sufficiency limitation is not really a limitation in its own right, but rather an effect of the spoilation proviso discussed above. He gives the example of an individual living under conditions of modest scarcity; such individual needs to appropriate resources for his needs but he realises that his appropriation will leave less for others who have a similar need to appropriate. If the sufficiency limitation is taken to its logical conclusion, does he sit back and starve? In the context of this example, Waldron explains that such a conclusion would be absurd and inconsistent with the

---

[53] J. Locke, 'Second Treatise of Government', para 27, in C.B. Macpherson (ed), *op cit*, at p 18.

[54] J.J. Thomson, *The Realm of Rights* (1990) at p 330. Thomson is not alone in making this point; J.H. Bogart, *op cit*, writes (at p 834): '[E]very acquisition worsens the lot of others – and worsens their lot in relevant ways'.

[55] J. Locke, 'Second Treatise of Government', para 36, in C.B. Macpherson (ed), *op cit*, at p 21.

[56] *The Right to Private Property*, *op cit*, at pp 211–213.

substance of Locke's theory of property. It would in effect mean that because everyone else in the world is in a similar position everyone has to starve. Waldron writes, 'all God's human creatures would perish notwithstanding the fact that He had provided resources for the sustenance of at least some of them. Such a result, dictated by the alleged proviso in conditions of scarcity, is absurd ... It follows, surely, that he who appropriated the food and shelter he really needs is entitled, even bound to use them – *irrespective of the needs of others*.'[57] The only limitation is that if he appropriates more than his needs then others have a right to be sustained out of his surplus.

Schmidtz provides a somewhat different response to the sufficiency limitation.[58] Schmidtz explains that appropriation is not what he calls a 'zero sum game'.[59] It is not plausible for philosophers on original acquisition, and for that matter subsequent readers of the theories provided by such philosophers, to maintain that all appropriation takes place by the first person to arrive. First appropriation is just the beginning of creating the resource in question, the real benefits to be enjoyed by later owners. Schmidtz neatly explains the point:

> '[O]riginal appropriation diminishes the stock of what can be originally appropriated, but that is not the same thing as diminishing the stock of what can be owned. On the contrary, in taking control of resources and thereby reducing the stock of what can be appropriated, people typically generate massive increases in the stock of what can be owned. The lesson is that appropriation is not a zero-sum game. It is a positive sum game. As Locke himself stressed, it creates the possibility of mutual benefit on a massive scale.'[60]

The question was raised above regarding the extent of labour needed before I can regard the thing in question as mine. This is different from the question under discussion so far – that is, how much private property can I acquire under Locke's theory? Whilst the amount of private property which can be acquired or appropriated is governed by the spoilation proviso and the sufficiency limitation, a question which is not directly tackled by Locke is the relationship of labour to the value added to the thing in question. It is this aspect of his theory which has been the subject of criticism. Nozick raises the following questions: even if labour can be owned and such labour is mixed with resources, does it automatically mean that the resource becomes the private property of the labourer?[61] For example, if I make the very first effort to extract the oil from the bottom of the seabed, am I entitled to the world's supply of oil? Nozick's primary concern is thus: where labour is expended by

---

[57] *Ibid*, at p 214.

[58] D. Schmidtz, 'The Institution of Property' in Frankel, Miller and Paul (eds), *Property Rights* (1994) at p 42.

[59] *Ibid*, at p 45.

[60] *Ibid*, at p 46.

[61] R. Nozick, *Anarchy, State and Utopia* (1974), p 175.

the labourer, why should the labourer be entitled to an exclusive right over the resource in question? His right should only extend in so far as to the added value to the resource in question. The potential problem with this line of attack by Nozick is, how does one practically discriminate between lesser and greater interests in resources in a simple state of nature? Waldron makes the point that only in a positive legal system can different estates and interests in the same object be recognised, distinguished and upheld in law.[62] A plausible explanation is that in a state of nature full and exclusive entitlements are only provisional and in any event 'could not operate as moral constraints on the activity of a subsequently instituted civil society which was determined to strike retrospectively and in rectification of the crudeness of the natural entitlements on a fair balance between the legitimate claims of the appropriator and those of the rest of mankind.'[63]

A second criticism directed at Locke's theory relates to the question: why should the mixing of labour with a resource give any entitlement at all? The much-quoted question which Nozick asks is, '[W]hy isn't mixing what I own with what I don't own a way of losing what I own rather than a way of gaining what I don't have. If I own a can of tomato juice and spill it into the sea so that its molecules ... mingle evenly throughout the sea, do I thereby come to own the sea, or have I foolishly dissipated my tomato juice?'[64] This question posed by Nozick is often taken to illustrate the shortcomings of the labour principle in Locke's theory. However, as one commentator explains, such criticism is inappropriate.[65] Duxbury gives two reasons: in the first place, Locke only recognises those activities which improve the resource as constitutive of labour; second, a person who does labour and makes no improvement to the resource in question or even diminishes its value is simply acting irrationally or out of ignorance.

How far is the natural right justification for private property relevant in modern property law? Critics of the natural law theory of private property reject it has having any significance in modern property law. In the first place, there appears to be the theological dimension to the theory and the resulting question as to how, and the extent to which, the Church continues to influence the legal policymaking process. Legal philosophers argue that private property must be justified by some greater social and economic objective rather than by reference to historical entitlement. As with the occupation theory the view is that such a theory, only explains the principle of original acquisition. The matter is perhaps best summed up by Simmons:

---

[62] *Op cit*, at p 191.

[63] *Ibid.*

[64] *Op cit*, at pp 174–175.

[65] N. Duxbury, *Theorising Private Property Rights*, University of Manchester Working Paper No 20 (1996), p 11.

'[T]here is a solid consensus among philosophers and legal and political theorists that attempted original acquisition justifications of private property, when presented in any even remotely plausible form, in fact have little or no interesting justificatory force. However compelling their intuitive underpinnings might be, they can justify nothing which helps much in our deliberation about the possible moral defences of private property in contemporary society.'[66]

Simmons, however, challenges this consensus by examining the idea of justification of private property. His main aim is to show that when philosophers talk of justifying private property, the concept itself is very vague. Justifications of private property can be one of two types: namely, 'optimality justifications' or 'permissibility justifications'.[67] The former justification looks to the wider social, moral and economic goals of having one type of property over another. Thus, an optimal justification of private property would sound something like this: it is better to have private ownership because it provides for the greater human happiness in society or it is the best means of efficient utilisation of resources. On the other hand, permissibility justifications simply look to what is morally permissible or morally legitimate. The everyday actions of an individual are not always done with the individual seeking to do what is optimal in the sense of the best alternative. Individuals do not necessarily do what is the best thing they can do in the circumstances; rather, they do things because they think they are morally permissible or otherwise legitimate, without any wider objective goal in mind. In this context, Simmons writes: 'the primary force of Locke's original justification of private property is to display private property rights as morally possible and permissible ... The permissibility arguments constitute an attempted justification of private property, they show that private property claims can be legitimate (i.e. morally acceptable), probably were once mostly legitimate and may still be legitimate in certain contexts.'[68]

Finally, the principles emerging from the labour theory continue to be reflected in intellectual property rights and in the law and policy concerning unfair competition.[69] Individuals who create, manufacture or invent things through their labour and intelligence seek to make these things theirs through their acts of labour. It has been said that the law of intellectual property 'is a branch of law which protects some of the finest manifestations of human achievement.'[70]

---

[66] A.J. Simmons, 'Original Acquisition Justification of Private Property' in Frankel, Miller and Paul (eds), *Property Rights* (1994) at p 65.

[67] *Ibid*, at p 66.

[68] *Ibid*, at p 73.

[69] See, for example, R.G. Hammond, *Personal Property Law* (1992) at p 51.

[70] W.R. Cornish, *Intellectual Property: Patents, Copyright, Trade Marks, and Allied Rights* (2nd edn, 1989), p 3.

UTILITARIAN THEORY OF PRIVATE PROPERTY: PROPERTY AS A POSITIVE RIGHT

The utilitarian theory of property regards property as a positive right created instrumentally by law to achieve wider social and economic objectives. Property is said to be a positive right as opposed to a natural right. The essence of a positive right is that it is prescribed by state; the right is both given and protected by state. The most influential utilitarian justification for private property is that of Jeremy Bentham contained in his *Principles of the Civil Code*.[71] The principal thrust of Bentham's argument is that the total or average happiness of society cannot be maximised unless there exist rights to appropriate, use and transfer objects of value or interest. In order to understand the utilitarian justification for private property it is necessary to understand exactly what is meant by the concepts of utilitarianism and positive law.

Jeremy Bentham rejected that there could be any notion of natural law and natural rights. In his words, 'natural rights are simple nonsense: natural and imprescriptable rights, rhetorical nonsense, –nonsense upon stilts.'[72] Bentham argued that all laws flowed from the state alone; states prescribed laws and such laws were positive laws. The principle upon which a law would be prescribed was the principle of utility. The concept of utility and utilitarianism is explained by one commentator in the following manner:

> '[T]he classical utilitarian theories (of Bentham, J.S. Mill ...) took the fundamental basis of morality to be a requirement that happiness should be maximized: the basic principle of utility required us to weigh up the consequences, in terms of happiness and unhappiness of various alternative actions, and choose that action which would, on balance, have the best consequences, in the sense of producing the largest net balance of happiness.'[73]

The principle of utility alone governs what we should or should not do; in other words, the principle is used by state and sovereign and its lawmaking authorities to command rules. Law and rights are not dependent on moral judgments and our actions cannot be simply justified on past facts.

In rejecting property as a natural or moral right of an individual, Bentham claimed that private property and law are born and die together. Without law there is no private property; thus, even where a person is to labour on a resource, his only entitlement to the resource is the guarantee that the law

---

[71] (1830); see his analysis of property in C.B. Macpherson (ed), op cit, at pp 41–59. The best edition is that contained in Jeremy Bentham, *The Theory of Legislation* (C.K. Ogden (ed), 1931).

[72] J. Bentham, 'Anarchical Fallacies' in Waldron (ed), *Nonsense Upon Stilts: Bentham, Burke, and Marx, on the Rights of Man* (1987) at p 53.

[73] N.E. Simmonds, *Central Issues in Jurisprudence: Justice, Law and Rights* (1986), p 15. There is no scope in this book for a complete analysis of utilitarianism; however, for further analysis, see J.J.C. Smart and B. Williams, *Utilitarianism: For and Against* (1973); D. Lyons, *Forms and Limits of Utilitarianism* (1965); Sen and Williams (eds), *Utilitarianism and Beyond* (1982).

will assure the enjoyment of his labour. In this sense laws perform the function of security, without which there would be misery and a denial of the
right to subsist. The positivist nature of the right to private property is clear
when Bentham writes,

> '[T]he idea of property consists of an established expectation; in the persuasion
> of being able to draw such or such an advantage from the thing possessed,
> according to the nature of the case. Now this expectation, this persuasion, can
> only be the work of the law. I cannot count upon the enjoyment of that which
> I regard as mine, except through the promise of the law which guarantees it
> to me.'[74]

Bentham argues that the greatest or total happiness in society in respect of
resources will only come about if such resources are in the hands of private
individuals; how does he apply the utility principle to private property? The
assumption is that acquisition of wealth is good, but good in what manner?
In respect of the utility principle Duxbury comments:

> 'the principle is inherently vague in that it is not entirely clear how it is sup-
> posed to be applied or how utility might be measured or – assuming satisfactory
> criteria for measurement are devised – how the utilitarian is expected to balance
> one person's gain in utility against a loss in that of another.'[75]

Bentham does not provide a precise way in which human happiness can be
measured; instead, in his work, Bentham identifies what he calls 'evils' resulting from violations of private property.

The first evil, which Bentham comments upon in *Principles of the Civil
Code*, is the evil of non-possession. The acquisition of a resource is a good
thing; non-possession, on the other hand, is an evil since the resource is
simply being wasted. Second, there is the pain of losing since, where I do
have private property and possession of things, such property performs different functions and represents to the individual different values. Property
may have an intrinsic value but it also has a value of affection: for example,
as an inheritance, as the reward of labour, of the provision for dependents.
Third, there is the fear of losing what one already has. Whilst individuals
have property, future acquisitions are necessary to supplement the property
which an individual already possesses. If the law does not guarantee private
property then there is a fear of losing what we already have; this is a bad
thing, since resources are not utilised properly. Instead they are hidden or
preserved and the enjoyment of them becomes 'sombre, furtive, and
solitary.'[76] Finally, there is what Bentham describes as the deadening of

---

[74] J. Bentham, *Principles of the Civil Code* (1830), in C.B. Macpherson (ed), *op cit*, at p 52.
[75] N. Duxbury, *Theorising Private Property Rights, op cit*, at p 4.
[76] J. Bentham, *Principles of the Civil Code* (1830), in C.B. Macpherson (ed), *op cit*, at p 54.

industry which arises from the insecurity of labour and the resulting fruits of labour. Bentham argues that the law alone can give security in respect of these four evils.

One of the shortcomings of Bentham's utilitarian justification for private property is that it does not address the question as to how people come to own resources and how initial distribution arises in the first place. Bentham's philosophy of property and law was written in a period witnessing the end of the medieval period and the beginning of a capitalist economy. Certainly his ideas were influenced by the industrial revolution and the rise of nation states anxious to assert total independence in an age of economic expansion. It may be that Bentham had no need to worry about how initial acquisitions of property occurred, instead justifying private property in this age of economic expansion. Land had become increasingly parceled into private ownership and rights in land more absolute.[77] In so far as the question of initial distribution of wealth and resources, it is commonly said that the utilitarian is not concerned with this question since his primary aim is the maximisation of welfare. Presumably this means that those who have the largest amount of property will have the greatest opportunity to maximise wealth. What about those who have nothing or very little? Is the utilitarian concerned about the distribution of welfare or is the divide between poor and rich not a concern for the utilitarian?

It is submitted that the distribution of welfare is a central concern for the utilitarian and thus an integral part of any utilitarian justification for private property. Distribution of welfare can take place on the theory of diminishing marginal utility which itself needs to be balanced with the objectives of maximisation of welfare. Simmonds[78] explains the theory of marginal utility with the following example: an extra £1 given to a millionaire will make a negligible contribution to his welfare, whereas £1 given to a very poor person might make a significant contribution to his welfare, enabling him, perhaps, to buy a meal which he would not otherwise have been able to afford. The £1 in the hands of the poor man has the effect of maximising welfare on a much greater scale than in the hands of a rich man. However, marginal utility needs to be balanced with the fact that high productivity requires resources to be placed in the hands of individuals who have strong incentives to work hard. Strict equality of resources will inevitably bring about a reduction in productivity and welfare in the long run. In this respect, Simmonds explains that a utilitarian can offer a plausible response to distributive issues; he identifies two main arguments which purport to show the distributive nature of utilitarian arguments.

---

[77] See, for example, C.B Macpherson, 'Capitalism and the Changing Nature of Property' in E. Kamenka and R.S. Neale (eds), *Feudalism, Capitalism and Beyond* (1975) at p 105.

[78] *Op cit*, at p 32.

'[F]irst the utilitarian can claim that his theory explains the way in which we do in fact trade off equality against productive and economic efficiency. This trade off is neither arbitrary nor hypothetical: it reflects the fact that the underlying concern is the maximization of welfare, that being a goal to which both redistribution and higher productivity can contribute. Secondly, the utilitarian can argue that he alone has offered a plausible explanation of why redistribution matters. When we take money from the rich and give to the poor, he may argue, we do this because we believe it will do more good relieving poverty than being spent on trivial comforts.'[79]

Seen in this way, like the Lockean natural right justification for private property, there are limitations on the extent of private property under a utilitarian justification. Under Locke's theory we identified the spoilation and sufficiency limitations; the utilitarian principle of maximisation of welfare does accommodate the need for distribution to others.

ECONOMIC JUSTIFICATIONS FOR PRIVATE PROPERTY

In more recent times philosophers have advanced economic justifications for private property. This has been part and parcel of a process whereby laws have been analysed from a purely economic perspective which, in substance, represents a scientific alternative to utilitarianism as discussed above.[80] Property underlies each and every aspect of economics, since by its very definition economics deals with all things of worth. Posner argues that the legal protection of property rights performs a very important economic function – that is, to create incentives to use resources much more efficiently.[81] Posner identifies three criteria for an efficient system of property rights. First, 'universality', that is, all resources should be owned by someone or capable of being owned, except those resources which are so abundant that consumption does not reduce the resource for others. Second, 'exclusivity', that is, to give owners the incentive to incur the cost required to make efficient use of resources which they own. Finally, 'transferability' – property rights should be able to be freely transferred since this is the only way that a resource can be shifted from a less productive use to a more productive one. In substance, this economic justification for private property argues that there are costs or disutilities when there is no ownership of resources. If these costs are much greater than the costs involved in having a private property regime, then a system of private property rights is justified by considerations of economic

---

[79] *Ibid*, at p 33.

[80] The economic analysis of law has generated a vast literature: see R. Posner, *The Economic Analysis of Law* (1972); A.M. Polinsky, *An Introduction to Law and Economics* (1989); and in the context of property rights, see B. Ackerman, *The Economic Foundations of Property Law* (1975).

[81] *Ibid*, at pp 10–13.

efficiency. The essence of the economic justification for private property is the minimising of cost and the resulting efficiency in distribution of resources.[82]

Demsetz argues, like Posner, that the general welfare will be better served if material resources are owned and controlled by private individuals.[83] A system of private ownership is much better than communal because under private ownership the full impact of ownership is greater. According to Demsetz, the 'primary function of property rights is that of guiding incentives to achieve a greater internalization of externalities.'[84] He gives the example of a communal ownership of land by a group of hunters. When this group of hunters hunts on the land, no individual hunter has any incentive to increase or maintain the stock of game. This is simply because the cost of doing so will go to others as well as himself. The consequence is that there will be over-intensive hunting and a reduction in the game stock which will not only affect his fellow hunters but hunters for generations to come. It is because the cost of one's use is not reflected in communal ownership that a private property regime is justified. A private scheme of ownership over game territory is much better because it 'will internalize many of the external costs associated with communal ownership, for now an owner, by virtue of his power to exclude others, can generally count on realizing the rewards associated with husbanding the game and increasing the fertility of his land. The concentration of benefits and costs on owners creates incentives to utilize resources more efficiently.'[85]

---

[82] The economic idea of efficiency is construed in one of two ways: Pareto efficiency and Kaldor-Hicks efficiency. A situation is said to be Pareto optimal if it is impossible to change it without making at least one person believe he is worse off than before the change. Thus, under this principle, an allocation of resources will be Pareto optimal if any other different system of allocation makes one person better off but only to the cost of another. A situation may be superior if a change produces a gain in one person but not at the expense of anyone else; in other words, one person is better off and no one else is affected in terms of loss. The difficulty with the Pareto standard applies when there are no losers; however, most rules and social policies produce both winners and losers. The Kaldor-Hicks test gets round this problem by allowing a situation to be optimal or efficient if someone is made better off by a change but losers are fully compensated for their loss. Thus, an allocation of resources will be efficient where those who lose as a result of the allocation are fully compensated. See J.L. Coleman, 'The Economic Analysis of Law' in J.R. Penncock and J.W. Chapman (eds), *Nomos XXIV: Ethics, Economics, and the Law* (1982) at pp 83–103.

[83] H. Demsetz, 'Towards a Theory of Private Property Rights' (1967) 57 American Economic Review: Proceedings and Papers.

[84] *Ibid*, at p 348.

[85] *Ibid*, at p 356.

4

CLASSIFICATION
OF PROPERTY

THE NEED FOR AND MEANS OF CLASSIFICATION

In Chapter 2 the idea of property as a right held by an individual in or over external things was examined. The idea of property consisted of an enforceable claim to a thing. However, property was not just a mere right in relation to a thing; it was better explained as constituting a bundle of rights. This simply means that a holder of a proprietary right has a number of rights and duties, liberties and powers enforceable against other individuals in respect of the external object in question. The most basic proprietary right an individual can have in a thing is the right of ownership;[1] it is, however, one of many proprietary rights that the law recognises.[2] This chapter examines the manner in which the English legal system classifies property rights.

The need for a rational system of classification of property is important for a number of reasons. First, many external objects such as land can sustain multifunctional property rights at the same time. In this respect, a system of classification of property is important in that it allows one to determine exactly what right a person has at any given time. Second, classification is important for the very fact that the types of resources or things in which people can have property rights are many and diverse in nature. Land is permanent in nature and indestructible and to be enjoyed by future generations. Other resources, such as cars, the contents of my house and so forth, are less permanent in nature. The question is whether the nature of a particular resource should say something about the manner in which a property right is classified. The English legal system, like other systems of law, makes a fundamental distinction

---

[1] The idea of ownership in property law is considered in more detail in Chapter 6.
[2] The use of the word 'law' is here used in the broad sense to include law and equity.

ₗween rights in land and rights in everything other than land. The third reason for the need for a system of classification of property turns to the question of enforceability. The law makes a fundamental distinction between rights that are recognised at law and those which are recognised in equity. A system of classification in respect of the enforceability viewpoint will help to determine the relative strength of one right as compared to another.

If classification is important, how does property law seek to classify property rights? The legal system does not provide a prescribed method by which property rights should be classified; instead, property rights have come to be classified through other criteria. These criteria have developed implicitly and look to the dominant factors that have influenced the development of property law. Jurists have attempted to classify property rights by looking to a number of factors that make certain property rights different from other property rights. The factors which jurists have looked to are first, the nature of the object in question, second, the sphere of enforceability of the property right in question, and finally, the function performed by the proprietary right in question. By looking at these factors, rights of property become classified in accordance with some rational criterion.

CLASSIFICATION ACCORDING TO THE NATURE OF THE OBJECT

Like most legal systems, English law makes a fundamental distinction between land on one side and everything other than land on the other. Rights in land are collectively referred to as real property, whilst rights in everything else are referred to as personal property. The distinction is also often said to be with rights in immovables (land) and movables. The basis of the distinction between rights in land and rights in things other than land turns primarily to historical factors. It is often said that land should be kept apart from other resources because of its very nature.[3] Land is permanent, it is indestructible, and it can serve the needs of future generations whilst at the same time serve a multitude of purposes. Moreover, land has a very important value attached to it. Despite these characteristics, this alone does not provide any justification as to why land and rights therein should be treated separately from other things. To say that one object such as land should remain the only important resource in society fails to recognise that the idea of property is not constant but is very dynamic. Land may have been an important asset in times gone by; however, other things in which property rights are capable of existing have superseded its relative exchange and use value.[4]

---

[3] Lawson and Rudden, *The Law of Property* (2nd edn, 1982), p 19.

[4] The idea of use and exchange value is examined in more detail in Chapter 5; however, the things to which people look for their security, liberty and ability to generate value are more diverse than land itself.

The historical factor, which does explain the distinction between real property and personal property, is one relating to procedure rather than the nature of the object itself. The procedure is that of the Middle Ages relating to the recovery of a thing in the event of loss or interference with the thing itself. In the event of a person being dispossessed of his land, the common law allowed the rightful owner of the land to bring a real action to recover his land.[5] A real action is described by one commentator as, '... an action which gives a right of recovery ... in the sense that the 'res' (or interest) can be recovered.'[6] In the case of land the common law courts would order the return of the land itself to the rightful owner. A real action is therefore restitutionary in character.[7] In the event of loss or interference with anything other than land, the right to the return of the thing was not as of right, but rather the defendant being personally liable to pay damages for the loss suffered by the plaintiff. It was not until 1854 that the '*res*' or thing forming the basis of personal property law could be recovered.[8] In this respect all property to which a personal action could be brought was termed personal property. What one can say for generalisation purposes is that in the event of loss of a thing, where a remedy of recovery as of right existed, such thing belonged to the realms of real property. Where the remedy of recovery was not as of right, the thing that had been lost belonged to the realms of personal property. The distinction between real and personal property is, therefore, historical. However, even today, whilst the common law recognises the right to the return of a chattel or good, such restitutionary relief is only available if the good in question is capable of being returned and even then it is at the discretion of the court.[9]

The view that rights in land are referred to as real property needs some qualification. The common law in the Middle Ages only recognised certain real actions, and despite the fact that there may be an interest in land, it could so happen that a real action did not exist. Perhaps the most obvious – and often difficult to understand – example is that of a lease. According to the common law procedure, a lease could not be recovered by a real action because real actions were only available in respect of freehold property. Thus, where someone other than the landlord dispossessed a tenant of his lease, he was entitled to compensation as opposed to the return of the land in the form of restitutionary relief. One of the reasons for this was that a lease was viewed by the law as a commercial transaction rather than as part of the feudal system pertaining to

---

[5] See Holdsworth, *A History of English Law*, Vol II, at p 3.

[6] See D.C. Jackson, *Principles of Property Law* (1967) at p 24.

[7] A restitutionary remedy is one that deprives the defendant of benefits which have been received in circumstances that make it improper for the defendant to retain the thing or benefit in question. The function of a restitutionary remedy is to restore the plaintiff to the position he or she was in before the wrongful acts of the defendant. See generally, P. Birks, *An Introduction to the Law of Restitution* (1994).

[8] Common Law Procedure Act 1854, s 78.

[9] Torts (Interference with Goods) Act 1977, s 3.

land.[10] It was not until the fifteenth century that the common law recognised the right to recovery of a lease following dispossession. It is because of this factor that a lease is still classified as personal property in the form of chattels real. The classification, however, is totally unsuitable today because a lease is firmly recognized as an estate in land by the Law of Property Act 1925. Indeed, the idea of a lease as a time in land is wholly consistent with the idea of an estate in land.

Given that some of the historical factors explaining the distinction between real and personal property have lost some of their justificatory force, what then is the significance of the distinction between real and personal property? At one time the idea of real actions and the recovery of the '*res*' or thing was regarded as paramount in distinguishing real and personal property. However, other factors contributed to the making of the distinction between the two types of property rights. One significant factor was the rule relating to succession and the transfer of property on death. In the case of real property, the rule of intestacy was that all land passed to the heir at law who was usually the oldest son. In the case of personal property, all property of this nature vested in the personal representatives who were obliged to distribute the property in accordance with the Statute of Distributions 1670. This, however, is no longer the case and the rules of intestacy are now the same for both real and personal property.[11] Despite this, there appear to be some factors that continue to suggest that the distinction between real and personal property should be firmly made. In the first place, the types of interests which are capable of existing at law in land are much more diverse than is the case with personal property. Personal property recognises absolute ownership; the next thing to this is possession and the very fact of possession makes it difficult for numerous concurrent rights in the same piece of personal property to exist. Second, the formalities required for the transfer and creation of rights in real property are very different from the formalities required for personal property.[12]

REAL PROPERTY

Historical foundations

The idea of real property consists of proprietary rights in land. The law of real property governs the rights and liabilities of persons who have such rights in land. The law is also concerned with the manner in which such rights are created and transferred. There is no doubt that the law of real property is a difficult branch of property law. The difficulty stems from the

---

[10] D.C. Jackson, *op cit*, p 25.

[11] Administration of Estates Act 1925. The rules of succession are briefly examined in Chapter 8.

[12] See Chapter 8.

very nature of land, which, unlike other resources in which property rights can exist, is unique in nature. Another reason for the inherent complexity in the modern law is that the law itself is deeply rooted in historical concepts and principles. Despite the fact that we live in the twenty-first century, the law of modern real property has its roots in concepts dating back to the Middle Ages and beyond. In this respect it is almost impossible to have any sensible discussion of real property law without first looking at its historical origins. One leading real property law commentator writes, 'it remains true that the law of today is heavily impressed with the form of ancient legal and intellectual constructs ... English law cannot be understood except in light of its history and it is in the doctrines relating to tenures and estates that the historical roots of English land law are to be found.'[13]

Fundamental to an understanding of the modern law are the doctrines of estates and tenure. It is not intended to revise a detailed history of such doctrines; such an exercise is not within the scope of this book.[14] Rather, the inquiry here is into the manner in which these doctrines have influenced the modern law. Where does one begin to explain the constituent elements of real property law with respect to historical doctrines? In an attempt to start defining the types of proprietary rights capable of existing in law, a law tutor once told his students that all land in England belongs to the Crown. On hearing this statement, one student asked, 'what, then, can people have in the land when everything belongs to the Crown?' It is often this sort of dialogue that seeks to set in motion a discussion which eventually leads to a number of conclusions about real property law. First, it confirms the idea of property in land as a legal right as opposed to property being a factual state of affairs such as absolute control of a thing. Second, it explains that real property consists of carefully defined estates and interests in land, such estates and interests being legally protected rights as opposed to tangible concepts.

The basis of the modern law of real property goes back to 1066 when the King acquired the radical title to all land in the country.[15] Even today, the principle, albeit artificial in nature, is that all land ultimately belongs to the Crown. The radical title of the Crown in the modern law has been described as '... a brute emanation of the sovereign power acquired through physical conquest. It denotes the political authority of the Crown both to grant interests in the land to be held of the Crown and also to prescribe the residue of unalienated land as the sovereign's beneficial demesne. The Crown's radical title is, in truth, no proprietary title at all, but merely an expression of the *Realpolitik* which served historically to hold together the

---

[13] K.Gray, *Elements of Land Law* (2nd edn, 1993) at p 51, (3rd edn published 2001).

[14] See generally, A.W.B. Simpson, *A History of the Land Law* (2nd edn, 1986).

[15] See, F. Barlow, *The Feudal Kingdom of England 1042–1216* (4th edn, 1988).

theory of tenure'.[16] Under the concept of feudal tenure, the Crown's radical title served as a means by which smaller rights of ownership could vest in other persons. These smaller rights were not absolute ownership but instead limited forms of ownership. The principle of feudal tenure worked on the basis that the Crown grants possession of land for a defined period of time in return for services of some kind.[17]

Initially the King could grant land to a lord in return for services of a military nature. The lord was regarded as the tenant of the Crown and in this respect held land from the Crown. The relationship between the Crown and the lord was one of tenure and the period for which the lord held the land was determined by the estate vested in him. The idea of the estate was a time in the land rather than a physical piece of land given to the lord. The doctrine of tenure allowed the lord to grant smaller estates to other people, a process called subinfeudation, in return for services. The net effect of the process of subinfeudation was that a pyramidal structure of land holding emerged with the King at the top of the pyramid and smaller, less powerful landowners at the bottom. Each person, apart from the King, held land for defined periods of time.[18] This pyramid structure of land holding was characterised by land being vested in powerful lords, the rest of the ordinary population being condemned to serfdom and being answerable to the lord who had been granted the land.[19]

The types of services rendered in return for the grant of land were determined by the type of tenure in question. The feudal doctrine of tenure recognised two main types of tenures, namely free tenure and unfree tenure. Free tenure was grants of land from the Crown in return for services of three main types. These were tenures in chivalry, which were grants of land in return for military services, tenures in socage, which were grants of land in return for agricultural services, and finally, spiritual tenures involving land in return for religious services. Unfree tenures were grants of land by a lord to the common labourer. Such tenures did not in fact give any possession to the labourer, instead the possession or 'seisin' being vested in the lord. The nature of the services to be rendered in return for land in unfree tenures varied according to the requirements of the lord. There were two main characteristics of this type of tenure. In the first place there was the doctrine of escheat, which simply meant

---

[16] K.Gray and S.F. Gray, 'The Idea of Property in Land' in Bright and Dewar (eds), *Land Law: Themes and Perspectives* (1988) at p 28.

[17] For a detailed examination of feudal tenure, see K. Gray, *Elements of Land Law* (1993) Chap 3, (3rd edn published 2001); also R. Megarry and M.P. Thompson, *Megarry's Manual of the Law of Real Property* (1993) at pp 19–23.

[18] See, S.E. Thorne, 'English Feudalism & Estates in Land' [1958] CLJ 195.

[19] It was in this context that one of the more important concepts of property law, the trust, was given birth to: see Chapter 7.

that if a person committed a felony he would lose his land to the superior lord. Second, if a tenant died without heirs, the land would vest back into the superior lord. Wealth in the form was thus concentrated at the top of the pyramidal ladder. Going down this ladder, the time for which each person held the land decreased since no superior tenant could grant a time in the land greater than the one already vested in him. The striking point from this idea of land holding was that no person had any absolute ownership or dominium in the land. Ownership that ultimately vested in the Crown could be said to have been fragmented amongst a number of people by the element of time and space. It is this idea of fragmentation that still plays an important role in property law and seeks to explain the idea of multiple rights capable of existing in land at the same time amongst more than one person.[20]

Whilst the doctrine of tenures explained the manner in which land could be acquired, the companion doctrine of estates explained the length of time for which the land had been vested in the tenant. The idea of an estate was simply time in the land as opposed to a physical abstract entity. Unlike the doctrine of tenures, the doctrine of estates still plays a fundamental role in the modern law of real property. The concept of the estate seeks to explain what a person can acquire in land if all land ultimately belongs to the Crown. The idea of an estate in land was explained in one sixteenth-century case in the following manner: '... the land itself is one thing, and the estate another thing, for an estate in the land is a time in the land, or land for a time, and there are diversities of estates, which are no more than diversities of time...'.[21]

Three main types of estate were dominant in the feudal system of land holding. The most common and basic estate was the estate in fee simple which was a grant of a land without an ending. In other words, a time in the land without an ending. The Crown was still the ultimate owner of the land but the tenant's occupation of the land or his seisin was not limited by time. In this respect, a fee simple estate is tantamount to absolute ownership. Indeed, the fee simple estate today is the ultimate right one can have in land and being vested in such an estate is conclusive of absolute ownership (or anything near it) in English law. The second type of estate recognised by the law was something called a fee tail or an entailed interest. Such an estate served the function of tying up land within the family because the duration for which land was held under such an estate was the lifetime of the original grantee and his linear descendants. The word tail was derived from the French expression *taillé*, which means to cut down; the cut down aspect being that land could only pass to direct descendants of the original grantee. Such an estate was rather controversial in that it conflicted with one of the fundamental axioms of property law – that land

---

[20] Fragmentation of ownership is considered in depth in Chapter 7.
[21] *Walsingham's Case* (1573) 2 Plowd 547 at 555, 75 ER 805 at 816.

should be freely alienable.[22] The final type of estate recognised at law was the life estate, which simply was a grant of land for the life of the tenant, the tenant in possession referred to as a life tenant and land being given to another (a remainderman) after his or her death.

In light of these historical principles and doctrines the modern law of real property places a heavy reliance on the doctrine of estates rather than the doctrine of tenures. Whilst the doctrine of tenures was capable of explaining a feudal system of land holding, with the passing of time such a mode of acquiring land became both impracticable and unsatisfactory. The main problem with the doctrine of tenures was the excessive subinfeudation that resulted from the system. Rather than create new tenures by subinfeudation, the practice of substituting one tenant for another was more practicable. The Statute Quia Emptores 1290 prevented subinfeudation and only the Crown could grant new tenures. The Tenures Abolition Act 1660 furthered the demise of tenures by transferring all tenures into free tenures of socage or simply freehold tenure. The modern day position is that, whilst it may be said that land is held of the Crown, the type of tenure which forms the basis of land holding is freehold tenure. It is worth noting here that the most modern form of tenure is that called a lease. Even though a lease did not find any space in the feudal doctrine of tenure, it is the clearest example of tenure in modern law. In contrast to the doctrine of tenures, the doctrine of estates still plays a pivotal role in the modern law of real property. The concept of time in the land is a powerful device that explains the ability of multiple rights to co-exist in land at the same time. The doctrine also seeks to explain the idea of property as a right rather than a physical abstract entity. What has changed is the type of estates capable of existing in law. The only legal estates capable of existing in law are the freehold and leasehold; all other estates must exist in equity behind a trust.[23]

The modern law: estates and interests in land

The modern day analysis of proprietary rights in land starts with section 1 of the Law of Property Act 1925 which attempts to list the types of proprietary rights capable of existing in land. The section draws a sharp distinction between four main concepts. In the first place it seeks to draw a distinction between estates and interests in land. Second, it seeks to distinguish between rights at

---

[22] In order to get round this problem, the common law allowed entails to be converted into a fee simple by a process called barring the entail: see Megarry and Thompson, *op cit*, at pp 40–42. It is not intended to discuss the entail in much depth in this book since in contemporary law such an interest has lost most of its significance. After 1925 such an interest was no longer an estate but one that could only exist behind a trust in equity; and after 1996, the Trusts of Land and Appointment of Trustees Act 1996 prohibited the creation of any new entails.

[23] The most obvious example is now a life estate, since (after 1996) the entailed interest is now prohibited.

law and rights in equity. The latter distinction is discussed in the next section; beforehand, consideration of the modern day position regarding estates and interests that can be created in law.

Section 1 of the Law of Property Act 1925 recognises two main types of estate capable of existing in law. The first estate is that called a *fee simple absolute in possession*. This is the largest estate that is capable of existing in the common law and, given the fact that it amounts to an indefinite period in the land, having been granted with a fee simple, is tantamount to having absolute ownership. The idea of a fee simple absolute in possession is therefore perpetual; the estate can be transferred inter-vivos, in which case the new owner simply steps into the shoes of the outgoing owner. In the event of the death of the estate owner, the estate vests in personal representatives of the deceased and the estate passes in accordance with the will of the deceased or the intestacy rules.[24] The meaning of the words fee simple absolute in possession are relatively simple. The use of the word 'fee' denotes that the estate is one that is capable of being inherited. The incorporation of the words 'absolute' and 'in possession' seeks to explain that the estate is one that accrues immediately as opposed to some time in the future. The right to enjoyment and possession is immediate.[25] It is important to note here that a person retains a fee simple absolute in possession even though he or she may have granted a lease to a tenant. The reason for this is that incidence of immediate enjoyment has not theoretically been take away from the estate owner who has voluntarily granted a term of years to another. The fee simple owner has the right to the receipt of rents and profits for the duration of the lease. The use of the word 'absolute' is specially included to explain that the estate is not cut down in any way and that it does have the characteristic of perpetuity.

The fee simple absolute in possession is the only fee simple estate capable of existing in the common law after 1925. There are, of course, cases where a fee simple estate can be modified in one way or another. Before the Law of Property Act 1925 the common law did recognise different types of fee simples existing in law. The reason for this was due to the very nature of the idea of estates, which allowed the co-existence of many estates in the same piece of land. The first example is the case where A grants to B a fee simple for the life of B and thereafter to C. The estate conferred upon B would be an estate in possession but not absolute since it was cut down by the life of B. This is called a life interest where B would be termed a life tenant and C as a remainderman. The obvious reason for this type of land holding arrangement would be, for example, to give land to one child followed by another. Although this type of land holding has lost its attraction in an age where family solidarity has

---

[24] See Chapter 9.
[25] See *Pearson v IRC* [1981] AC 753 at 775, *per* Viscount Dilhorne.

decreased,[26] it nevertheless provided an example of a lesser fee simple than an absolute fee simple in possession.[27]

Another way in which a fee simple can be modified is by allowing it to retain its characteristic of absoluteness – that is, being principally perpetual in nature; however, restricting the possession entitled thereunder. The principal way in which this can be done is by referring to an event that might or might not happen, and one that will determine the fee simple and vest it elsewhere. For example, A can grant a fee simple to B until such time as C qualifies as a doctor. The event here is one that might or might not occur, so whilst the fee simple is principally perpetual in nature, it can be cut down by the determinable event. A determinable fee simple is to be contrasted with a conditional fee simple, which is essentially a fee simple controlled by a condition precedent or a condition subsequent. An example of such a fee simple is where A grants a fee simple to B provided B qualifies as a doctor. This is a fee which is again principally perpetual in nature, but possession and enjoyment are delayed until the satisfaction of the condition precedent. Another example is where A grants a fee simple to B provided B does not qualify as a doctor, in this case a condition subsequent – that is, not qualifying as a doctor will operate to forfeit the interest of B.[28] The task of deciding whether a determinable fee or a conditional fee has been created is very difficult in practice. There is a very fine line between the two and the matter is essentially one of construction.[29]

The majority of the modified estates mentioned above are incapable of existing in the common law today.[30] Such estates are deemed as interests existing in equity behind the concept of a trust. The idea of the trust is considered in Chapter 7; it is sufficient to say here that the trust allows these types of estate to co-exist with the fee simple through law and equity.[31] One rather strange situation in real property law is that a conditional fee simple is capable of existing in the common law by virtue of the Law of Property Act 1925.[32]

---

[26] See generally Chapter 10.

[27] This type of land holding usually existed behind a strict settlement governed by the Settled Land Act 1925; however, since the Trusts of Land and Appointment of Trustees Act 1996 such settlements are no longer permitted and any such land holding must exist behind a trust of land. It is not intended to examine life interests in depth in this book partly because of their decreasing importance in real property law.

[28] The types of conditions that may be inserted in a conditional fee vary in nature. What is important to note here is that such conditions are subject to control by the courts, which will strike down conditions which are illegal, contrary to public policy or are otherwise capricious. See K. Gray, *Elements of Land Law* (1993), pp 89–92, (3rd edn published 2001).

[29] The idea and differences between conditions subsequent and precedent and the determinable interests are discussed in Megarry and Thompson, *Megarry's Manual of the Law of Real Property* (1993) at pp 34–39.

[30] Law of Property Act, s 1.

[31] The obvious advantage of this is from a conveyancing point of view, where a purchaser need only deal with one legal title, equitable interests being protected through the system of registration. These matters are explored in more depth in Chapter 6.

[32] Law of Property Act 1925, s 7(1). Section 7 holds that all fee simple grants that have rights of re-entry should be regarded as fee simple absolute estates, and given the fact that a conditional fee will by its very nature have a right of entry in the event of the forfeiting condition, such conditional fees simple are thus legal.

The only other estate capable of existing in law is the *term of years absolute*, otherwise commonly known as a leasehold estate.[33] The idea of a lease as an estate in land did not originate from feudal doctrines of estates and tenures. The concept was instead part of personal property law which viewed a lease as a commercial transaction, the breach of which gives rise to a personal remedy as opposed to a real one. However, given the fact that a lease represents no more than a time in the land, that is a term of years, it is difficult to set it aside from the idea of estate ownership.[34] Moreover, the fact that it represents land holding based on a landlord and tenant relationship, it is perhaps in modern times the only realistic form of tenure. The term of years absolute is a concept employed to utilise land for a variety of reasons. The most important of these are the provision of residential occupation and the provision of land for commercial purposes. The idea behind the term of years absolute is the grant of occupation and enjoyment of land for a fixed period of time. The use of the word absolute in the words 'term of years absolute' is not the same as in the context of a fee simple absolute in possession. In the case of a lease it simply means that the maximum duration of the lease is fixed in years.[35] One of the essential requirements of a term of years is that the tenant be granted exclusive possession of the land forming the subject-matter of the lease.[36] This means that the tenant must have the right to exclude others, including the landlord, from the land for the entire duration of the lease. Like a freehold estate, a lease is capable of being transferred to another person. The process is one of assignment of the term of years, which is to be distinguished from a subletting of the lease which is another lease carved out of the head lease.

Section 1 of the Law of Property Act 1925 also deals with interests in land. Interests in land are the other type of proprietary rights capable of existing in land. Whilst an estate grants some form of ownership in land, an interest confers no absolute ownership in the land. The idea of an interest in land is a right over some other person's land which seeks to draw some advantage from that other person's land. In this sense, an interest is usually a

---

[33] Law of Property Act 1925, s 1(1)(b).

[34] A lease is both a contract and an estate in land; it is because a lease lies between contract and property that it often becomes a difficult and controversial matter as to whether a lease is governed by principles of contract law or by property. These difficulties present themselves to the courts in many manifestations: for example, see the recent complexities presented to the House of Lords in *Bruton* v *London & Quadrant Housing Trust* [1999] 3 WLR 150. This matter is discussed in Chapter 10.

[35] See P. Sparkes, *A New Land* (1999) at p 392.

[36] *Street* v *Mountford* [1985] AC 809. The requirement of exclusive possession is indeed the main indicia of whether a lease has been granted. It often happens that in substance a lease may have been created but the landlord may seek to negate that lease through pretence or a sham in order to avoid certain landlord and tenant legislation. Where this happens the courts will look to see whether in substance exclusive possession has been granted so as to find a tenancy in the face of pretence or a sham: see *Aslan* v *Murphy* (No 1) [1990] 1 WLR 766; see Chapter 10.

ᵣₓght in or over an estate such as freehold or leasehold. An interest may be seen as conferring some aspect of the estate owner's ownership to another person enabling that other person – that is the holder of the interest – to take advantage of the right given to him. The matter is perhaps best explained with specific examples. The Law of Property Act recognises, amongst others, the following legal interests capable of existing in land. The first one identified is called an easement,[37] which is effectively a right to utilise another person's land. The best examples of easements are rights of way, rights to light and rights to water. The basic idea behind an easement is that a right is annexed to one piece of land, usually called the dominant land, which allows the holder of that right to make use of land belonging to another, called the servient land. The function of an easement is not to give any personal benefit to the grantee of an easement; rather, the purpose is one which relates to the better use of the dominant land. It is often said that the easement must accommodate the dominant land, which is no more than saying that the easement must benefit the land to which it is annexed.[38]

Another type of interest recognised and capable of existing in land is a rentcharge.[39] A rentcharge is a charge on the land entitling the holder of the charge to a specified sum to be paid periodically. A rentcharge is an interest existing independently from a lease; in other words, the holder of a rentcharge owes no rights or duties to the person who has created the charge. A landlord who collects rents from a tenant owes his tenant duties in relation to the land that is the subject-matter of the lease. A rentcharge simply entitles the holder to money without any correlative obligations. Rentcharges are uncommon in modern property law, and since the Rentcharges Act 1977, no new forms of rentcharges are capable of being created.[40] A typical example of a rentcharge is where a person charges his own land with a payment of £500 in favour of another person. Initially the function of a rentcharge was to facilitate the transfer of land to another where the purchaser could not make full payment of the purchase price. In this instance a purchaser could buy the land and create a rentcharge in favour of the vendor to facilitate the full payment of the price. The demise of rentcharges was facilitated by the growth of mortgage finance and any remaining rentcharges have now only nominal values as a result of inflationary pressures.

A common legal interest in land is a mortgage; it is a security interest which gives the mortgagee a charge on the mortgagor's land.[41] Mortgages have been an important mechanism for the purchase of residential occupa-

---

[37] The section actually states 'easement, rights and privileges'.
[38] See *Re Ellenborough Park* [1956] Ch 131 and also *Keppel v Bailey* (1834) 2 My & K 517. For an example of a purely personal benefit, see *Hill v Tupper* (1863) 2 H & C 121, ER.
[39] Law of Property Act 1925, s 1(2)(b).
[40] Rentcharges Act 1977, s 2(1).
[41] Law of Property Act 1925, s 1(2)(c).

tion and commercial activity. The advantages of a mortgage are that a lender can advance money to a borrower and obtain security which will enable him to recover the monies in the event of the insolvency of the borrower. From the point of view of the borrower, he remains the owner of the property and has a contractual obligation to pay the borrowed money. In modern property law, the most typical way of creating a mortgage over land belonging to another is by way of legal charge.[42] This is a charge made by deed which is expressed to be by way of legal mortgage. The advantage of a charge by way of mortgage is that the charge acts as a conveyance of a legal interest in the land with provision for redemption.[43] In other words, the borrower (the mortgagor) transfers some aspect of his ownership to the lender (the mortgagee) with a right to redeem that aspect of ownership on full payment of the mortgage monies. The effect of a charge is to give the mortgagee the same protection as he would have if he were vested with a lease for 3,000 years. Since the mortgagee is theoretically the tenant of the land, it has the right to possession that becomes important on default by the mortgagor. The right to possession is a step towards selling the property and realising the monies lent under the mortgage.

PERSONAL PROPERTY

Nature of personal property and relative conceptual underdevelopment

Unlike real property law, personal property has not been rooted in historical doctrines and principles. Rights in movables have never been subjected to the doctrines of tenure and estate simply because of the nature of movables, which, unlike land, are destructible, generally not of a permanent nature and usually incapable of serving the needs of multiple users at the same time. Proprietary rights in movables are relatively less complex in structure; the law recognises only two types of proprietary rights in or over movables, namely, ownership and possession.

It is often said that personal property is 'conceptually underdeveloped'[44] and the reasons for this appear to be the lack of historical influences on the law and also the fact that proprietary rights in movables have not been subject to rigorous theoretical doctrine until recent times. In this respect, Sir

---

[42] *Ibid*, s 87.

[43] It is important to understand that the matter is essentially one of substance. Whilst a mortgage in strict terms requires conveyance of the subject-matter of the mortgage to the mortgagee, a charge does not actually vest any ownership in the chargee. It is, however, difficult to maintain any real distinction between a charge and a mortgage since the vesting of rights and powers in the chargee equivalent to those of a tenant under a 3,000-year lease is similar to giving ownership to a mortgagor.

[44] M. Bridge, *Personal Property Law* (2nd edn, 1996), p 11.

William Holdsworth, commenting on the history of movable property in
English law, once wrote: 'early law does not trouble itself with complicated
theories as to the nature and meaning of ownership and possession. The law
must have been peacefully administered for many years before the materials
for such theories are collected. In fact the earliest known use of the word
"owner" comes from the year 1340; and the earliest known use of the word
"ownership" from the year 1583.'[45] The same cannot be said for rights in
land. Moreover, much of the history of the law relating to movables does not
indicate that such objects were within the domain of property law. For example, the common law did not recognise a right of recovery of movables as it
did in the case of land. There was no proprietary remedy for wrongful interference with movables; rather the law of tort sought to protect possession by
the award of damages. This procedural distinction still applies in the modern
law save that the courts now have discretion to order delivery of goods back
to the rightful owner.[46]

It is fair to say that personal property – that is, rights in movables – has
never been regarded as a fundamental part of the law of property. Instead,
given the fact that personal property usually, although not always, finds itself
in dealings and transactions of a commercial nature – such as the sale of
goods, negotiable instruments and factoring of debts – discussion of the rules
of personal property is often left to commentaries on commercial law.
Commentators on commercial law sometimes say that '... land is governed
primarily by property law concepts, goods and choses in action by commercial law concepts'.[47] It is also often concluded that due to the procedural
matters relating to recovery, personal property does not represent property in
the true sense because of the lack of a proprietary remedy. Remedies for
interference with movables are personal as opposed to proprietary. This,
however, is not entirely correct.

It is not altogether clear why the ability to recover the thing in question
should be the criterion for deciding whether a right in the thing is proprietary
or personal. Surely in both cases of land and movables, wrongful interference
with rights does avail the holder of the right to a remedy. What differs is not
the presence or absence of a remedy; rather it is the extent of the remedy in
each case. Moreover, to suggest that the mode of recovery alone should
determine the difference between proprietary and personal interests results
in, as explained by Jackson, 'the ridiculous conclusion that so far as any
object other than land is concerned there are no proprietary interests save
where the object of a trust can be followed, for as a court has a discretion in

---

[45] Sir William Holdsworth, *A History of English Law*, Vol II at p 78.
[46] Torts (Interference with Goods) Act 1977, s 3.
[47] R. Goode, *Commercial Law* (1982) at pp 51–52.

any action to recover an interest whether to order delivery or compensation, adopting the criterion of recovery, no such interest can be proprietary.'[48]

In the context of movables the two main legal proprietary rights are ownership and possession. Unlike land, movables consist of a wide diversity of things such as tangible objects and intangible objects. The manner in which personal property has come to be classified is rather different from the way in which property rights in land have been classified. Property rights in land have been defined in the sense of the right itself, that is an estate or an interest. In contrast, personal property has been classified by looking at the type of personal property in question rather than by emphasising the particular right in question. This is understandable in the sense that the types of property right capable of existing in law in personal property are only two: ownership and possession, usually for a limited period of time. By looking at the types of personal property, the law makes a distinction between chattels real and chattels personal. Chattels real consist of leasehold interests in land since, as mentioned above, leases were never subjected to the doctrines of feudal tenure and estates. However, nowadays the Law of Property Act 1925, s 1 includes a lease as an estate in land and, therefore, the idea of chattels real is one which is historical and one which does not carry much importance in the modern law. Chattels personal are those items of personal property which are not chattels real, and thus include everything left once land and leases are removed from the spectrum of things capable of sustaining proprietary rights.

Choses in action and choses in possession

Chattels personal are divided into two main types, depending on whether they are tangible or intangible.[49] Where a thing representing personal property is tangible – such as a car, a book and a pen – it is described as a chose in possession or simply a chattel, the use of the word 'chose' meaning 'a thing'. Where the thing in question is intangible – such as shares in a company, a debt or a copyright in a book – it is described as a chose in action. Sometimes the distinction is said to be between things that are corporeal and things that are incorporeal. A chose in possession is essentially a tangible thing which is capable of being in actual possession. A chose in action refers to those things which are intangible and thus incapable of being in actual possession.

One of the more noticeable features of modern property law is the growth of intangible personal property; in other words, the ever increasing types of intangible things in which proprietary rights are capable of existing. Whilst at

---

[48] D.C. Jackson, *Principles of Property Law* (1967) at p 85.
[49] *Colonial Bank* v *Whinney* (1885) 30 Ch D 261.

one time land was seen as the most prized resource in society, coupled with tangible things of value, modern society places much emphasis on things which are intangible in nature.[50] In this respect, Bridge writes, 'the expansion in modern times of forms of intangible property means that many commercial entities operating in post-manufacturing industries have intangible property rights greater in value than their tangible property.'[51] Choses in action can be broken down into two main types, namely, pure intangibles and documentary intangibles. The best examples of pure intangibles are a debt,[52] copyright and goodwill.[53] Documentary intangibles are documents which are said to embody choses in action. The main idea behind a documentary intangible is that such a document evidences a right to the receipt of something such as money or goods. Furthermore, it not only evidences the right to the receipt of something, but also embodies that right in the document. The consequence of this is that the document not only entitles the holder to demand something, it also allows the holder of the document to transfer the right to another by delivery of the document followed by any necessary indorsement.[54] The best example of a documentary intangible is a bill of exchange, which is described as a negotiable instrument. Such a bill represents a promise to pay by a drawee of the bill a specified sum of money to a payee. The payee can be any person to whom the bill has been delivered.[55]

There are some things forming the subject-matter of personal property which call for special attention. First, there is a group of personal property which is commonly referred to as intellectual property. Intellectual property is often regarded as a third branch of property law alongside real

---

[50] This theme is developed in much more depth in Chapter 5, where the changing nature of property and limits on property are examined.

[51] M. Bridge, *Personal Property Law* (2nd edn, 1996) at p 4.

[52] The idea of a debt as proprietary in nature lies in the fact that it is assignable.

[53] These are examples of legal choses in action which should be distinguished from equitable choses in action. The idea of equity in property law is examined in the next section. However, it is important to note that certain intangible things, which are proprietary in nature, exist only in equity. There are two good examples of equitable choses in action which are essentially equitable in nature: the beneficial interest under a trust, and the interest of a person entitled in the estate of a person who has died. A beneficiary under a trust has an equitable interest in the subject-matter and also a proprietary right to the due administration of the trust. The latter obligation is a chose in action which can be transferred when the equitable interest in the property is transferred to another. In the case of the administration of the deceased person, persons entitled to any interest in the estate have a right to the due administration of the estate; again, this is a chose in action recognised in equity.

[54] See Chapter 9.

[55] Other examples of documentary intangibles include rights under an insurance policy. In international trade arrangements a bill of lading is used as a document obliging the carrier of goods aboard a ship to release them to the lawful holder of the bill of lading. Such a bill of lading is capable of being indorsed in favour of another person (which may be a bank or another purchaser) even when the goods are in transit. The indorsement of the bill is sufficient to transfer the title in the goods. See J. Wilson, *Carriage of Goods by Sea* (2nd edn, 1993) p 143.

and personal property. Intellectual property consists of copyright, patents and trademarks, which are essentially rights in ideas.[56] Patents are rights to technological inventions and designs in mass-produced goods. The basic idea behind a patent is the temporal protection given to a person who is the inventor of a design or an idea.[57] At the heart of the patent system lie two competing problems. The first relates to the fact that a patent gives some degree of monopoly power to the holder of a patent, which in turn does not encourage competitiveness and economic efficiency in the market. However, on the other hand, within property law there are sound justifications for a patent system. The justification for a patent system can be found in most of the justificatory theories of property examined in the previous chapter. From a Lockean point of view, the reward of labour is perfectly compatible with the idea of a patent system. Moreover, from a utilitarian perspective, patents act as a medium for technological advance by providing an incentive to the individual to invent and innovate.[58] Copyright gives protection of a much longer duration than patents to literary, artistic and musical creations. Trademarks are protected against imitation so long as they are used in the course of trade. Intellectual property rights are thus proprietary rights in intangible concepts and therefore choses in action.

The second aspect of personal property which calls for special attention, is money. Money is often classified as either a chose in possession or a chose in action since it has characteristics of both. A coin is a physical tangible object and thus something like a chose in possession. On the other hand, the effective enjoyment of money lies not in its mere possession but by virtue of its exchange value. The concept of exchange is not tangible but intangible. Perhaps more acute is the example of a bank note, which is nothing more than a paper with a promise to pay the specified sum by the Bank of England. However, unlike a bill of exchange, a bank note can be exchanged and its value received from people other than the Bank of England.[59] Title to money passes with delivery to anyone who takes money in good faith. In this respect, one leading commentator on the legal aspect of money writes, '... in law, the quality of money is to be attributed to all chattels which, issued by the authority of the law and denominated with reference to a unit of account, are meant to serve as universal means of exchange in the State of issue.'[60] Money is better classified as negotiable chattels to which title passes by delivery and receipt for consideration in good faith.

---

[56] See W.R. Cornish, *Cases and Materials on Intellectual Property Law* (3rd edn, 1999).

[57] The Patents Act 1977, s 25 gives a 20-year duration for a patent.

[58] See, generally, Taylor and Silberston, *The Economic Impact of the Patent System* (1973).

[59] See *Banque Belge v Hambrouck* [1921] 1 KB 321.

[60] F.A. Mann, *The Legal Aspect of Money* (5th edn, 1992) at p 8.

Choses in action and choses in possession: the basis of the distinction

Whilst the legal system makes a distinction between tangible and intangible personal property in the form of choses in action and choses in possession, what is the rationale behind this? At one level of analysis the basis of the distinction appears to be related to the question of how such property is protected. In other words, how does one maintain ownership in tangible and intangible things? Choses in possession are things which are capable of actual possession. What makes my car mine, or my book mine, is the fact that I continue to exercise control over them. Control is only exercised when I have possession thereof.[61] It is evident from this line of reasoning that tangible things are choses in possession because it is through possession that I assert my ownership against others. On the other hand, intangible property or choses in action, such as a debt, cannot be protected by physical possession. The only way in which ownership rights therein and ultimate entitlement to such things can be asserted is by taking action against the wrongdoer.[62] In one case Chanell J explained that 'a chose in action is a known legal expression used to describe all personal rights of property which can only be claimed or enforced by action and not by taking physical possession.'[63] In an earlier case Lord Blackburn emphasised that the distinction between a chose in action and a chose in possession lay between the type of personal property which could be stolen and that which could not be.[64] In this respect Jackson comments, 'a chose in action could be either "the right to bring an action in respect of" a chose in possession or "that which is sought to recover" if that is itself intangible as, for example, a patent.'[65]

CLASSIFICATION ACCORDING TO THE SPHERE OF ENFORCEABILITY OF THE RIGHT

English law, like many other common law traditions, makes a fundamental distinction between proprietary rights enforceable at law and proprietary rights enforceable in equity. Rights of property that are recognised at law are said to be legal interests; they are also said to be rights *in rem*. In contrast, rights of property recognised and enforced in equity are said to be equitable interests, and generally are said to be rights *in personam*.

---

[61] The idea of possession and actual possession of chattels is considered in Chapter 6.

[62] The early common law did not recognise actions for the recovery of choses in action; the matter was left to equity – see Chapter 9.

[63] [1902] KB 427 at 430.

[64] *Colonial Bank* v *Whinney* (1886) 11 App Cas 426 at 439.

[65] D.C. Jackson, *Principles of Property Law* (1967) at p 29.

Common law

An understanding of the existence of property rights at law and property rights in equity is not sufficient unless one examines some important historical factors shaping modern English law. The origins of the common law go as far back as 1066 when the Norman Conquest introduced a new system of law for England. Towards the end of the thirteenth century two main types of court were responsible for administering law in the country. First there were the local courts, which were courts set up within the feudal structure and administered by the feudal lords. Second, there were the Royal Courts, also known as the Courts of Common Pleas consisting of the King's Bench, Court of Common Pleas and the Exchequer. A litigant who felt that he did not receive justice in the local courts had a right to petition the King and ask for his case to be heard in one of the royal courts. The right to petition the King arose out of the fact that the right to justice was a royal prerogative. Maitland explained that each of the royal courts at one time had a separate sphere of interest but soon the plaintiff had a choice as to which court heard his complaint, since each court began to administer the same law in the same manner.[66] The Exchequer was more than a court of law; it had the responsibility for fiscal matters as well as legal. Alongside the Exchequer was the Chancery department headed by the Chancellor (who was normally a bishop). The Chancery at this stage was not the court of equity that developed much later on, administering equitable principles and doctrines on the basis of unconscionable conduct. Rather, it was a secretarial office answerable to the King's permanent Council. The Chancellor, by way of delegation from the King, dealt with many of the petitions made to the King for justice in individual cases.

The law administered by the medieval courts was partly traditional and partly statute. Traditional law was that based on precedent and it was termed the common law in that it was common to all areas of England and all its subjects.[67] A plaintiff wishing to commence an action in the Court of Common Pleas or the King's Bench needed a royal writ, which was a sealed authorisation to commence proceedings. The office of issuing a writ was given to the Chancellor who had at his disposal a number of established writs, but also had a limited power to invent novel writs. It is important to note that at this point in history the Chancellor did not act in a judicial manner; his role was simply to hear the plaintiff's application and issue the appropriate writ. The grant of a writ did not mean that the plaintiff was

---

[66] F.W. Maitland, *Equity: A Course of Lectures* (J. Brunyate (ed) 1936), p 2.
[67] See, generally, S.F.C. Milsom, *A Historical Foundation of the Common Law* (2nd edn); Holdsworth, *A History of English Law* (7th edn, 1956), Vol I and also J. Baker, *An Introduction to English Legal History* (2nd edn, 1979).

successful, since the courts could quash the writ as being contrary to the law of the land. The power to invent new writs presented a real threat to the feudal lords and barons since new writs meant new remedies, which in turn created new rights and duties. As a result the Provisions of Oxford 1258 disallowed the issuing of new writs without the permission of the King's Council. The result was that a number of new cases requiring new remedies would not be resolved at common law.

Apart from the fact that the common law became unable to redress new legal problems, there was also the fact that the common law lacked appropriate remedies in many cases. The most predominant remedy at common law was, and still is today, the award of monetary damages. Thus, in the case of typical civil wrongs – for example, a breach of contract or the commission of a tort such as negligence – the injured party was entitled to compensation in the form of monetary damages reflecting the loss suffered. Whilst this remedy may be appropriate in many cases of civil wrongs, the award of monetary damages is not always appropriate when there has been interference with proprietary rights. For example, in the case of a trespass to land the award of damages may be appropriate; however, in the case of a persistent trespasser the appropriate remedy would be an injunction restraining the continued commission of the tort. Another example is that of a contract for the sale of a valuable painting. In this case, failure to perform the contract by the vendor results in a breach of contract entitling the plaintiff purchaser to damages. However, given the fact that special significance is attached to the painting in that it is a chattel that is not readily available on the market, the more appropriate remedy here would be the compulsion to perform the contract. The common law does not have a remedy that compels performance of the contract.

Having looked at the idea of common law, what then is the position of proprietary rights in the common law? In the modern law, for most purposes proprietary rights are recognised and enforced in the common law, which is administered by the modern civil courts. The ownership of my house evidenced by legal title – either documentary or in the form of a registered title[68] – is a legal proprietary right recognised by the common law. The same applies to other things over which I have ownership, such as my car, my watch and book, and so forth. Interference with such ownership gives rise to legal remedies such as a common law action for possession in the case of land, or the award of monetary damages for wrongful interference with personal property. An important thing to note about the common law is that it simply looks to questions of form rather than substance. The underlying concern of the common law is not so much with the intentions of the parties to a dispute; rather, the concern is whether the correct form has been complied

---

[68] The idea of title, and in particular registered title to land, is considered in Chapter 6.

with in so far as the dispute in question. In property matters this simply means, for example, in the case of acquisition of a proprietary right, has the correct formality been observed? So in the case of a transfer of ownership in land by way of sale, the common law requires the execution of a contract followed by a conveyance in the form of a deed.[69] Nothing short of this will transfer ownership at common law and it matters not what the conduct of the parties was and what their intentions were.

Equity

Like in many legal systems, proprietary rights can exist in equity as well as in the common law. One of the reasons for the complexity of property law is the fact that similar rights may exist in the same thing, and at the same time, but in two different systems of law – that is, law and equity. This duality of rights in law and equity, whilst imposing some difficulties in the understanding of the spectrum of proprietary rights, does, however, bring into the law of property remarkable flexibility. It allows a number of social and economic needs of the legal system to be met by the recognition of two sets of jurisdictions and the ability of proprietary rights to run side by side therein. Unlike the common law, equity looks to substance as opposed to form; this allows equity to recognise proprietary rights which correspond to legal proprietary rights in their nature – for example, ownership. Thus, whilst there can be legal ownership in a chattel or a piece of land, this does not inhibit the finding of equitable ownership in the same thing. However, equity is much more creative than the common law; there are proprietary rights which do not exist in the common law but only in equity. In other words, there are rights in equity which have no equivalent in the common law. The most celebrated example here is the restrictive covenant from real property law. It is used to restrict the manner in which land can be used and thus performs an important function in the control of the use of land. In the case of personal property the same is true – certain rights in equity have no real equivalent in the common law. It is perhaps more marked in the case of personal property simply because of the limited proprietary rights recognised by the common law.

What is equity and why are property lawyers, perhaps unlike most other lawyers, so concerned with the idea of equity? It is true to say that when compared with many other areas of civil law, such as contract and tort, equity plays a much more significant role in property law. This is not to say that contract lawyers are not concerned with equity; the fact is that property transactions often find themselves governed by equitable principles. English

---

[69] See Chapter 9.

law has a particular history of the development of equity in the Court of Chancery.[70] The idea of a body of rules called equity is not something that is peculiar to English law. Most legal systems, whether common law based or civil law based, have had to entertain notions of equity.[71] So, what then is equity? In the context of law, the word equity is susceptible to more than one meaning. In one sense the word equity means what is fair and just, and in this sense equity is a theme that runs through all legal systems in that all laws should strive for fairness and justice. Another sense of the word is that equity consists of a body of distinct rules which seek to introduce ethical values into the legal norms. In respect of the latter definition, Maine once explained equity to consist of 'a set of legal principles entitled by their intrinsic superiority to supersede the older law.'[72] It is the latter definition that we are concerned with here. The idea of equity as a distinct body of rules and principles founded on different juridical foundations is that body of law which is separate from, yet part of, the legal norms of a legal system.

Equity in English law is that body of rules developed by the Court of Chancery in the medieval ages. The need for a separate court arose from the deficiencies of the common law at this period of time. The common law failed to redress emerging legal problems simply because of the lack of a writ to initiate proceedings, and, even when a writ was obtainable, the lack of an appropriate remedy. It was not simply the fact that a remedy was inappropriate; in many cases a remedy was not forthcoming even though it existed. The principal reason for this was the fact that in many cases rich, powerful people could influence both the courts and the jury – in such cases justice was simply not forthcoming for the weak.

Equity was administered by the Chancellor who, when unable to give an aggrieved person an appropriate writ, could demand that the defendant appear before him to answer the charges made against him. The complainant needing a legal solution to a problem presented a bill to the Chancellor. Having considered the bill, the Chancellor ordered the potential defendant to appear in person before him. The writ, called a *subpoena*, ordered the man to appear upon pain of forfeiting a sum of money, eg *subpoena centum librarum*.[73] This writ was very different from the types of writ available to commence proceedings in the common law courts, since it simply asked the person against whom the complaint was made to answer to the Chancellor the complaints made against him.

---

[70] See, generally, *Snell's Principles of Equity* (28th edn, 1982).
[71] For an excellent discussion, see R.A. Newman, *Equity in the World's Legal Systems: A Comparative Study* (1973).
[72] Sir Henry Sumner Maine, *Ancient Law* (1905) at p 44.
[73] See Maitland, *op cit*, at p 5.

What started out as a mere secretarial office of government answerable to the King's Council, now took on shape as a court administering law. What law did the Chancellor administer? He did not introduce any novelty into the law making process; he did not introduce laws so different in their juridical nature from the ordinary laws of the land. What the Chancellor had recognised was the inability of the common law to grow and meet the social and economic challenges put to the lawmakers of the country. Given the fact that the Chancellor was an ecclesiastic, a man of the Church and learned in civil and canon law, he was ideally situated to deal with legal problems put to him. The basis upon which he exercised his power was on the simple premise of what was right in any given case. The question turned primarily to the merits of every case. If there is any one word that describes how the Chancellor exercised his power to relieve aggrieved parties, that word is conscience. The early court of equity was essentially a court of conscience. The Chancellor decided every case on its merit, not by way of precedent. Given that Chancellors would change from time to time, each Chancellor would exercise greater or lesser power depending on his own notion of justice. In this respect most accounts of equity in English law talk of the length of the Chancellor's foot, which was simply another way of saying that some Chancellors went further in the administration of justice than others.

The idea of conscience being the primary basis of equitable intervention in the court of equity is well explained by Lord Ellesmere in the famous *Earl of Oxford's Case*[74] in 1615, when he said: '...[M]en's actions are so diverse and infinite that it is impossible to make any general law which will aptly meet with every particular and not fail in some circumstances. The office of the Chancellor is to correct men's consciences for fraud, breaches of trust, wrongs and oppression of what nature so ever they be, and so soften and mollify the extremity of the law.' The Chancellor, in administering equitable relief, did so not by interfering with the common law, but rather by asking the defandant to personally appear before him. A judgment was said to be given *in personam*, which is another way of saying that *equity acts in personam*. The idea that *equity acts in personam* is a fundamental maxim of equity. The Chancellor would order the plaintiff to do something; failure to comply would make him liable to imprisonment for contempt of court. The flexibility of the early court of equity was that it was not constrained by precedent and moreover the Chancellor could make a number of orders which were not essentially monetary awards. In the modern day world of remedies the types of equitable remedies emanating from the Court of Chancery include specific performance of an obligation, injunction, rescission and rectification.

---

[74] (1615) 1 Rep Ch 1 at 6.

The types of complaints petitioned to the Chancellor at the initial stage of the development of equity were predominantly property based and centred on the most prized resource at the time, which was land. A few examples of the types of problems presented to the Chancellor can be given to illustrate the development of the Court of Equity as a judicial court in the form of the Court of Chancery.[75] One of the most common complaints brought to the attention of the Lord Chancellor was the abuse of trusts.[76] The predecessor of the modern trust was a use, a concept used to set up a particular form of land holding in the age of feudalism. Thus, A, the holder of an estate in land could put the land upon use for B, appointing trustees (called feoffees). There were a number of reasons for the creation of a use. If A was going on a crusade, then he could put land upon use to someone else to collect the feudal dues. The more important reason for the creation of a use was to avoid feudal dues. Under feudal law, the heir of a deceased was required to pay feudal dues before taking the land belonging to his father. Moreover, a person did not have freedom of testation in this period of time; that is, freehold land could not be devised to designated persons. These problems could be avoided if the land, before the death of the owner of the land, was put upon use for the benefit of the heir or the person whom the deceased wished to take his land after his death. Thus, the legal title to the land would be conveyed to the feoffees for the benefit of another. At common law the feoffee was regarded as the absolute owner, and the persons for whom the land was put on use – called *cestui que use* – had no entitlement at law. However, given that the feoffees had agreed to hold the land for another, their conscience would bind them in equity. The Chancellor would compel the feoffees to recognise the equitable rights of the *cestui que use*.[77]

Another notable example of the intervention of equity in property matters was the protection afforded to a mortgagor. A mortgage is a proprietary right in the form of security over a thing. The common law regarded the agreement to create a mortgage as an ordinary commercial one; however, equity intervened in a number of ways to stop the mortgagee (the lender) getting more out of the transaction than the security for his money.[78] Moreover, equity regarded the right of the mortgagor to get his property back on repayment of the loan as fundamental to the mortgage agreement. This right to the return of the property, termed by equity as the mortgagor's equity of redemp-

---

[75] The dominant types of property problems argued in equity will be considered in more depth below.

[76] The idea of the trust is considered in Chapter 7.

[77] These issues are discussed in more detail in Chapter 7; see, however, Hanbury and Martin, *Modern Equity* (15th edn, 1997) at pp 8–11.

[78] J. Derek Davies, 'Equity in English Law' in R. Newman (ed) *Equity in the World's Legal Systems* (1973) at pp 159–185 provides an excellent account of the development of equity in English law.

tion, prevailed over the contractual provisions purporting to restrict it. The need for equity to intervene in mortgage transactions in the eighteenth and nineteenth centuries was influenced by the inequality of bargaining power between lender and borrower. The typical mortgage transaction at the time was in the form of money raised for a commercial venture or as a last resort for the poor person.[79]

Some equitable maxims and equity acts *in personam*

An important concept, which needs to be appreciated in order to understand the modern day position regarding property rights at law and in equity, is that equity *acts in personam*. As the Court of Chancery began to administer equity doctrines and principles, albeit initially on the premise of conscience, what emerged was a series of principles or maxims on which the Chancellors sought to exercise equitable relief.[80] At the heart of exercising equitable relief was the equitable maxim *equity will not suffer a wrong to be without a remedy*. This simply meant that, where possible, wrongs should be redressed by equity in the form of an appropriate remedy. Thus, even though the common law did not recognise the rights of a beneficiary under a trust (or at that time the rights of the *cestui que use* under a use), equity compelled the trustee to recognise such rights. Again, a contract may be perfectly recognised at common law in that it satisfied all requirements as to form. However, if such a contract had been entered into on grounds of fraud, mistake or undue influence, equity would allow the party influenced by the fraud, mistake or undue influence to escape contractual liability. Unlike the common law, equity could put an end to the contract in the form of rescission.

Another maxim of equity – one which students of law become accustomed to more than any other – is that *he who comes to equity must come with clean hands*. Unlike the common law, which is based on precedent and essentially looks to questions of form, the Chancellors exercised early equity jurisdiction in a discretionary manner. This is still true today: the grant of an equitable remedy is discretionary. The court will look to the conduct of the complainant before a remedy is awarded. If the complainant has himself acted wrongfully in the dispute complained of, equity will generally not assist such a person. The best example given here is that of a lease and the relationship of tenant and landlord. Although a lease is an estate in land, it is also contractual in nature. Any attempt by the landlord to remove the tenant contrary to the terms of the lease agreement amounts to a breach of contract; the

---

[79] See K. Gray, *Elements of Land Law* (2nd edn, 1993) at p 949, (3rd edn published 2001).

[80] A detailed account of these maxims can be found in standard texts on equity: see R. Pearce and J. Stevens, *The Law of Trust and Equitable Obligations* (2nd edn, 1998) at pp 17–24; and also Hanbury and Martin, *Modern Equity* (15th edn, 1997) at pp 25–29.

tenant can ask for specific performance of the lease. However, it is quite clear that equity will not grant such a remedy where the tenant is at fault, for example, by not observing the covenants in the agreement. The wrongful conduct of the complainant must have a direct nexus with the dispute in question in order for the clean hand maxim to apply. In *Argyll (Duchess)* v *Argyll*[81] the fact that the wife's adultery was the sole reason for divorce proceedings did not prevent her from obtaining an injunction stopping her former husband from publishing confidential information.

The most important maxim for our purposes is that *equity acts in personam*. The method by which a Chancellor would seek to redress a legal wrong complained of by a plaintiff was by demanding that the defendant appear before him. The Chancellor would not interfere with the common law rule or judgment awarded by courts administering common law. Instead, the Chancellor would make a decision and enforce it by means of a personal order against the defendant. Thus, where a contract was capable of being performed, the order would be one to perform the contract. Where a trustee refused to recognise a trust, the order was one which compelled the trustee to recognise the trust and the rights of the beneficiary. Failure to comply with the order amounted to a contempt of court, which would lead to imprisonment; thus there was every incentive to comply. What is clearly apparent from the idea of acting *in personam* is that the Chancellor and, therefore, equity did not interfere as such with the property in the hands of the defendant. For example, equity could not say that the beneficiary was the legal owner of the property subject to the trust, but could compel the trustee to recognise such trust and if appropriate transfer the title in the appropriate common law manner so as to make the beneficiary the real owner.[82] The idea of equity acting *in personam* is to be distinguished from the manner in which the common law acts. A judgment of the common law courts is essentially a judgment *in rem* which attaches to the specific *res* or thing in question rather than to a specific person. Thus, the legal ownership of my house is a right *in rem* in that my ownership binds the whole world; the persons who are to respect my ownership are not limited by number.

---

[81] [1967] Ch 302; see also *Tinsley* v *Milligan* [1994] 1 AC 340 where a lesbian partner had joined her co-partner in the purchase of land but did not put herself on the title so that she could make dishonest claims for social security benefits. The House of Lords confirmed that the maximum, *he who comes to equity must come with clean hands*, only applied where the wrongful conduct of the plaintiff was the purpose of setting up her entitlement in the first place. In this case, although there had been wrongful conduct by the plaintiff, her right to an interest in the property purchased was not influenced by the wrongful conduct put before the court.

[82] The Court of Justice of the European Community in *Webb* v *Webb* [1994] QB 696 recognised that equity acting *in personam* was sufficient to give jurisdiction over a person abroad and it made no difference that the order related to property situated abroad. Given the fact that the order related to the person and not the property there was no conflict with the laws of the foreign country regarding ownership of the disputed property. The order simply related to the person and not the property. In *Webb* v *Webb* a son was held to hold a flat in the Antibes on a resulting trust for his father who had paid for the flat but did not take the legal title.

The Judicature Acts 1873 & 1875

The idea of two sets of courts, that is the common law courts ,
of Chancery, gave rise to procedural problems for potential l.
common law courts did not have equity jurisdiction; the Court (
did not have the right to interfere or change a decision given by th   ..non
law courts. If a litigant had no redress at common law he would have to present a bill to the Lord Chancellor for his complaint to be heard in the Court
of Chancery. This was so even where the common law courts acknowledged
that there might be redress in equity; because of their limited jurisdiction,
they could not award an equitable remedy such as injunction. The same was
true of the Court of Chancery, which could not award damages although it
could grant an equitable remedy.[83] This meant the lodging of a new action in
a separate court.[84] However, it was not just the problem of procedure itself;
by the nineteenth century the work of the Court of Chancery had increased
considerably and this inevitably resulted in numerous delays. The famous
Judicature Acts of 1873 and 1875 overcame this problem by restructuring
the court system in England. The Acts had the effect of abolishing the old
courts and establishing one unified single court, the Supreme Court, which
was divided into a number of divisions. Initially these divisions were the
Court of Chancery, King's Bench, Common Pleas, Exchequer, Probate and
the Court of Admiralty. The Supreme Court could administer law and equity
at the same time.

The modern position is re-enacted in the Supreme Court Act 1981,[85]
which divides the Supreme Court into the Court of Appeal and the High
Court, the High Court consisting of the Queen's Bench, Chancery and Family
Divisions. These divisions are to administer law and equity together; where
there is a conflict between law and equity, the rules of equity are to prevail.[86]
The relationship between law and equity in light of the Judicature Acts is
best explained with the concept of a lease. A lease which has a duration
exceeding three years needs to be created by deed.[87] Failure to comply with
the requirement of a deed has the effect that no legal lease is created since no
legal estate has been created in the tenant. At most, where the landlord pur-
ports to act inconsistently with the terms of the lease, the purported tenant

---

[83] F.W. Maitland, *Equity: A Course of Lectures* (J. Brunyate (ed) 1936), pp 14–15.
[84] There were limited reforms in the form of the Common Law Procedure Act 1854 which gave
the common law courts power to grant equitable remedies. The Chancery Amendment Act 1858
gave power to the Court of Chancery to award damages.
[85] s 49 (1).
[86] The rule that equity prevailed over the common law was found in s 25(11) of the Supreme
Court of Judicature Act 1873.
[87] Law of Property Act 1925, s 52. See Chapter 8, which deals with the issue of acquisition of
proprietary rights.

...y has a right to damages for breach of contract. However, given the fact that a lease is a contract, where all the other requirements of the lease have been met, there seems to be no reason why equity should not intervene to compel performance of the lease. After all, as a matter of substance, as opposed to form, a lease has been granted. Equity has long recognised that a lease, which failed for formality at common law, could take effect in equity as a contract to grant a lease. Although it was not a legal lease, the contract to grant a lease was for all practical purposes a lease taking effect in equity. Equity could compel the purported landlord to perform his obligation to grant the lease by means of a decree of specific performance.[88] Until such time of a decree of specific performance equity recognised the lease in equity on the maxim that *equity regards that as done which ought to be done*.[89] Thus, the substantive lease, which was purported to be created in law, would be recognised in equity. In this respect one can see the reason for the intervention of equity in the case of a lease which fails on grounds of formality.

Recognition of the lease in equity did not mean that the tenant was vested with a legal estate. At common law, the lease would still be merely contractual in nature, unless it could be construed as a different lease – for example, one not requiring formalities in the nature of a deed. Where the tenant, pursuant to a long lease,[90] moves into possession of the land, he may well be construed at common law as a periodic tenant under a periodic tenancy. This is particularly so in the case where a tenant is paying a periodic rent, that is, month to month or quarter to quarter. A periodic tenancy needs no formality even though it may continue for a long period of time.[91] Thus, a periodic tenancy can be created at law even though the intentions of the parties were to create a longer lease.[92] It is at this point in the example that one can see the potential conflict between law and equity. What is the position where a long lease fails at common law but is recognised in equity, and at common law the long lease is construed as a legal periodic tenancy? In other words, which one takes supremacy in the event of a dispute?

The matter is both shown and resolved in the famous case of *Walsh* v *Lonsdale*,[93] which preserves the supremacy of equity. On the facts, a landlord had agreed in writing to grant a seven-year lease of a mill to the tenant but failed to grant the lease by deed which was necessary to give it effect at

---

[88] See *Parker* v *Taswell* (1858) 2 De G & J 559.

[89] Recognition of a lease in equity, which fails for formality in law, will today only exist if the lease is in writing, containing all the terms: Law of Property (Miscellaneous Provisions) Act 1989 s 2(1) (see Chapter 8).

[90] Exceeding three years.

[91] See K. Gray, *Elements of Land Law* (2nd edn, 1993) at p 737, (3rd edn published 2001).

[92] *Alder* v *Blackman* [1952] 2 All ER 41.

[93] (1882) 21 Ch D 9.

common law. One of the terms of the lease was that the tenant pay rent in advance. The tenant paid no rent in advance, instead having moved in and paid rent quarterly. The payment of quarterly rent was sufficient to find a legal periodic tenancy in the tenant. When the landlord demanded a year's rent in advance the tenant refused to pay. The landlord sought to exercise the right of distress which entitled him to distrain the tenant's goods in order to meet the rent demanded. The tenant complained that the distress was illegal since the periodic tenancy, which arose at common law, did not contain any provision for payment of rent in advance. The landlord counter argued that the distress was not illegal because it was the seven-year lease, which had a provision for payment of rent in advance, that determined the rights of the landlord and tenant. There was no doubt that the seven-year lease took effect in equity as a contract to grant a lease, whilst at common law there was a mere periodic tenancy. The tenant's action failed since the contract to grant a lease, in other words the equitable lease, prevailed over and above the legal periodic tenancy. The distress by the landlord, pursuant to the terms of the seven-year lease, was therefore not illegal at all but entirely consistent with the terms of that lease.

RELATIVE NATURE OF PROPRIETARY RIGHTS IN LAW AND EQUITY

Once the property lawyer becomes accustomed to the fact that proprietary rights can exist in law and equity, the next line of inquiry is that which deals with the significance of the distinction between rights in law and equity. The common law looks to form and as a result will recognise all property rights that have been created in accordance with the appropriate form. The legal ownership to my house, evidenced by title deeds or, as in contemporary practice, as registered proprietor[94] will suffice to give me a legal right of property. Likewise, the purchase of my watch followed by taking legal possession will give me a legal title to my watch. Equity will intervene to protect and recognise proprietary rights in a number of situations. In particular equity will recognise proprietary rights corresponding to those recognised in law when there has been informality in the creation of such rights at law. Thus a lease that fails for formality at law will nevertheless be recognised in equity. The same applies to the informal creation of mortgages and easements.

Equity is a much broader jurisdiction than one that simply seeks to protect informally created proprietary rights. There are some proprietary rights which are essentially the creation of equity and without a legal equivalent. The most

---

[94] The idea of a registered title to land is considered in detail in Chapter 6.

notable is the concept of the trust; however, others include an estate contract,[95] restrictive covenants and to some extent the mortgage. Although the mortgage may be a legal interest, the nature of a mortgage and the rights and duties of the parties under such a concept have been subject to the rigour of equitable rules alone. Finally, there is the equitable doctrine of estoppel which, when applied in property contexts, can give rise to equitable rights of property.[96]

In Chapter 1 the idea of property centred on the notion of rights in relation to things. The idea of property is a right in a thing, the thing itself constituting the foundation or subject-matter of that right. The idea of a right is that it is a two-way process, in that the right generates claims and duties amongst persons. Thus, rights cannot exist between people and things simply because things cannot have claims and duties and nor can they be bound by and recognise legal rules. Instead the appropriate analysis of property is that it is a right in a thing, which consequently gives rise to mutual relations between people – that is, rights and obligations – in respect of external resources or simply things. In this background, what is the distinction between legal rights and equitable rights of property?

At the heart of the matter is the traditional distinction between rights *in rem* and rights *in personam*.[97] The basic idea is that rights *in rem* bind the whole world, that is to say, that such rights are exercisable against everyone. In contrast, there are certain rights which do not bind the whole world; they are only exercisable against a particular person or a closely defined group of persons. The typical examples of rights *in personam* include rights arising under a contract, for example a contractual debt; also included is the right to damages in tort for injury caused. In both of these examples the right is merely personal and exercisable against a particular person, that person being the contracting party of the wrongdoer. The right does not avail against the whole world; instead it is restricted to a particular person or persons. The application of this juridical analysis of rights to proprietary rights does cause some problems.[98] Legal proprietary rights are classified as rights

---

[95] The estate contract arises where a person enters into a contract to purchase a legal estate in land, such as the estate of freehold, but has no conveyance by deed in his favour. The absence of the deed's formality does not inhibit equity finding equitable ownership in the purchaser on the maxim that *equity regards that as done which ought to be done*. The estate contract is one to which equity can give the remedy of specific performance; the contract must satisfy the need for writing (see Chapter 9).

[96] The doctrine of estoppel in the context of property law is considered appropriately in Chapter 10 in the discussion on the distinction between personal and proprietary rights.

[97] The idea that rights can be classified as rights *in rem* and rights *in personam* is not unique to rights of property but extends to the notion of rights in general: see J. Stone, *Legal System and Lawyer's Reasonings* (1964) at pp 149–157.

[98] The idea of rights as rights *in rem* and *in personam* has been the subject of much jurisprudence. See A. Kocourek, *Jural Relations* (1927) at pp 189–202; W. Hohfeld, 'Fundamental Legal Conceptions as Applied in Judicial Reasoning' (1917) 26 Yale LJ at p 710; and also J. Stone, *op cit*.

in rem whereas equitable proprietary rights are classified as rights *in personam*. At first glance this does look rather strange in that only legal rights of property are truly property rights since to describe equitable rights as rights *in personam* is to reduce them to mere personal rights. This does seem rather contradictory in the sense that at one level of analysis we describe equitable rights of property (for example, the rights of a beneficiary under a trust) as proprietary, then on another level of analysis as rights *in personam*, which are merely personal. They can only be one or the other. Much of the confusion centres on the context in which the words *in rem* and *in personam* are used. These words are often used to describe rights *in rem* and *in personam* and actions *in rem* and *in personam*, which, of course, are two separate things altogether.

Legal proprietary rights: rights *in rem*

The general principle is that legal proprietary rights, such as legal ownership, are good against the whole world. Legal proprietary rights are rights *in rem*. There are two meanings to the use of the phrase that they bind the whole world. In the first place, legal rights prevail over any subsequently created legal or equitable interests. A legal right, for example, affecting land will bind anyone who subsequently acquires the land irrespective of the lack of knowledge of its existence.[99] Thus if A, the owner of a piece of land, leases it to B for a term of 25 years and subsequently sells the land to C, then C, although the owner of the freehold title, cannot take possession of the land because he will be bound by the legal lease created in B. He will, however, be entitled to the receipt of rent.

The idea that legal rights bind the world in this sense of the meaning needs one qualification in the context of rights in things other than land. Title disputes in personal property do not always result in the legal right taking priority over any subsequently created legal rights. Unlike title to land which is often documentary and subject to a sophisticated system of registration, title to movables such as goods depends on the concept of possession.[100] It may so happen that a legal right may be lost to a subsequently created legal right under what are known as the exceptions to the *nemo dat* rule – a rule in property law that finds itself applicable in the context of personal property and is expressed in Latin as *nemo dat quod non habet*. This property law principle holds that a person cannot give a better title to a thing than he has himself. Thus, if I

---

[99] In the case of land, certain legal rights may be subject to registration where the title to land is registered. Registration of legal rights in this context is an integral and normal part of the registration process; such registration does not alter the common law principle that legal rights bind the whole world.

[100] The concept of title and its various manifestations is considered in Chapter 6.

borrow a car from my friend, I cannot sell that car to another and give a good legal title to it, simply because I have no title in the car to give. This is a sound principle which seeks to protect the private property rights of individuals. However, an unlimited application of this principle can cause hardship in a purely liberal market involved with exchange. A pure market economy requires conditions which facilitate exchange; one of those conditions is security in contractual dealings.[101] If in our previous example, I had not borrowed the car from my friend but rather unlawfully dispossessed him of it and then sold it to C, if C purchased the car from me in good faith and for value, should the law protect the original owner or C? In other words, which legal right prevails? Although the common law holds that legal rights are rights *in rem*, the rules relating to exceptions to the *nemo dat* rule hold that in some circumstances a pre-existing legal right can be lost to a new legal right.[102] The policy of the law here is to balance the two competing interests, of the private individual and his property with that of the market and exchange.[103]

The second aspect of the phrase that legal rights bind the world in the context of property relates to the fact that the right is held within a thing and not against a person or persons. In this respect the right is good against anyone who interferes with the thing in which the right is held. The ownership of my house is good against anyone in the world and it matters not who has trespassed on my land; I can bring an action against any person who commits such trespass. Whilst this may be true, it is not quite true to say that the only reason that a right is a right *in rem* is that it is a right in a thing as opposed to a person or persons. It has already been mentioned that the significance of having rights of property is that they are rights between people in respect of things. A right *in rem* is a right which binds the whole world and is exercisable against persons generally. In this respect Austin once wrote, 'rights in rem may be defined in the following manner – rights residing in persons and availing against other persons generally.'[104] It is more appropriate to conceptualise the idea of a right *in rem* as a right binding per-

---

[101] See M. Bridge, *Personal Property Law* (1996) at pp 95–115, where he comments on the competing interests of the market and private individual. The author then provides a very concise analysis of the modern exceptions to the *nemo dat* rule.

[102] The exceptions are found in the common law and statutes in the form of the Factors Act 1889 and the Sale of Goods Act 1979. It is outside the ambit of this chapter to discuss these rules in depth; however, one example can be given to illustrate the nature of such title disputes. A person who sells goods to another can pass title to such goods by virtue of the sale of goods contract. However, although the seller can pass title to the purchaser, he can retain possession such as where the goods have not yet been delivered to the buyer. If the seller sells the identical goods subject to the former sale to another purchaser, the latter purchaser can obtain a better title to such goods even though the seller did not have any title in the goods to convey. This is often described as the seller in possession exception and is now found in s 24 of the Sale of Goods Act 1979.

[103] See *Bishopsgate Motor Finance Corp v Transport Brakes Ltd* [1949] 1 KB 322.

[104] Austin, *Jurisprudence* (4th edn) at p 381, quoted in A. Kocourek, *op cit*, at p 189.

sons in general rather than a right in a thing. This is important because the violation of a right *in rem* (for example, the legal ownership to my car) does not always give rise to an action *in rem* – that is, the specific recovery of the thing itself. It does, however, give me a right to bring an action against any person who wrongfully interferes with my car.

Equitable proprietary rights: rights *in personam* or rights *in rem*?

Equitable property rights are said to be rights *in personam*. The initial suggestion that they are such rights does cause some conceptual problems in property law. The typical idea of a right *in personam* is that it is a right held by a person and exercisable against another person or specific persons as opposed to people in general. The example given already is that of a right of a contracting party under a contract. The right *in personam* in this context means that the holder has a mere personal right to the performance of an obligation. The right binds only those parties to the contract and no one else. When this legal reasoning is applied in the property context, it does cause some problems because to hold equitable property rights as rights of a purely personal nature is of course absurd. The property rights of persons in equity, like that of a beneficiary under a trust, are essentially proprietary as opposed to personal. The fact that equitable property rights are rights *in personam* arises from the historical basis that *equity acts in personam* rather than from the orthodox sense of the phrase which relates to mere personal rights. Historically, the method of enforcement of a judgment of the Court of Chancery was by a personal order restraining or ordering the defendant to do something. The court did not interfere with the common law judgment in respect of the same dispute and neither did it interfere with the defendant's property. Despite this, there have been many voices in the history of equity and property law which seem to suggest that the equitable rights of a person, in the context of property, are essentially personal as opposed to proprietary.[105] Professor Langdell once wrote that an equitable right, 'may be defined as an equitable personal obligation. It is an obligation because it is not ownership.'[106] Professor Langdell is not the lone voice in the jurisprudence of equitable rights; other leading commentators on equity have taken a similar view on equitable property rights.[107]

---

[105] See, for example, W. Hart, 'The Place of Trust in Jurisprudence' (1912) 28 LQR at p 290 where the author examines the idea of a right *in personam* in the context of the trust and the rights of the beneficiary thereunder.

[106] Langdell, 'Brief Survey of Equity Jurisdiction' (2nd edn) at p 6, quoted by W. Hart, *ibid*, at p 291.

[107] See J.B. Ames, *Lectures on Legal History* (1913) at p 76 and also F.W. Maitland, 'Trust and Corporation' in 3 *Collected Papers* (1911) at pp 349–350 and *Equity: A Course of Lectures* (J. Brunyate (ed) 1936) at p 47.

It is submitted that equitable property rights, albeit classified as rights *in personam* are proprietary rights in the true sense of the word. The answer is arrived at by putting to one side the juridical analysis of rights and then asking the simple question of the enforceability of the right. Where a right has the ability to bind a potentially large class of persons it looks more proprietary than personal. Equitable rights are not mere personal rights as under a simple contract; they are rights which are enforceable against not just one person but a potentially large class of persons. They are rights in things and exercisable against what may constitute a large class of persons. The fact that they have the ability to bind a large group of persons makes them more like rights *in rem*. It is the aspect of enforceability, and in particular the extent of enforceability, which is decisive of whether a right is proprietary or not. Although the orthodox opinion suggests that rights *in rem* are rights in a thing rather than persons, the real value of the right lies in the fact that it is exercisable against persons in general. The thing in question merely sustains the right; violation of the right does not lead to specific recovery in all cases. When one looks at the substantive nature of equitable property rights, there may be very little in the difference between legal rights to the extent that both are rights in things exercisable against persons. Even though equity acts *in personam* the range of persons bound by the right can be large. In this respect Megarry and Thompson write, 'Equitable rights ... look less and less like mere rights *in personam* and more and more like rights *in rem*. Although it is still possible to regard them as rights *in personam*, it is perhaps best to treat them as hybrids, being neither entirely one nor entirely the other. They have never reached the status of rights *in rem*, yet the class of persons against whom they will be enforced is too large for mere rights *in personam*.[108]

Equitable proprietary rights and the doctrine of notice

Equitable proprietary rights are governed by the doctrine of notice. This means that such rights are binding on all persons except a bona fide purchaser of a legal interest without notice of the pre-existing equitable interest.[109] Equity, acting *in personam*, clearly binds the conscience of the party against whom an equitable right is granted. It goes further and binds all those persons who subsequently acquire the legal title to the property in which the equitable right is granted with notice of the equitable right. Thus, where a trustee transfers the legal title to another person, the equitable rights of the beneficiary may bind the transferee if she or he has notice thereof. Likewise in the case of land, a pur-

---

[108] R. Megarry and R. Thompson, *Megarry's Manual of the Law of Real Property* (7th edn, 1993) at p 57.
[109] See *London and South Western Company v Gomm* (1882) 20 Ch D 562 and *Pilcher v Rawlins* (1872) 7 Ch App 259.

chaser of the fee simple estate may be bound by a contract to grant a lease, which as discussed above will be afforded protection in equity, if he has notice of such a contract to grant a lease.[110] It must, however, be stressed at this point that the doctrine of notice in relation to land has been largely superseded by a system of registration of land interests which include equitable rights.[111]

The doctrine of notice requires the purchaser to be a bona fide purchaser. This is no more than saying that the purchaser must be one who is innocent, and where there is an absence of notice, this requirement is easily satisfied. The purchaser must have given value, that is, consideration. Consideration includes the common law meaning as well as that in equity, thus money or money's worth and marriage consideration[112] will suffice. A purchaser for value need not, however, show that the consideration was adequate.[113] The doctrine of notice does not extend to a person who has not furnished consideration, thus a mere donee will be bound by existing equitable interests irrespective of notice. Equity has long established that it will not assist a mere volunteer. The purchaser must be a purchaser of the legal estate. In real property this means that the purchaser must purchase either the estate of fee simple absolute in possession or the term of years.[114] In personal property the purchaser must be purchaser of the legal title to the thing in question. It is clear that the doctrine of notice does not extend to the purchase of an equitable estate or interest in property. Here the equitable maxim 'where the equities are equal the first in time prevails' normally seeks to give priority to equitable rights in the order of creation as opposed to notice of such rights.[115] A purchaser of an equitable estate will not, however, be subject to what are commonly called 'mere equities' if he purchases the equitable estate without notice of the mere equity. Mere equities are different from equitable rights and interests. They are not rights in things themselves; rather they are personal rights[116] recognised in equity which allow a person, for example, to set aside a contract on grounds of fraud[117] or to rectify or rescind a contract on grounds of mistake.[118]

---

[110] This is, of course, subject to the principles of registration of title and charges (discussed below) by the Law of Property Act 1925, Land Registration Act 1925 and the Land Charges Act 1972.

[111] The system of registration of land interests in whatever form they may be in is, however, not watertight. There is a residual category of equitable interests which do not find themselves catered for in the system of registration of interests and as such the doctrine of notice in its fullest sense applies in such cases. The most obvious example is beneficial rights under a trust concerning unregistered land: see *Kingsnorth Finance Company Ltd v Tizard* [1986] 1 WLR 783, discussed below.

[112] A future marriage is recognised as consideration in equity.

[113] *Midland Bank Co Ltd v Green* [1981] AC 513.

[114] Purchaser includes a legal mortgagee who, by operation of the Law of Property Act 1925, s 87(1), is deemed as being vested with an estate in land.

[115] *Re Morgan* (1881) 18 Ch D 93: *McCarthy and Stone Ltd v Harding* [1973] 1 WLR 1547.

[116] *National Provincial Bank v Ainsworth* [1965] AC 1175 at 1258.

[117] *Ernest v Vivian* (1863) 33 LJ Ch 513.

[118] *Shiloh Spinners Ltd v Harding* [1973] AC 691 at 721.

The central requirement of the doctrine of notice relates to the question of what constitutes notice.[119] Three types of knowledge have been identified for the purposes of the doctrine of notice. The most obvious type of notice attributable to a person is actual notice. This refers to a situation where the purchaser is consciously aware of the equitable interest in property at the time of the purchase. Actual notice is to be distinguished from constructive notice which refers to knowledge which would have come to the attention of the purchaser had he carried out a reasonable inspection of the title to the thing in question. It is trite law that a person buying land should carry out a reasonable inspection of the land and title that he is purchasing. The purpose of such inspection is to establish whether the land is affected by, for example, a right of way or other persons in occupation of the land other than the vendor. Thus in *Kingsnorth Finance Company Ltd* v *Tizard*[120] a husband held the legal title of a matrimonial home on trust for himself and his wife. After they had separated the wife discontinued to live with her husband but did visit the house on a daily basis to look after the children. The husband arranged a mortgage with the mortgagee, which was duly given after an inspection on a Sunday afternoon. The husband told the surveyor that he had been separated from his wife long ago and that she had no interest in the house. When the husband later absconded with the mortgage monies, the court held that the equitable rights of the wife under the trust bound the mortgagee. The inspection by the mortgagee was simply insufficient and they were affixed with constructive notice. The final type of notice is imputed notice, which arises when an agent of the purchaser has notice, actual or constructive, which is imputed to the purchaser.

The effect of a successful claim that a purchaser purchased the legal title without notice of the equitable interest is to give him an 'absolute, unqualified, unanswerable defence'[121] against the holder of an equitable interest in property. The doctrine of notice not only gives the purchaser an unqualified defence against the purchaser; the doctrine operates in a destructive way so that the equitable interest in the property is completely destroyed. It cannot be revived against a subsequent purchaser of the legal title who may have notice of the fact that the equitable interest once existed.[122]

Equitable proprietary rights in the modern law: registration, over-reaching and different rules for personal property

The above discussion is not complete without an examination of how equity, equitable rights and the doctrine of notice work in the modern law of property. In the case of real property the doctrine of notice has been largely

---

[119] See Law of Property Act 1925, s 199.
[120] [1986] 1 WLR 783.
[121] *Pilcher* v *Rawlins* (1872) 7 Ch App 259 at 269.
[122] *Wilkes* v *Spooner* [1911] 2 KB 473.

superseded by the system of registration of interests in land. What is typically referred to as the 1925 legislation, culminating in the Law of Property Act 1925, Land Charges Act 1925 (now the Land Charges Act 1972) and the Land Registration Act 1925, provides a framework for governing various legal and equitable interests in land. The primary objective of the legislation was the free alienability of land coupled with the protection of the various legitimate interests, legal or equitable, in land that may be vested in a person. What is of importance here are the registration of equitable interests as land charges and the doctrine of overreaching. These two things had the effect of replacing or modifying the doctrine of notice which was applicable to the operation of equitable interests in land.

In so far as unregistered title to land, the Land Charges Act 1925, replaced by the Land Charges Act 1972, introduced a system of registration of equitable rights as land charges. The obvious attraction of this system is that the purchaser's task of investigating title is made easier by the provision of a register of equitable rights in land. On the other side of the coin is the protection afforded to the holder of an equitable right in that registration of the right on the land charges register gives notice to the whole world. Absence of registration as a land charge will not bind a purchaser even if he has notice of the equitable right in the land.[123] The types of rights registrable as land charges include a contract for a lease or fee simple,[124] a restrictive covenant and an equitable easement. Where the title to land is one that is registered,[125] equitable interests are subject to registration as minor interests unless they fall under the grouping of interests that are overriding.[126] Overriding interests will bind a purchaser in the absence of registration. Overriding interests are usually those interests that are readily discoverable upon inspection of the land. With respect to the system of registration, one can appreciate how equitable property rights are more akin to rights *in rem* as opposed to rights *in personam*. The system of registration and the consequential effect of registration, in so far as giving notice to the whole world, makes the extent of their binding force extremely large.

Remaining with real property, the 1925 legislation introduced the doctrine of overreaching which had the effect of diminishing the role of notice under conditions which had the effect of lifting the equitable rights of certain individuals in land and replacing them in the proceeds of the sale of land. Thus,

---

[123] Law of Property Act 1925, s 198.

[124] This is referred to as an estate contract and is registered as a Class C(IV) charge in the Charges Register under the Land Charges Act 1972.

[125] The system of registration of title introduces a degree of certainty in title and makes the task of inspection of title easier by the guarantee of a title on a central register; the Land Register is fragmented into appropriate districts.

[126] Land Registration Act 1925.

even where an equitable property interest existed in land and the purchaser of the legal title had notice thereof,[127] the right would not bind the purchaser if the conditions of overreaching applied. So why and when does this doctrine apply? In order to make land more freely transferable it is important that title to land is not hampered with many separate and often competing interests. The purchaser needs to make sure that he gets a clean title and not one which is subject to the rights of others. Inevitably, there are certain interests such as easements and restrictive covenants which will bind the purchaser. These interests are protected and allowed to run with the title to land in order to make the best utilisation of land.

However, the truth of the matter is that the very nature of land and the purposes that it can serve makes it a resource in which many other interests can co-exist at the same time. It is quite possible for the title to land to become fragmented, as where two or more people acquire ownership in the land concurrently.[128] Where title to land has become fragmented, such land is subject to a trust of land[129] and the legal owners of the land, being vested with the legal estate, are trustees for the beneficial owners (whom they themselves may be some of). Thus, where two people take title to land at the same time, this poses few problems since the two owners are trustees at law but beneficial owners under the trust of land. Whilst this is quite simple, in practice there may be beneficial owners under a trust of land who do not appear on the title to the land. Such persons can be those who have made some contribution to the purchase price of the land or those who understood by means of a common intention that, although they for some reason do not appear on the legal title, they have an interest in the land.[130] It is clear that these interests are interests recognised by equity and theoretically binding upon the purchaser under the doctrine of notice. They are interests that are not generally covered by the system of registration. If the purchaser of the land is aware of these interests – and in practice a careful inspection of the land will so disclose – he will be bound by the interests of the beneficiaries under the trust of land. He is unlikely to purchase title which is hampered with the equitable interest of the beneficiaries. At the same time, if he has no notice, the vendor or vendors of the legal title can give a clean title to the purchaser. The only question remaining is, what happens to the interests of the beneficiaries?

Overreaching has the effect of transferring the rights of beneficiaries under a trust of land to rights in the proceeds of sale, providing that the purchaser pays to two trustees.[131] It matters not that he has notice of the interests of

---

[127] Whether by registration or otherwise.

[128] Fragmentation of ownership is considered in Chapter 7.

[129] Trusts of Land and Appointment of Trustees Act 1996.

[130] These matters are appropriately discussed in Chapter 7.

[131] Law of Property Act 1925, s 2(1).

the beneficiaries under the trust of land. The beneficiaries' rights are shifted to the proceeds of the sale of the land.[132] Overreaching will not apply where there is sale by one owner of the legal title to land, in which case the doctrine of notice will apply in its strict sense.[133]

The final point to note about the doctrine of notice in the modern law is that there is a difference in the manner in which it applies to personal property. Unlike real property, where it is trite law that a purchaser of land must carry out a detailed inspection of the title that he or she is purchasing, the same does not apply to personal property. Personal property has never been subject to rigorous inspection of title simply because there are no means, such as elaborate title deeds or a system of registration, by which the purchaser can inspect the title to the property in question. Thus, a purchaser of goods, shares or a person exchanging goods for money, does not generally carry out an inspection of the title that he is purporting to acquire. In this respect it is questionable whether the doctrine of notice in the strict conveyancing sense applies to personal property. The view for a long time has been that the doctrine of notice does not apply to personal property in the same way that it does with real property.[134] It is clear that a purchaser will be bound with actual notice; however, the extent to which constructive notice will apply depends on whether there is a proper procedure for investigation of title or if there are other factors which raise suspicion about the vendor's title.[135] In recent times litigation has arisen in the commercial context where attempts have been made to fraudulently transfer monies belonging to beneficiaries under pension funds or where there has been a fraud instigated by a director or other agent of a company.[136]

CLASSIFICATION ACCORDING TO THE FUNCTION PERFORMED BY THE RIGHT

Another means by which proprietary rights can be classified is by examining the function performed by the right. This idea is developed by Bell,[137] who identifies a number of functions performed by proprietary rights.[138] The idea

---

[132] *City of London Building Society* v *Flegg* [1988] AC 54.

[133] *Kingsnorth Finance Company Co Ltd* v *Tizard* [1986] 1 WLR 783. In relation to registered title to land, beneficial interests under a trust of land may bind the purchaser even where he has no notice thereof and even where there is a complete absence of registration of such an interest. See *Williams & Glyn's Bank* v *Boland* [1981] AC 487, where it was held that beneficial interests under trusts of land may constitute overriding interests, which are interests that bind the purchaser of a registered title to land irrespective of notice. They are literally overriding and include amongst the class of such interests, interests of those persons in actual occupation of the land. See, R. Smith, *Property Law* (2nd edn, 1998) at p 226.

[134] See *Manchester Trust* v *Furness* [1895] 2 QB 539, *per* Lindley LJ at 545.

[135] *Macmillan Inc* v *Bishopsgate Investment Trust plc (No 3)* [1995] 1 WLR 978.

[136] See S. Panesar, 'Financial Institutions and Misdirected Funds' (1997) 12(5) Journal of International Banking Law at p 175.

[137] A.P. Bell, *Modern Law of Personal Property in England and Ireland* (1989).

[138] *Ibid*, at pp 4–5.

here is that proprietary rights are multi-functional – that is, what they can do for the holders of such rights varies from right to right. In this book the function of property is considered in two contexts. The first is the function of a particular right such as the right of ownership, an easement or mortgage. This is the approach taken by Bell, which basically deals with the question, what function does a particular right perform? This is different from the second meaning, which looks to the broader question of the function of property in general. In other words, what function does the institution of property serve in society? In respect of the latter, property serves two main functions, the relative importance of which changes with time. These functions relate to the exchange and use value of property, and are more appropriately examined in the next chapter. For the time being the function of particular rights is examined.

Bell explains that property rights can perform a number of functions: in particular security, beneficial and managerial. Certain rights perform a security function, that is, they seek to guarantee performance of an obligation such as to pay money. In the case of land, a mortgage would be classified as a security right since the function of a mortgage is to secure the obligation to pay money lent by a mortgagee. In respect of things other than land – for example, goods – a pledge is another example of such a security right. A pledge involves a transfer of possession from a pledgor, who is a debtor, to a pledgee creditor. The transfer of possession is pursuant to the loan made by the pledgee to the pledgor. Default in payment by the pledgor will allow the pledgee to sell the property to realise the debt that it is owed. Similarly, a lien allows a person to retain goods until payment has been made under a contract – for example, until payment for the repair of a car the garage may have a lien on the car. Common law pledges and liens are not always a satisfactory security because they involve the retention of possession by the person who is owed money. In commercial practice, money may be provided upon security of assets without having to transfer the assets to the creditor. It is quite possible to have what is commonly described as non-possessory security in the form of a charge or mortgage. A mortgage usually involves the conveyance or assignment of title in something to the mortgagee although the mortgagor may retain possession of the mortgaged property. A charge, on the other hand, does not convey anything to the chargee but allows the chargee to appropriate property in default of payment under the terms of the charge.[139]

Apart from security rights, property rights may be either beneficial or managerial. A beneficial right literally allows the holder of the right to benefit from the thing in question. Sole ownership vested in a person entitles that person to enjoy that thing within the prescribed limits of law. Another exam-

---

[139] Possessory and non-possessory security is excellently accounted for in M. Bridge, *Personal Property Law* (2nd edn, 1996) at p 141.

ple here is the right of a beneficiary under a trust, who has a right to enjoyment of a thing which is held upon trust. Thus, beneficial rights exist both in law and in equity. A right may give a person no enjoyment to the thing but, instead, oblige the holder of it to manage the thing on behalf of another. A trustee has no rights to enjoyment but must manage the property for the beneficiary; in this respect a trustee has a managerial right. Another example is a conferment of a power to another person to dispose of property on behalf of that other.[140]

CLASSIFICATION AND PROPERTY LAW

Understanding classification of property is an important part of understanding property law for a number of reasons. It seeks to redefine our understanding of the idea of property law; in particular, where property rights come from and why property rules come about. More importantly it seeks to explain the reasons for the divisions that are inherent in the law. It is more important to understand the basis for the various divisions in property law rather than simply assume or be told that land is different and personal property is something confined to commercial law. This involves a movement away from simple compartmentalisation of rights and things and an attempt to understand the basis of why certain things are treated differently from others. Such an exercise shows that despite compartmentalisation into real and personal property law, compartmentalisation is often artificial from the viewpoint of the study of law. The common theme is that rights in things form the basis of property, and once this is appreciated the divisions in property law are literally divisions of what forms a unifying idea of the law of property.

---

[140] See Chapter 7.

5

THE CHANGING NATURE
OF PROPERTY

PROPERTY AS A DYNAMIC RELATIONSHIP

In the previous chapter property was classified according to a number of factors such as the nature of the objects, the sphere of enforceability of the right
and the function performed by the right of property. Such classification maps
out the types of things that are capable of being the subject-matter of property
and also explains the nature of property itself. Classification of property is
important in property law; however, it is equally important to appreciate that
classification of property in one era of time is not necessarily the same as that
in another. In other words, the idea and nature of property change from one
period of time to another. Any classification of property in one period of time
must be understood within the social, economic and political context of that
era. This chapter seeks to examine, *inter alia*, how the idea and nature of
property has changed with time and how it continues to change, why the
nature of property changes, and, finally, what limits there are on the legal
concept of property.

At a broad level of discussion, it has long been recognised that the concept
or institution of property is dynamic. Property is dynamic because it is influenced by social, economic and political ideas. One commentator writes that
'the meaning of property is not constant. The actual institution, and the way
people see it, and hence the meaning they give to the word, all change over
time ... The changes are related to changes in the purposes which society or
the dominant classes in society expect the institution of property to serve.'[1]
The idea of property changes with time so that what was understood as

---

[1] C.B. Macpherson, *Property: Mainstream and Critical Positions* (1978) at p 1.

property in ancient law is not necessarily the same as that in medieval law or in the modern law. Moreover, the idea of property changes from one political thought to another. Ideas of property and ownership in western law traditions are not necessarily the same as in communist based traditions. The amount of private property in comparison to communal and state property varies with different political regimes. For example, the idea of property in a capitalist system differs from that in other systems of political and economic thought.[2] Property comprises control of material resources, and every system of state makes its own decisions as to who should control such material resources. Friedmann writes: 'in socialized systems, the function – and to some extent, the concept – of property differs fundamentally from that of the systems in which property is the foundation of private enterprise. The transfer of the major means of production into the hands of the state, and the direction by a central economic plan, removes property as an instrument of power from private ownership.'[3] This book is essentially concerned with the concept of private property and, therefore, it is the changing nature of private property that is examined in this chapter.

CHANGES IN PRIVATE PROPERTY AND LIMITATIONS

The changing aspects of property

It has been said above that the idea and nature of property changes with time: this statement, however, requires some clarification. The legal idea of property consists of a right held by a person in a thing of value. The right in a thing generates rights and duties between other persons in the legal system. The right of property is better understood as emanating from a property relationship between a subject and an object. The right is held for a particular purpose or function. The idea of property, in so far as it consists of a claim or claims to material resources of value, remains fairly constant throughout time. What do, however, change are the ingredients of the property relationship. This simply means that the subjects and objects of the relationship and the function performed by the right change with time. It is because of these changes that property is said to be a dynamic concept.[4] Gray and Symes, commenting on the property relationship, write:

> 'the content of the relationship is liable to change. The subjects of property may be differently determined in one social era as compared with another. The objects of property are likewise liable to fluctuate with the passage of time and

---

[2] See, for example, C.B. Macpherson, 'Capitalism and the Changing Concept of Property' in E. Kamenka and R.S. Neale (eds), *Feudalism, Capitalism and Beyond* (1975) at p 105.

[3] W. Friedmann, *Law in a Changing Society* (1959) at p 105.

[4] See K. Gray and P. Symes, *Real Property and Real People: Principles of Land Law* (1981) at p 10.

the emergence of new economic conditions. Above all, the ideology of property is profoundly influenced by much wider factors of social, political and economic philosophy.' [5]

At one time the most important object in the property relationship was land; however, with the passage of time, whilst land still retains a dominant position in the spectrum of material resources, other forms of tangible and intangible resources are becoming objects of property. The changing subjects, objects and functions of property are examined in more detail later on.

Limits on property

Conceptualising property as a dynamic concept presupposes that property law is also dynamic, or, in other words, capable of adapting to changes in the property relationship. If we are to say that the nature of property changes with time, we are also saying that the law changes in order to accommodate different types of subjects, objects and functions of property. In this respect, two important questions arise when discussing the changing nature of property and the adaptability of law to changes in the property relationship. First, is property law readily capable of admitting new types of subjects, objects and functions of property? Second, are there any limitations on the extent to which the idea of property can change? The answers to these questions are important in assessing how far the nature and idea of property can change and be accommodated for in law.

Invariably, new social, economic and technological advances will cause the property relationship to change over time. Land may have been the most prized resource in times gone by; however, an increasing amount of new resources have raised the question whether they are capable of being the objects of property. Material resources such as information and body parts have in recent times begged the question whether they are capable of being the subject-matter of ownership. There are also debates as to whether benefits of a very intangible nature can be regarded as objects of the property relationship. Given that property is an important aspect of individual liberty and security, can forms of wealth which flow from the government in the form of welfare benefits be regarded as property of an individual? These are just some of many different forms of resources or objects that continue to raise debates as to whether they fall into the category of property.[6] In order to make sense of the extent or limits of private property one needs to establish whether property law has a defined notion of what constitutes property and its extent.

---

[5] *Ibid.*

[6] The property debate surrounding these resources is examined later under the section on changing objects of property.

The House of Lords in *National Provincial Bank Ltd* v *Ainsworth*[7] explained the hallmarks of a property right. Here, in assessing the rights of a wife in the matrimonial home where title was solely in the name of her husband, Lord Wilberforce made a statement, which to a large extent continues to provide the model upon when a right will be regarded as property. Lord Wilberforce commented that 'before a right or interest can be admitted into the category of property, or of a right affecting property, it must be definable, identifiable by third parties, capable in its assumption by third parties, and have some degree of permanence or stability.'[8] There appears to be one central characteristic of property from this statement and that is transmissibility. The hallmark of a property right is that it should be capable of transmission from one person to another. Transmissibility seems to be an elementary aspect of property; indeed, much of the law of property is concerned with rules governing how property is transferred from one person to another.

The transmissibility hallmark of a property right, although elementary, has however become controversial in modern property law. Gray, for example, writes that, 'the dogma which requires that a property interest be both identifiable by, and capable of transmission to, third parties may well represent an increasingly obsolete conception of property in the context of the modern world. As a dogma it is pervaded by an image of property as something commercial – as something belonging essentially in the world of exchange relationships.'[9] This is an important observation in the attempt to understand property, not only as dynamic concept, but also concerning its primary function. Gray points to the types of resources which form the basis of security in the modern world and many of these resources have no aspect of transmissibility. For example, certain security claims in the form of residential security, pension security and employment security are much more important in many cases than the security of ownership of a piece of land. To deny property significance to these types of resources is to raise the question, what is the most basic function of property? In the American legal literature there have been strong voices claiming that pensions and welfare benefits and a wide number of other intangible sources of wealth, such as jobs and residential security, should be accorded the status of property.[10] English law, on the other hand, has been more reluctant to entertain security kinds of the nature discussed here as property in the traditional sense. One reason for this is the transmissibility nature of property, which does not fit into such security claims. Another reason lies in the constitutional importance attached to property in

---

[7] [1965] AC 1175.

[8] *Ibid*, at 1247–1248.

[9] K. Gray, *Elements of Land Law* (2nd edn, 1993) at p 926, (3rd edn published 2001).

[10] The most powerful of the discussions has been by Professor C. Reich in his seminal article, 'The New Property' (1964) 73 Yale LJ 733. The idea of 'new property' is examined in more depth later.

America. For example, Twinning writes that 'debates in the American literature in recent years on the scope of property and the recognition of new property ... naturally reflect the entrenched constitutional significance of the property label.'[11]

Another crucial hallmark of a property right is that it should grant the person in whom it is vested the right to exclude others from the enjoyment of the material resource which sustains the right. For example, the ownership of a house vests in its owner a right to exclude others from interference with the enjoyment of the right. In Chapter 2 it was emphasised that such excludability formed a basic element of property and it was taken as a test of whether a new right could be admitted as property. The right of ownership of a house easily fits into the category of property; however, the right of ownership to a view, as observed in Chapter 2, is a little more problematic. Similarly, to subject resources such as oxygen and seawater to private property and ownership is impracticable.

Although certain resources are incapable of being subjected to private ownership, Harris explains that it does not mean that they can never be subjected to private property for certain purposes.[12] Harris gives the example of a lighthouse beam, which for practical purposes cannot be subject to trespass rules. Any vessel sailing around the lighthouse beam cannot be prevented from using it. However, Harris suggests that there is no reason why shipowners could not be taxed for using a coastal state's property because they had seen the beam of light. In *BBC Enterprises Ltd v Hi-Tech Xtravision Ltd*[13] (a case example used by Harris) BBC Enterprises entered into an agreement with a company to manufacture decoders that would allow television programmes that were beamed by BBC Enterprises to be received by viewers in Western Europe. It was agreed that the company would sell the decoders and pay £100 to BBC Enterprises for each one sold. The defendants decided to manufacture decoders themselves and sell them at a much-reduced price to European customers. BBC Enterprises sought an injunction to prevent the defendants from selling the decoders. They based their claim on the grounds that the recipients of the television programmes received using the defendants' decoders had no right to receive the programmes. The defendants had manufactured apparatus designed to enable such improper receipt of the programmes and this was clearly contrary to section 298 of the Copyright, Designs and Patents Act 1988.[14] At first instance Scott J rejected the claim of

---

[11] R. Cotterrell, 'The Law of Property and Legal Theory' in W. Twinning (ed), *Legal Theory and Common Law* (1986) at p 86.

[12] J.W. Harris, *Property and Justice* (1996) at p 334.

[13] [1991] 3 All ER 257.

[14] This section provides civil remedies against any person making apparatus for the fraudulent reception of broadcast by wireless telegraphy and also includes broadcasts in encrypted form.

BBC Enterprises, having found no property belonging to them in the waves in the ether.[15] The House of Lords, confirming the decision of the Court of Appeal to reverse the decision at first instance, held that reception of programmes broadcasted by BBC Enterprises without their consent was wrong. Although the language used in the judgments did not centre entirely on property law principles, the ether waves broadcasted by BBC Enterprises belonged in substance to them and in the end were subject to trespass rules, albeit enforced through the Copyright, Designs and Patents Act 1988.

THE CHANGING SUBJECTS OF PROPERTY

The types of person who can be the subjects of the property relationship can change over time. In modern society most people have some control over material resources of one kind or another. However, given that property involves an element of control, control is impossible without power, and power itself may determine the distribution of property amongst the subjects of a legal system. In primitive law, power may be analysed as force: for example, the stronger person capable of exercising control to the exclusion of others. In the modern world, in an age of exchange and bargain, power may be analysed in the form of financial power. It is such power that may determine when and how much property a person may gain. Land is generally an expensive asset; however, with the aid of mortgage finance and earnings a larger proportion of society has become capable of having some form of ownership in land.

Slaves

Historically, certain persons have been generally excluded from having property in some form or another. Instead such persons have been regarded as objects or material resources in which other persons may have property rights such as ownership. The most notable example is that of a slave, who was incapable of having property but instead was the property of his master. In one American case, Judge Crenshaw commented that 'a slave is in absolute bondage; he has no civil right, and he can hold no property, except at the will and pleasure of his master.'[16] A slave could neither give nor receive gifts, he could make no will, nor could he by will inherit anything. In ancient Greece and Rome as many as 80 per cent of the population were slaves.[17]

---

[15] *BBC Enterprises Ltd v Hi-Tech Xtravision Ltd, The Times*, 28 Nov 1989.
[16] *Brandon et al v Planter's and Merchants' Bank of Huntsville* (1838) 1 Stewarts Ala Rep 320, quoted in S.M. Elkins, *Slavery: A Problem in American Institutional and Intellectual Life* (1959) at p 59.
[17] See E.K. Hunt, *Property and Prophets: The Evolution of Economic Institutions and Ideologies* (7th edn, 1995) at p 2.

The denial of property rights to such a large proportion of the population did inevitably bring about gross inequality of distribution of wealth. The idea of slavery has long been rejected in the English law and it is quite clear that human inviolability takes precedence over the sanctity of property. In *Sommersett's Case*[18] it was held that a slave's right of freedom prevailed over his owner's right to his property. In more recent times the courts continue to repudiate conditions that are akin to slavery. For example, in *Eastham* v *Newcastle United Football Club*,[19] Wilberforce J commented that the retain and transfer rules governing the employment of professional footballers constituted an unjustified restraint of trade. In the course of his judgment, Wilberforce J held that 'the transfer system has been stigmatisd by the plaintiff's counsel as a relic from the Middle Ages, involving the buying and selling of human beings as chattels.'[20]

Married women

Until the enactment of the Married Women's Property Act 1882, a married woman had no right to own property; everything she had belonged to her husband. Despite the 1882 legislation, which changed that rule, the husband usually continued in practice to be the sole owner of property.[21] It is not altogether clear why the common law denied property rights to married women. Holcombe explains that historians attribute the common law rule on grounds such as religion.[22] The medieval church regarded marriage as sacramental and the idea that two persons became one flesh justified the husband's dominion over his wife and any property she may have. Other justifications simply concentrate on the social and economic reality of the position of women in the Middle Ages. The extent of the common law rule prior to 1882 is neatly explained by Holcombe:

> '... the property that a woman possessed or was entitled to at the time of the marriage and any property she acquired or became entitled to after her marriage became her husband's to control. Moreover, if a woman who accepted a proposal of marriage sought, before the marriage took place, to dispose of any property without the knowledge and consent of her intended husband, the disposition could be set aside as a legal fraud.'[23]

---

[18] (1772) *State Trials*, Vol 20, p 1.

[19] [1964] AC 413.

[20] *Ibid*, at 427.

[21] See B. Roshier and H. Teff, *Law and Society in England* (1980) at p 173.

[22] L. Holcombe, *Wives and Property* (1983) at p 19.

[23] *Ibid*, at p 18. The approach of the common law to the property rights of married women was not followed by equity jurisdiction. Equity contributed to law reform by using equitable principles, notably the trust and marriage settlements, to protect the rights of married women in property they might acquire after marriage.

The denial of property to married women was not something peculiar to English law; other systems of law and state followed similar patterns. [24]

Corporations

Subjects of the property relationship need not be human beings but can be artificially created persons such as corporations.[25] A company has its own separate legal identity and as such can own property in its own right. A company can enter into property transactions such as the sale, lease or mortgage of assets that belong to it. The property relations of corporations are, however, rather different from the traditional notions of private property. They are different because of the very nature of a corporation and the way it functions. Whilst a corporation in the form of a company limited by shares can both hold and dispose of property in its own right, the corporation itself forms an object or material resource through which revenue is generated. In this respect, the corporation is subject to ownership and the owners are generally those persons who supply the capital in the form of shareholders. However, traditional private property law notions of ownership do not easily explain the ownership of corporations.[26] Not only is the nature of ownership vested in the owners of companies different from ownership vested, for example, in an owner of land or goods; the function of ownership is rather different.

In their classic work on corporations and private property, Berle and Means[27] pointed out how traditional notions of ownership did not easily explain the ownership of corporations. Whereas traditional notions of ownership involved not only the right to determine what uses an object was put to, but also the right to benefit from the use, in the case of a corporation there was almost a complete divorce between these aspects of ownership. In the case of the modern corporation there is a shift of power from those who own the corporation to those who control it. Whilst shareholders are the owners of a corporation, the ownership vested in them does not carry with it the incident of management and control. Control and management of the corporation is vested in a few in their capacity as directors and managers or corporate executives. It is they who decide what uses the corporation is put to. This is in sharp contrast to the position that existed prior to the rise of the

---

[24] See E. Sullerot, *Women, Society and Change* (1971) at pp 19–28.

[25] Corporations can be of two main types: corporations aggregate and corporations sole. A corporation aggregate is an incorporated group of several existing members, such as in the case of a limited company. On the other hand, a corporation sole is an incorporated series of successive persons: for example, a person serving in public office such as Minister of Education (see *Salmond on Jurisprudence* (12th edn, 1966) at p 308). It is the corporation aggregate that is the subject of discussion here.

[26] See Chapter 6 for the discussion of ownership in private property.

[27] *The Modern Corporation and Private Property* (1932).

modern corporation: the owner of industrial property had both the right of use and enjoyment vested in him simultaneously. The emergence of stocks and shares and the consequential limited company has the effect of giving its owners an interest in the corporation, but without the element of control that normally goes with ownership. In this respect, Scott writes, '... when the two aspects of property rights (use and benefit) are disassociated, it is possible to distinguish nominal ownership, which is the right to receive revenue as a return for risking one's wealth by investing in a company, from effective ownership, which is the ability to control the corporate assets.'[28]

The divorce between ownership and control in the context of the modern corporate system has a number of ramifications. In the first place, the shift in control of the system of production from individual entrepreneurs to directors of the company has remarkable features akin to property relations in the age of feudalism. The idea that control be vested in a few powerful persons whilst others receive benefit from their control of the resource is not too far from the concept of land being vested in feudal lords who had governmental functions. Julius Stone writes that '... the corporate system shows fascinating analogies to the feudal land system at its best, where control of landed property went with performance of governmental or other social functions.'[29] A second feature of the modern corporate system and its property relations is the function of property. The nominal ownership vested in the shareholders is usually held for the purpose of receiving income, whereas the effective ownership vested in those who manage the activities of the company is usually for power. Commenting on the divergence of interest between the owners and managers of a company, some commentators write that, 'the shareholder is interested more in income and capital appreciation of his investment rather than the company as an enterprise. Management is interested in the enterprise for a diversity of motives ranging from professional pride to the most naked self-interest in the pursuit of power.'[30]

THE CHANGING OBJECTS OF PROPERTY

Just as the persons who can claim proprietary rights in things of material value change, so too the things or objects of property change over time. The modern law of property seeks to protect a diverse range of things which have a value attached to them. These things range from tangible things such as land and goods to intangible things such as shares, debts, designs and ideas. The objects of the

---

[28] J. Scott, *Corporations, Classes and Capitalism* (1979) at p 32.
[29] J. Stone, *Social Dimensions of Law and Justice* (1966) at p 250.
[30] J.H. Farrar, N. Furey, B. Hanningan, *Farrar's Company Law* (2nd edn, 1988) at p 9.

property relationship continue to evolve along with changes in technological advances. For example, advances in the biotechnology industry have in recent times raised the issue whether body parts and human tissue can be the subject-matter of private property. Other advances such as the ability to make data and information readily accessible have likewise questioned the ability of property law to protect such resources from wrongful interference. Consequently, the system of property rules is constantly under pressure to extend the protection it affords to novel types of objects. However, it is not just technological advances alone that contribute to the ever–changing types of resources which demand property law protection. Changes in social and economic patterns are also responsible for changes in the types of resources to which people lay claim for things like basic subsistence and wealth. For example, many people do not place emphasis for their survival, wellbeing and security on resources such as land. Instead things like jobs, pensions and social security may be the significant things that form the basis of a person's wealth in modern times. The following paragraphs look at some of the traditional objects or things of value which property law protects through property rules; thereafter, the next section addresses those objects that in recent times have pleaded for admission into the category of objects which deserve property law protection, but which have not succeeded for a variety of reasons, ranging from practicality to ethics and morality.

Tangible property: land and goods

In the words of Gray and Symes, '... for centuries the most highly prized object of property in the common law world was land.'[31] The importance of land in property law cannot be ignored and, despite its relative declining importance as compared with other types of objects in modern times, land dominates the discussions in property law. Until the end of the nineteenth century land was both a key to political power and wealth.[32] However, as Professor Birks has pointed out:

> 'for institutions and individuals with serious wealth, land has lost its central role. The managed fund has displaced the rolling acres. Land used to be the pre-eminent form of wealth. Landed property was the focus of dynastic ambition. Land opened the door to high social status and political power. A landed family had by that fact alone a stake in governmental power. Keeping land in the family mattered. That has changed. Land, important as it is, has lost its pride of place. For the mega-wealthy, land has become just one species of investment, just as agriculture has become just one more industry.'[33]

---

[31] K. Gray and P. Symes, *Real Property and Real People* (1981) at p 11.

[32] W.R. Cornish and G. de N. Clarke, *Law and Society in England 1750–1950* (1989), p 121.

[33] P. Birks, 'Before We Begin: Five Keys to Law' in S. Bright and J. Dewar (eds) *Land Law: Themes and Perspectives* (1998) at p 457.

Whereas from early times land was the dominant object in which proprietary rights could be sustained, the same was not true for goods. In comparison with other objects that make up a person's wealth, goods do not generally appear at the top in terms of value. It is for this reason that the law relating to goods, as compared with that of land and intangibles, until relatively recent times remained underdeveloped. It certainly did not form the subject-matter of property law curriculums in law schools and neither did the library shelves boast volumes of literature on the subject. One commentator writes, 'this traditional legal distaste for the law of goods has often been ascribed to the fact that goods, except when traded *en masse*, are relatively low in value compared to land and intangibles ... However, a more accurate way of putting it might be to say that, except where goods are treated as commodities, the law of goods is poor people's law'.[34] Things changed in the latter part of the twentieth century. Not only is there now a growing recognition that the law of goods represents a substantial part of the law of property and is not something confined to the realms of commercial law, but also there is a steadily growing body of literature on the subject-matter. At one time the law of goods was governed by the Sale of Goods Act 1893, which for all purposes governed the market transactions of goods. The Act did not govern many of the other types of property interests that were capable of existing in goods, such as bailment, security transactions, hire purchase and other matters relating to title by finding lost and abandoned objects and treasure trove. Although the Sale of Goods Act 1979 went some way to redressing these matters, the essence of the 1979 statute again was to govern the sale of goods. Instead the common law covered matters such as bailment and so forth. More recently, the types of property interest that are capable of existing in goods have expanded. For example, it is now recognised that where goods form part of a bulk and are unascertained, buyers of the goods are capable of acquiring co-ownership interests until such time as the goods are ascertained to the particular contracts in question.[35]

Intangible property

A person's wealth today is comprised of an increasing amount of intangible rather than tangible property. By this it is meant that the types of resources, assets or objects to which claims are made are represented in an intangible form. It is not unusual for a person to acquire shares in a public company; indeed, many of the employees of such companies today have schemes that allow them to acquire such shares at discount prices. A company share enti-

---

[34] A. Clarke, 'Property Law: Re-establishing Diversity' (1997) 50 Current Legal Problems at p 148.
[35] Sale of Goods (Amendment) Act 1995; see Chapter 9.

tles the owner to share in the profits of the company. By its nature a share is an intangible form of property that is not dependent on possession. Other examples of intangible forms of wealth include claims under an insurance policy, debts and claims to money. A debt is an intangible thing in which a proprietary claim can be sustained; furthermore, it is capable of assignment. On a related matter, further examples of intangible property include documentary intangibles: these are instruments or documents embodying an obligation on a person to pay a specified sum of money on presentation of the document. For example, a bill of exchange obliges the drawee of the bill to pay a specified sum of money on presentation of the bill. [36]

A very special class of intangible property consists of what is commonly known as intellectual property. It includes items such as patents, copyright, trademarks, and registered industrial designs and know-how. The significance of these forms of wealth cannot be underestimated as they form a substantial medium through which revenue is generated. These forms of wealth demonstrate that the nature of value in property no longer lies in its use value but rather in its exchange value.

EMERGING PROPERTY FORMS

Although the English law of property has a fairly rigid approach to what can and cannot constitute the objects of property, changes in social and economic patterns exert pressures on the categories of property to be extended.[37] Admitting new objects and resources into the category of property is not an easy task. It often happens that the types of resources to which people wish to make proprietary claims differ in their nature from land and chattels. The changing nature of these resources consequently affects the manner in which the traditional rules of property – and here we are essentially concerned with trespassory rules – are capable of extension to such resources. Given these problems, the effect has often been that systems of law may simply decline to extend the objects of the property relationship, basing their justifications on the premise that these novel objects do not fit into the traditional notions of property. However, it is not entirely clear why this should be the case. Such an approach fails to appreciate law as operating in an ever-changing society. In this respect one is often reminded of the precious words of the then Honourable Mr Justice Devlin who, despite writing in a commercial law context, once wrote:

---

[36] See Chapter 9.
[37] See B. Edgeworth, 'Post Property? A Post Modern Conception of Private Property' (1998) 11 University of New South Wales Law Journal at p 87.

'it is only with much effort that law and practice upon any subject can be kept together; and that is because, though they have the same origin, they are in their motions attracted by different objects. Rigidity and a regular pattern are pleasing to the legal mind, and so soon as he can the lawyer sets up a system of principles and rules from which he is reluctant to depart. He may start close to his subject, but because it is alive, illogical and contrary, it is likely to slip and slither out of the pattern he devises for it. The danger in any branch of law is that it ossifies.'[38]

Reich and new property

In his seminal article Reich identified how a person's wealth had changed over time.[39] In particular, he emphasized how governments had become a major source of wealth for persons, thereby displacing more orthodox forms of wealth in the form of tangible objects. The types of resources to which Reich referred in his work consisted of welfare benefits, salaries for those in public service, pensions for retired persons, licences and other forms of government subsidies and franchises. In some cases these formed the very basis for a person's wellbeing and liberty. Reich's main contention was that these forms of wealth should be accorded the same degree of protection as traditional forms of wealth such as land and chattels. Reich's ideology of property is certainly not easy to accommodate in traditional property thought. Whether claims to, for example, welfare benefits can be the subject-matter of property rights is a very difficult issue to determine. Such types of resources are not really vested in persons absolutely but are held conditionally upon fulfilment of obligations imposed by the state. When such obligations are not fulfilled the government may deny the right to such benefits. Furthermore, claims to welfare benefits and other forms of government benefit do not empower the claimant with a right to exclude others in the traditional sense of property ideology. For example, as observed in Chapter 2, the right to exclude others empowers the holder of a property right with a right to exclude the whole world from interference with the right that is vested in him. Claims to a welfare benefit often entitle a claimant who satisfies the criteria with a right not to be excluded from enjoyment thereof rather than a general right *in rem*. In this respect welfare benefits constitute a form of common property rather than a strict form of private property.

The thrust of Reich's work points to the government as a provider of wealth in the form of a welfare benefit system. Such a system seeks to redress the imbalance of wealth that arises through capitalism. Redistribution of

---

[38] P. Devlin, 'The Relationship Between Commercial Law and Commercial Practice' (1951) 14 MLR 249 at p 250.
[39] C.A. Reich, 'The New Property' (1964) 73 Yale LJ 733.

wealth in the form of welfare benefits simply seeks to give what should already belong to a person for his liberty and security. Reich argued that property, as a legal institution, formed the function of protecting certain private rights in wealth of any kind. Without property a person would lack independence and dignity. Therefore, resources flowing from the government constituted the private property of an individual. This is a theme with which other property theorists would agree. Murphy and Roberts write that 'those deprived of property are at the same time deprived of citizenship – the stateless have no place of their own. Private property can be seen as a basic human right, because it guarantees the reality of place which is necessary in order to ground the possibility of becoming a fully active citizen.'[40]

A much-cited famous American case, which is said to have influenced Reich's work, is that of *Flemming* v *Nestor*.[41] On the facts of this case the Secretary for Health, Education and Welfare appealed to the United States Supreme Court from a decision of the District Court for the District of Columbia. The appellee, an alien, had immigrated to the United States from Bulgaria in 1913. In November 1955 the appellee became eligible for old-age pension payable by the state; however, this entitlement was withdrawn in July 1956 when the authorities discovered that the appellee had been a member of the Communist Party between 1933 and 1939. Pursuant to section 241(a)(6)(C)(i) of the Immigration and Nationality Act the appellee was deported for having been such a member. Alongside his deportation, his old-age benefit was also withdrawn under section 202 of the Social Security Act.[42] The District Court for the District of Columbia had concluded that section 202 was unconstitutional and that the appellee's right to old-age benefit was wrongfully terminated. Mr Justice Harlan, delivering the opinion of the United States Supreme Court, held that the District Court had erred in holding that section 202 of the Social Security Act deprived the appellee of an 'accrued property right'. Therefore, because the appellee had no property rights in the old-age benefit, termination of such entitlement did not offend the Due Process Clause of the Fifth Amendment of the United States Constitution. The Due Process Clause provides that '... No person shall ... be deprived of life, liberty and property without the due process of the law; nor shall private property be taken away for public use without just compensation.'

In his work, Reich found the decision of the United States Supreme Court to have profound implications. Reich pointed to the fact that no form of government benefit is more personal and individual than the old-age benefit. Not only does the recipient contribute to the social security fund during the years

---

[40] W.T. Murphy and S. Roberts, *Understanding Property Law* (1998) at p 8.
[41] (1960) 363 US 603.
[42] 68 Stat 1083, as amended, 42 USC s 402.

of his employment, but also such benefit is a compulsory substitute for private property. It certainly carries with it all the functions of private property in that the recipient relies on it for his own self-independence and security. However, unlike traditional notions of private property, wealth that flows from the government in the form of benefits of various kinds is held conditionally, subject to confiscation by the state for other paramount reasons. In this respect Reich viewed claims to welfare benefits as a form of new feudalism where, as observed in the previous chapter, claims to land in England were dependent on the provision of services of various kinds.

The idea that welfare benefits and other entitlements flowing from government should be accorded the same degree of protection as traditional forms of property has attracted strong support since Reich's work. The United States has been more receptive to the idea than England, for as observed above[43], the idea of new property has been closely argued in the context of the Due Process Clause and the constitutional significance attached to property. Other commentators, such as Professor Glendon, have explained support for the recognition of new property in a historical context.[44] Glendon argues that the idea of new property should be understood in a historical context, in particular the decline in the importance of the family and the relative increase in claims to jobs and government benefits as sources of independence, dignity and economic wellbeing. This is a very important observation and one that cannot be ignored in the need to understand contemporary notions of property. Up and until the nineteenth century the father of the family was normally the person who had the main role of providing for his family; his wife, as observed above, could not really hold property in her own name. The children of the family looked to the father as the provider for their economic wellbeing. Indeed, the idea *paterfamilias* linked property closely to the family and economic wellbeing that flowed from it. However, the breakdown of the family from the middle of the twentieth century, and its continued breakdown, has resulted in a number of changes in the types of claims that now perform the functions of economic wellbeing and dignity.[45]

---

[43] See note 9.

[44] M. Glendon, 'The New Family and the New Property' (1979) 53 Tulane LR 697.

[45] It is not just the breakdown of the family that has called for a re-thinking of property law; the actual ideology of *paterfamilias* does not seem to apply neatly in modern property law. For example, the idea of husband as provider and the wife enjoying inferior status, has formed the basis of certain property rules that have been questioned as to their relevance in the modern law. One principle of property law holds that a purchase of property in the name of another has the effect that the legal title to such property is presumed to be held on a resulting trust for the person providing the purchase money on the basis that equity assumes bargains and not gifts: see *Dyer* v *Dyer* (1788) 2 Cox Eq Cas 92 at 93. However, where the person advancing the money is a husband to a wife or a father to a child, the presumption is that the husband or father has a donative intent. This presumption does not apply to a wife giving to a husband or to a mother giving to a child. In *Pettitt* v *Pettitt* [1970] AC 777 Lord Diplock, at 824C, strongly questioned these presumptions and he went on to say that they belonged to a propertied class belonging to a totally different social era.

Glendon notes that jobs or welfare entitlements may be the only source of wealth for a person in the modern world, and that such forms of wealth should be accorded the status of property just as land and other things were accorded property in the age of *paterfamilias*.[46] Glendon argues that new property has increasingly been accorded legal protection; for example, it is becoming increasingly difficult to terminate a person's job without just reason. Although English lawyers have been less receptive to the idea of new property, Gray and Symes explained that 'the contemporary emphasis on the need for residential security' was linked with the fact that people generally were living in an age of insecurity and that, 'there is a very real sense in which the right to live in a house or flat free from the threat of arbitrary eviction, free from the unrestricted impact of normal market forces, has itself become a new form of proprietary right.'[47] It is interesting that, unlike other conventional textbooks on real property law, Gray in his first edition of *Elements of Land Law*[48] was to devote a whole chapter to homelessness. More recently, in their excellent work, Cowan and Fionda explain that issues such as homelessness ought to feature in land law themes more predominantly.[49] In particular, they question the approach of land lawyers who simply look to land law themes from a consumerist point of view. The idea that land law is concerned with issues of those who are included as consumers fails to address issues of social inclusion. They write that 'the preoccupation with consumerism is at odds with the more traditional socialist view of citizenship as social inclusion – a preoccupation with the most marginalized and poverty-stricken in society in order to ensure their inclusion in the mainstream of society; that is empowerment through social unity.'[50]

Although the idea of new property has sound social justifications underlying it, if one is to accept new property as property, there is a need to redefine the idea of property in law. The characteristics of new property do not fit neatly into the exclusionary nature of the traditional notion of private property. Furthermore, the idea of new property does not fit into the idea of ownership in private law that is discussed in the next chapter. Indeed, new property and the claims that are comprised within it seem to exist independently of ownership of resources in the strict sense. The idea that persons have proprietary claims to things such as welfare benefits, jobs and rights to residential security does not rely on the exclusionary control of a particular resource. Instead these claims depend on the right to be admitted to a particular resource which serves the function of human development.[51]

---

[46] *Op cit*, at 708.

[47] K. Gray and P. Symes, *Real Property and Real People* (1981) at p 13.

[48] 1st edn, 1987.

[49] D. Cowan and J. Fionda, 'Homelessness' in Bright and Dewar (eds) *Land Law: Themes and Perspectives* (1998) at p 257.

[50] *Ibid*, at p 261.

[51] For a more recent analysis of new property, see S. Bowles and H. Gintis, *Democracy and Capitalism: Property, Community and the Contradictions of Modern Social Thought* (1986).

Property rights in body parts and human tissue

The idea that body parts and human tissue may form part of property relationship is not something that is new; indeed a large body of literature is steadily growing on the question of how far such 'things' should be capable of ownership.[52] On a philosophical level there is no reason to suggest why a person may not own himself. Indeed, as examined in Chapter 3, John Locke's justification for private property was underpinned by the very notion of self-ownership.[53] However, the debate is not simply an academic one; nor is it philosophical for that matter. In contemporary society we are not concerned so much with the question of whether property rights exist in human corpses;[54] instead, the pace of medical research has presented modern society with a host of new legal and ethical issues over the control of body parts. Various organs of the body are now capable of transplant into other bodies and blood is capable of transfusion. However, even more recently, rapid advances in the science of genetics and its applications present new and complex issues for individuals and society. In particular, the commercialisation of products manufactured through genetic engineering raises issues such as who owns a gene, the property rights over genetically manufactured products and the control of trade secrets. Whatever moral and ethical arguments there may be for the rejection of holding body parts as capable of ownership – and for that matter as capable of being subject to market or other transactions – there are some real pressures from various individuals that they be accorded proprietary status. The significance of attaching proprietary status to such objects lies in the consequential property law protection given to the owner of such body parts. Where such body parts are used, for example, for commercial exploitation, it is paramount that property law principles can protect the owner's commercial interests in such body parts or products made from such parts.

Property issues in body parts may arise in a number of contexts. One popular context is criminal law. In particular, in relation to the Theft Act 1968, s 1(1), which requires that for theft there must be an appropriation of 'property belonging to another', the question arises as to whether appropriat-

---

[52] Amongst the most cited works, see S. Munzer, 'An Uneasy Case Against Property Rights in Body Parts' in Paul, Miller and Paul (eds), *Property Rights* (1994) at p 259; P. Mathews, 'Whose Body? People as Property' (1983) 36 Current Legal Problems at p 193; R.S. Magnusson, 'Proprietary Rights In Human Tissue' in Palmer and McKendrick (eds), *Interests in Goods* (1993) at p 237; P. Skegg, 'Human Corpses, Medical Specimens and the Law of Property' (1975) Anglo-American Law Review 412 and also J.W. Harris, 'Who Owns my Body' (1996) 16 OJLS at 55.

[53] J. Locke, *Second Treatise of Government* (1690); see, generally, Chapter 3.

[54] Recognition is, however, one step towards recognising property in body parts. The general common law position is that the corpse of a human being cannot be the subject of property; this rule applies even though the person who is under a duty to dispose of it has a right of possession which, as explained in the next chapter, is one of the fundamental incidents of ownership. The rule has, however, been criticised as being based on very weak authorities: see P. Skegg, *op cit.*

ing body parts belonging to another can amount to a theft.[55] What counts as property for the purposes of the statute is not defined, this being a matter for the common law. Although there appears to be no general rule that for the purposes of the Theft Act 1968 body parts constitute property, there are a handful of authorities which suggest that for particular purposes body parts may constitute property so as to bring the offence of theft. In *R v Herbert*[56] the defendant, under the old larceny charge, was convicted of theft for cutting some hair from the head of a female passenger in his car. Unfortunately this case was only decided at magistrates level and it is not entirely clear upon what basis the magistrates arrived at their decision. In a later case, *R v Welsh*,[57] the defendant was convicted of theft of a urine sample which he had provided pursuant to section 9 of the Road Traffic Act 1972. Having initially provided the sample, the defendant poured it down a sink while the duty officer was absent from the police station room. Although the defendant later appealed against the sentence, the Court of Appeal did not comment on the appropriateness of the conviction itself. Presumably, therefore, the urine sample constituted property belonging to the police.

A much more convincing authority on the question of whether body parts can constitute property is that of *R v Rothery*[58] in which the defendant provided a blood sample in a capsule belonging to the police. He later removed the blood capsule when the police officer's back was turned and took it away when released. The defendant was convicted both for theft and for failing to provide a specimen under section 9 of the Road Traffic Act 1972. On appeal, his conviction for not providing a specimen was quashed on the basis that he had provided a specimen, albeit one which he later appropriated. The conviction for theft was upheld and the Court of Appeal did not question its appropriateness.

The above authorities do recognise the need for the recognition of property analysis to body parts. If the police in the latter two cases discussed above were found to have property in the samples of body parts provided by the defendants, then it naturally follows that such ownership must have flowed from the defendants themselves. The defendants must have had property in their body parts which then was gratuitously transferred to the police. Tissue samples, blood donations and DNA samples should be accorded proprietary status to avoid abuse and improper profit through commercial uses of such products. Property analysis to body parts, however, does raise secondary, yet important, questions as to whether such parts should be subject to the whole spectrum of property law. For example, in relation to the transfer of blood and human tissue, are such things 'goods' for the purposes of the Sale of Goods Act

---

[55] See, generally, A. Smith, 'Stealing the Body and its Parts' [1976] Crim LR 622.
[56] *The Times*, 22 Dec 1960; (1961) Journal of Criminal Law 163.
[57] [1974] RTR 478.
[58] [1976] RTR 550.

and therefore subject to the implied terms of quality in a contract of sale? For example, can blood which is sold on the open market, which then turns out to be contaminated, give rise to liability under the Sale of Goods Act 1979 for not being fit for its purpose? The American and Australian courts have tackled this issue for some time now and suggest approaches that may be followed in the English courts.[59] In the American decisions the approach appears to suggest that the matter may be decided on the basis of whether the blood was given voluntarily by a hospital or commercially by a blood bank.[60] In the former case the view is that the transfer of the blood is regarded as a provision of a service rather than a sale of goods. In the latter, where a profit-making organisation transfers blood it has been characterised as a sale of a good.[61]

A more recent and controversial context in which property law principles have been and will continue to be questioned is that of genetic engineering. Modern biotechnology has created a number of advances in modern medicine, but at the same time it has raised controversial questions that remain unresolved. Genetic engineering refers to that process whereby scientists can change the DNA of a living organism. Biotechnology on a broader scale involves things such as the transfer of genetic materials such as ova and sperm, and human tissue transplants. The splitting up of and customisation of genes that belong to individuals have allowed scientists to develop products that can aid in the cure of many diseases. The rapid discoveries made by the Human Genome Project (which consists of scientists on both sides of the Atlantic) and private genetic engineering companies, mean that scientists have almost deciphered the human genetic code. The advantages of this discovery include the manufacture of products that will revolutionise the diagnosis, prevention and treatment of most human diseases.[62] Such discovery has, however, provoked concerns from almost all parts of society. There is the moral concern as to whether individuals should interfere with what God has created. Public interest groups worry about the long-term effects genetic engineering will have on the human race.

For the commercialist involved in using genetic engineering to make money, there is the question of how discoveries made from genetic engineering and products manufactured thereby can be protected by law. The most obvious way is for patent protection to be given to genes and products made from genetic

---

[59] The American and Australian authorities are considered by R.S. Magnusson in 'Proprietary Rights In Human Tissue' in Palmer and McKendrick (eds), *Interests in Goods* (1993) at p 254.

[60] See *Perlmutter v Beth David Hospital* (1954) 123 NE 2d 792 and *Carter v Inter-Faith Hospital of Queens* (1969) 304 NYS 2d 65.

[61] This distinction may not be of particular significance in English law since to characterise blood given in a hospital and without profit as a provision of a service rather than as a sale of a good would nevertheless attract liability because the Supply of Goods and Services Act 1982 imposes similar warranties in the case of a supply of a service. There is, of course, the defence under s 4(1)(e) of the Act which allows the supplier to escape liability if the defect could not have been detected given the current state of technological and scientific knowledge.

[62] See B. Macintyre, 'Opening the Book of Life', *The Times*, 27 June 2000.

engineering. To attach proprietary significance to genetically engineered products, however, raises a number of important questions, such as who owns genetic information and who owns the products engineered from cell line discoveries from human tissue belonging to another. For example, where a person voluntarily or involuntarily contributes DNA samples that result in the production of a novel cell line that can cure a certain disease, who owns the novel cell line? The answers to this question, certainly in so far as English law is concerned, remain unclear. Statutory regimes such as the Human Organ Transplants Act 1989 and the Human Fertilisation and Embryology Act 1990 impose certain duties and prohibitions in respect of the storage and transfer of organs and embryos without making any assumptions about ownership rights therein. Litigation in the United States has, however, not only shown the potential for property protection to be accorded to genetically engineered products, but also has shown the difficulties faced by the courts when dealing with such matters.

The California courts in *Moore v Regents of the University of California*[63] were faced with the issue of whether a donor of human tissue was entitled to share in the proceeds of sale of a biotechnological product made from the donor's tissue. On the facts of the case, the defendant, Dr Golde, diagnosed Moore as suffering from hairy cell leukaemia and advised Moore that his spleen would have to be removed. The operation was duly carried out and Moore thereafter, in the course of his treatment, continued to visit the medical centre where Dr Golde was based. Moore supplied Dr Golde with a series of body fluid samples, which were initially intended for monitoring his progress. Dr Golde and his associates at the University of California Medical Center developed a unique cell line, capable of therapeutic value, using Moore's body tissue. This cell line was duly patented and licences were sold to drug companies. The commercial use of the cell line generated considerable revenue for Dr Golde, the University of California Medical Center and the drug companies. Moore initially had no knowledge that Dr Golde was using his human tissue for the production of the cell line. When Moore did find out that his human tissue was responsible for the production of the cell line Moore sued Dr Golde and the University for the tort of conversion. This property tort requires the plaintiff to show that somebody else has dealt with goods in a manner inconsistent with the rights of the true owner – for example, exercising possession of goods without the true owner's consent.

In the California Court of Appeal, Moore succeeded on the grounds that his spleen, which contained the cells used in the production of the cell line, was something over which Moore had an unrestricted right to use. The Court of Appeal explained that this right was akin to a property interest.[64]

---

[63] 249 Cal Rep 494 (1988) (Court of Appeals); 271 Cal Rep 146 (1990) (California Supreme Court).
[64] *Ibid*, at 505. The Court explained that 'the right of dominion over one's own body, and the interests one has therein, are recognised in many cases. These rights and the interests are so akin to property interests that it would be subterfuge to call them something else'.

However, on further appeal to the California Supreme Court, the decision of the Court of Appeal was overruled. The Supreme Court held that the finding of a property interest in human tissue and products generated thereunder would have a negative impact on medical and biotechnological research.[65] Furthermore, that scientist would be under a tort duty to investigate the consensual pedigree of each human cell used in research. Although Moore was denied a property interest in his human tissue, the Supreme Court did not deny that there could ever be property interests in human tissue or products generated from human tissue. The majority clearly felt that a property interest in the cells belonged to the Medical Center so that if somebody stole these cells a conversion action would lie against the thief.[66]

The litigation brought by Moore in California illustrates the difficulties in applying property principles to body parts and human tissue. Attaching property significance to body parts and human tissue is influenced by a number of factors. For example, whilst it may seem unfair that the person who genetically engineers a product using human tissue extracted from another can make a substantial amount of money, scientific research would be negatively affected if property rights were accorded to the owner of the tissue. However, there is no reason why the inventor of a genetic product cannot gain property rights in the product; after all, this is the only way his or her commercial interest in the product can be protected. The proprietary nature of body parts and human tissue will continue to be a controversial question for property lawyers. Leaving aside the scientific and commercial merits or de-merits as the case may be, there will always be strong moral and ethical doubts as to the appropriateness of according proprietary significance to separated body parts in whatever form they may be.[67] In his work, Munzer reviews the literature which discusses the arguments against property rights in body parts. In his own conclusions, based on the Kantian premise of dignity, he argues that 'it is morally objectionable for persons to sell their body parts if they offend dignity by selling for a reason that is insufficiently strong relative to the characteristics of the part sold'.[68] Dignity is an unconditioned and incomparable worth, thus having no market value. Other philosophers have objected on the grounds that property in body parts amounts to commodification, which is said to be morally wrong.[69]

---

[65] 271 Cal Rep 146 (1990) at 162.

[66] See the judgment of Broussard at 168.

[67] For an excellent discussion on this point, see S. Munzer, 'An Uneasy Case Against Property Rights in Body Parts' in Paul, Miller and Paul (eds), *Property Rights* (1994) at p 259.

[68] *Ibid*, at p 285.

[69] H. Hansmann, 'The Economics and Ethics of Markets for Human Organs' (1989) 14(1) Journal of Health Politics, Policy and Law.

Confidential information

In recent times there has been a great surge in the types of information that persons possess. In the age of industrialism, technical know-how is information that provides the very basis of commercial profit. If such information generated by a person or persons is wrongfully used by another to his or her advantage, the original owner of the information has a resource taken away from him just like any other tangible resource. More recently, the pace of scientific and technological research has led to the production of information that can be used for a number of commercial purposes. It has already been noted above that aggressive competition exists in the attempt to find scientific knowledge about human nature and how human genes function so as to produce products in medicine. Clearly the persons who acquire such knowledge will attempt to patent any product that is acquired through use of the information. However, before such products or designs are patented, does the information acquired belong to the persons who discover it in the form of a property right so that wrongful interference amounts to an infringement of a property right? Moreover, does it matter whether information is classified as property? The increasing nature of western societies to become information societies has raised the question whether information is a resource in which persons can acquire proprietary rights protected by principles of property law.[70]

Unlike the new property arguments initiated by Reich and the debates about property rights in body parts, which have been discussed above, the case for arguing property in information does not appear to be compelling at first glance. English law, like many other Commonwealth countries, has a fairly well-established law preventing the misuse of confidential information. The equitable action for breach of confidence protects the unauthorised use of confidential information. The equitable action lies irrespective of any contractual relationship between the confidant and discloser.[71] The remedy most often sought to protect the plaintiff's right is that of an injunction with an account for profits that may have been made with the unauthorised use of the information.[72] What is, however, unclear is the extent to which a plaintiff may be entitled to damages; this confusion stems from the very uncertainty over whether the equitable action for breach of confidence protects a property right in the true sense or concerns a duty of good faith arising in equity alone.

---

[70] See, generally, N.E. Palmer and P. Kohler, 'Information as Property' in Palmer and McKendrick (eds), *Interests in Goods* (1993) at p 187; and also J. Stuckey, 'The Equitable Action for Breach of Confidence: Is Information Ever Property' (1981) 9 Sydney Law Review 402.

[71] See *Saltman Engineering Company Ltd* v *Campbell Engineering Company Ltd* (1948) 65 RPC 203, where Lord Greene MR explained (at 466) that 'if the defendant is proved to have used confidential information, directly or indirectly obtained from the plaintiff, without the consent, express or implied, of the plaintiff, he will be guilty of an infringement of the plaintiff's right'.

[72] See, for example, *Peter Pan Manufacturing Corporation* v *Corsets Silhouette Ltd* [1963] RPC 45.

The English law authorities on the question of whether information is property or otherwise are not entirely consistent. Two often cited authorities rejecting that information is property are *Boardman* v *Phipps*[73] and *Oxford* v *Moss*.[74] In the former case, where a solicitor had used confidential information belonging to a trust, Lord Upjohn strongly dissented that information was property.[75] In the latter case, where a student misappropriated an examination paper, it was held that such student could not be guilty of theft under section 4 of the Theft Act 1968 since information was not property. However, dicta in other cases have suggested that information is property just like any other property. In *Rolls Royce Ltd* v *Jeffrey*[76] Lord Radcliffe could not see how confidential information was different from other forms of corporate assets. Although the equitable action for breach of confidence protects the holder of such information from wrongful use of it by another, commentators suggest that there are strong merits for treating confidential information as property. The basic claim is that, whilst the equitable action for breach of confidence protects against the wrongful use of information, a proprietary analysis of information would afford the original holder or possessor of such information with much better legal protection. In other words, the protection afforded by property law, and in this case personal property, would be far more extensive. For example, Palmer and Kohler identify two main areas where a proprietary analysis of information would be much more beneficial.[77] The first relates to remedies and the second to third parties who may acquire confidential information from the discloser.

Whilst the equitable action for breach of confidence opens the way for the plaintiff to seek an injunction against the discloser with the possibility of account for profits made, the question of whether the plaintiff is entitled to compensation is more difficult. The principal problem with the action for breach of confidence is, given that such action seeks to protect a purely equitable right, can monetary compensation be awarded? Although the Chancery Amendment Act 1858, commonly known as the Lord Cairns' Act, gave equity a power to award damages in addition to, or in place of, an equitable remedy, the question is whether damages will be awarded pursuant to a purely equitable right and in circumstances where no injunction has been granted.[78] It is clear that damages may be given to the plaintiff where the plaintiff is also seeking an injunction and that such damages would compensate for past actions of the discloser.[79] However, if the only likely breach has occurred so that there is

---

[73] [1967] 2 AC 46.

[74] (1978) 68 Cr App Rep 183.

[75] Ibid, at 127–128.

[76] [1962] 1 All ER 801.

[77] *Op cit*, at p 189.

[78] The provisions of the Lord Cairns' Act are now found in s 50 of the Supreme Court Act 1981.

[79] See generally *Jaggard* v *Sawyer* [1995] 1 WLR 269.

no case for an injunction, there is no question of the plaintiff suing for damages under the principle of the Lord Cairns' Act. Given this problem, it is more appropriate to analyse wrongful interference with information as an interference with property of another. Such information would, if likened to an interference with a chattel, entitle the plaintiff to sue alongside the grounds of conversion of a chattel. Palmer and Kohler identify a further advantage: they explain that if the information, which is wrongfully appropriated, has a special or personal significance, then it may be possible for the plaintiff to sue for special damages to represent distress occasioned by the discloser.[80]

The role of third parties in the disclosure of confidential information is another area in which a proprietary analysis of information would prove appropriate. The position under the equitable action for breach of confidence is far from clear in respect of third parties. Here one is dealing with the case where B wrongfully appropriates information from A and that information comes into the possession of C who may be dishonest, negligent or entirely innocent. In so far as concerns third parties who deliberately or recklessly acquire information, there is no question that they would be liable. This liability could arise under tort for inducing or procuring a breach of contract, interference with business or conspiracy. However, given that liability for breach of confidence is not necessarily based on contract, mere bad faith on the part of the third party would be sufficient to impose liability.[81] What remains unclear is whether a negligent or innocent third party becomes liable to the original owner of the information if the third party uses such information. Given that bad faith imports a subjective test requiring the defendant to be fixed with a state of mind, it is doubtful whether negligent and innocent third parties would be liable to the plaintiff.[82]

The apparent advantages of employing a proprietary analysis of information are that third parties would be liable under the established property law principles that govern third parties. The recognition of information as the legal property of a person would make it a right *in rem* and thus bind the whole world. Moreover, the application of the *nemo dat* rule would mean that third parties could not acquire any rights in such information.[83] Alternatively, it may be possible to construe information as equitable property of the person who originally possesses such information. Construing information as equitable property would make third parties liable on the principles of notice that apply to equitable rights in personal property.

---

[80] *Op cit*, at p 189.

[81] See W.R. Cornish, *Intellectual Property* (2nd edn, 1989) at p 232.

[82] In *Wheatley v Bell* [1982] 2 NSWLR 544 liability was imposed on an innocent volunteer once that volunteer was informed of the breach of confidence.

[83] See Chapter 3 for the difference between the legal and equitable rights of property and an explanation of the *nemo dat* rule.

Innocent volunteers would be liable since equity would not aid them with assistance[84] and negligent third parties would not satisfy the *bona fide purchaser for value test* that applies to third parties. This does seem tempting since it would not detract from the historical origins of the breach of confidence action, which is equity. However, equitable property is typically associated as arising, for example, under a trust where there is separation of legal and equitable ownership. It cannot be said that such a situation would arise if information were to be treated as equitable property. However, this is not an obstacle since there are occasions in property law where an equitable interest exists without an equivalent interest in law. The obvious example is that of a restrictive covenant in real property law. Other jurisdictions have rejected that the equitable action for breach of confidence grants the plaintiff an equitable right in the property sense.[85]

THE CHANGING FUNCTIONS OF PROPERTY

The reasons for claiming proprietary rights in things of value change with time; in other words, the function of property changes with time.[86] For example, the reasons for claiming ownership in land in the sixteenth and seventeenth centuries are not necessarily the same as those arising during the emergence of capitalism. Further still, with the emergence of the welfare state, the institution of property has yet undergone changes in its functions. Property lawyers often distinguish between the use value and exchange value of property. The use value or function of property lays emphasis on security claims that allow individuals to survive in society. The use value of land, for example, entitles individuals to draw such benefits from the land which promote that individual's wellbeing. The exchange value of property places emphasis on capital; an individual who relies on the exchange value of property is looking to the benefit of generating capital and revenue.

Before the emergence of capitalism, the predominant function of property lay in its use value. The emergence of capitalism, however, resulted in a gradual shift away from the use value of property to its exchange value. In particular, the purpose of ownership in land in the modern capitalist system is not simply subsistence and survival; rather the function of ownership is to generate wealth. The changing function also affects the ideology of property. Claims to resources in a capitalist system are claims to incorporeal things such as a corporation. It has already been observed how ownership claims to

---

[84] On the general equitable maxim that equity will not assist a volunteer.

[85] *Wheatley* v *Bell* [1982] 2 NSWLR 544; see the judgment of Helsham CJ at 549–550.

[86] An excellent account of the functional transformation of property is provided by K. Renner, *The Institutions of Private Law and Their Functions* (1949) at p 81. See also W. Friedmann, *Law in a Changing Society* (1959) at p 93, where the author examines the changing concepts of property.

corporations differ from traditional notions of ownership. The emergence of the welfare state suggests that the function of property is not necessarily exchange oriented; rather, claims to welfare benefits emphasise a use value of property. Again, as noted above, the ideology of property in the welfare state is fundamentally different from that in a pure system of capitalism. It is because social and economic conditions change that the function of property changes and so must its ideology. Lawyers on the whole do not wish to see significant changes in the ideology of property despite the changes in economic and social conditions. It is, therefore, for this reason that claims to certain resources are not admitted into the category of property when they should be on the grounds that conditions have changed.

Gray and Symes identified three major phases in the conceptual development of property in England.[87] The ideology of property – and included here is the function of property – changes from one phase to another. The first phase identified by Gray and Symes is the 'age of feudal solidarity'. In this phase property functions in a self-supporting society, in particular with the head of the family. The head of the household, the father, is the person who engages in property relations for the purpose of providing the basis of subsistence for his family. Otto Kahn Freund writes that in this period of time, 'property ... the central institution of private law, fulfilled, in the system of simple commodity production, the functions of providing an order of goods and, in part, an order of power.'[88] In this period property is vested in the head of the household or *paterfamilias* and it is that person who exercises power over others. The *paterfamilias* is not concerned with trade and revenue generation; rather, the function of property is essentially in the use of things for the existence of the family. In this respect, Friedmann writes: 'in a broadly accurate simplification, the owner of a farm or a workshop in such society owns the land, the stock and the tools, which he needs to live or to produce in exchange for certain elementary commodities. Hired labour and trade in commodities are generally ancillary rather than essential complements of property. Property and enjoyment of property and the capacity to work are not too far apart from each other.'[89]

The second period of time in which the idea of property changed is described by Gray and Symes as the 'age of commercialism'. The predominant function of property here is to generate income and capital; it can be said that the emphasis in this period is on the exchange value of property rather than the use value. In this period there is a movement away from basic commodity production based around the *paterfamilias*; furthermore, the

---

[87] K. Gray and P. Symes, *Real Property and Real People* (1981) at p 14.

[88] Otto Kahn Freund, 'Introduction to K. Renner' in K. Renner (ed), *The Institutions of Private Law and Their Social Functions* (1949) at p 26.

[89] W. Friedmann, *Law in a Changing Society* (2nd edn, 1959) at p 99.

power aspect of property is now extended to cover a much more diverse range of things than just land. With the emergence of the industrial revolution, the importance of land becomes displaced with the factories that are built upon it. Individual wealth is now contained in intangible things such as shares in a company and wages, in addition to land and other assets such as machinery. The importance of the exchange value of land is reflected in the Law of Property Act 1925 which had as one of its main aims the free alienation of land.[90] Just as other assets could be freely transferred on the open market, land too should be freely alienable.

The final stage identified by Gray and Symes is the 'age of social welfare' where the function of property has once again changed to reflect its use value rather than exchange value. In an age of social welfare, where people's claims depend not so much on the ability to share in the profits of a company or the ability to sell labour, but rather on welfare benefits, property performs the function of allowing individuals to belong to a kind of society.[91] It is in this context that debates about 'new property', which have been discussed above, have argued for property to be extended to such things as welfare benefits and other claims to residential security. Macpherson writes:

> 'If property is to remain justified as instrumental to life, it will have to become the right not to be excluded from the means of such a life. Property will, in such circumstances, increasingly have to become a right to a set of social relations, a right to a kind of society. It will have to include not only a right to a share in political power as instrumental in determining the kind of society, but a right to that kind of society which is instrumental to a full and free life.'[92]

---

[90] See S. Anderson, 'The 1925 Property Legislation: Setting Contexts' in S. Bright and K. Dewar (eds), *Land Law: Themes and Perspectives* (1998) at p 107.

[91] See C.B. Macpherson, 'Capitalism and the Changing Concept of Property' in E. Kamenka and R. Neale (eds), *Feudalism, Capitalism and Beyond* (1975) at p 121.

[92] *Ibid*, at p 121.

6

OWNERSHIP, POSSESSION AND TITLE

THREE FUNDAMENTAL CONCEPTS IN PROPERTY LAW

This chapter examines three fundamental concepts of property law: namely, ownership, possession and title. Although the underlying idea of property revolves around the idea of rights in things and that such rights can be multi-functional, the most predominant right a person can have in a thing is the right of ownership. Ownership usually carries with it a number of incidents, the most common of which is the right to possession of the thing in which ownership is held. Ownership is a *de jure* relationship between a person and a thing. This simply means that ownership is a question of law. Whether A is the owner of a piece of land is dependent on whether he can furnish necessary evidence of his ownership therein. In the case of land this will usually involve evidence of title deeds or as registered proprietor of the legal title to the land. Possession, on the other hand, is a *de facto* relationship between a person and a thing. Possession is a question of fact; it does not necessarily mean that a person in possession is the owner of the thing in question. Although it is quite normal for ownership and possession to go hand in hand, it need not be the case. A person may have possession without having ownership in the thing in question. For example, it is quite possible for a thief to have possession without ownership, or an agent to have possession without ownership. Possession without owner-ship can occur lawfully, for example, in the case of a bailment of goods.[1]

---

[1] A bailment arises where goods are entrusted to another, called the bailee, who is either to hold or do something with the goods for the bailor. Bailment is a concept used in a number of situations, most commonly, commercial. Examples of bailment include mere storage of goods for another and hire of goods. The relationship between the bailee and bailor is one of bailment and is subject to rights and duties. See, generally, M. Bridge, *Personal Property Law* (2nd edn, 1996) at pp 26–33.

The first objective of this chapter is to examine the nature and idea of the concepts of ownership, possession and title. The second objective is to examine the relationship between the three concepts. This is basically an inquiry into whether the concepts are inter-related and, if so, what does that relationship tell us about property law. At the outset of the discussion it can be said that, at least in so far as English law is concerned, possession is a much more important and wider concept than ownership. The importance is reflected in the fact that the courts have been much more troubled with the concept of possession rather than ownership. Ownership is rarely a concept that has called for much judicial deliberation. The law prescribes the various methods of how ownership can be lost or acquired, and disputes are resolved accordingly without much juridical analysis of the concept of ownership itself. Furthermore, ownership, as will become apparent in the course of the chapter, has not been met with the same degree of theoretical rigour as the concept of possession. There are both historical and legal reasons for this development. In early law, ownership did not play an important role in the control of things. The earliest use of the word ownership did not, according to Pollock and Maitland, come about until 1583.[2] Certainly, in so far as the English law of land was concerned, the right to remain in control of land depended on a better possession, or otherwise known as *seisin*, rather than on any notion of abstract title. Factual possession was the nearest to ownership in land a person could have; it was certainly the evidence of ownership in the medieval structure of rights in land.[3]

The legal reason, which suggests that possession retains a more superior importance than ownership, relates to the manner in which ownership has been construed in the common law tradition. Unlike Roman law, which was to provide the basis for many of the civil law systems, the common law does not treat ownership as an absolute concept. The Roman law analysed ownership and possession as an absolute jural relationship between a person and a thing.[4] Interference with ownership gave the owner a remedy in damages known as *vindicatio*, or simply damages in trespass. English law never based its remedies for trespass on the abstract notion of ownership, instead possession being the basis of such remedies. The question of whether a remedy was forthcoming depended on the better entitlement to retain or obtain possession rather than ownership *per se*. In so far as the property torts, this still remains the position today.

Again, unlike Roman law, the idea of ownership emerged in a different way depending on the type of object in question.[5] In so far as land was concerned, the idea of ownership emerged from the feudal structure of land

---

[2] Pollock and Maitland, *History of English Law*, Vol II at p 153.
[3] See K. Gray, *Elements of Land Law* (2nd edn, 1993) at pp 61–63, (3rd edn published 2001).
[4] See J.W. Jones, 'Forms of Ownership' (1947) 22 Tulane LR at p 82.
[5] See R.W.M. Dias, *Jurisprudence* (1985) at pp 292–298.

holding, which was examined in Chapter 3. The entitlement to land depended on feudal tenure – that is, the grant of land in return for services of some form or another.[6] The grant of land in a person was to vest him with an estate in the land, which was no more than a time in the land. The resulting possession, or *seisin*, was the interest that was to be protected by the remedy of a real action. In this sense ownership was no more than a better title in land, which in turn was a question of better possession. As regards chattels, it is questionable whether early law ever treated such objects as capable of ownership.[7] They were never subjected to the doctrines of tenure and estate and they never enjoyed the same social, economic and political significance attached to land. Furthermore, given their non-permanent nature and the fact that they could be readily replaced with similar chattels or monetary compensation, the idea of ownership was more difficult to comprehend in such objects. However, if any notion of ownership was to be attributed to them, remedies such as detinue and trover once again, as in the case of land, turned to questions of better possession.[8]

The importance of possession as opposed to abstract notions of ownership still continues to govern the modern law of property, which places an emphasis on the notion of relativity of title. These matters must now be looked at in a little more depth in order to appreciate what has been said at the outset.

OWNERSHIP

Conceptual problems: abstract notion or social reality?

Although ownership plays a pivotal role in property law, it is a concept which, at least in English law, is extremely difficult to refine into one single idea. As mentioned above, it has never been equated to the idea of *dominium* as in Roman law, which simply treats the idea of ownership as the right to enjoy and dispose of something in an absolute manner.[9] Instead, the idea of ownership in English law has been influenced by a number of factors. The

---

[6] For more detail, see Chapter 3.

[7] Pollock and Maitland, *op cit*, at p 153.

[8] Detinue and trover were the old property torts protecting unlawful detention and unlawful taking respectively.

[9] See J.H. Merryman, 'Ownership and Estate' (1974) 48 Tulane LR at p 916 where the author describes the difference between Roman ownership and Anglo-American ownership in land. He writes, '[the] basic difference between Romanic ownership and the Anglo-American estate or interest in land can be illustrated by a simple metaphor. Romanic ownership can be thought of as a box, with the word ownership written on it. Whoever has the box is the owner ... as long as he keeps the box he still has ownership even if the box is empty. The contrast with the Anglo-American law of property is simple. There is no box. There are merely various sets of legal interests.' For an excellent account of Roman ideas of property in the context of land, see J. Getzler, 'Roman Ideas of Land Ownership' in Bright and Dewar (eds), *Land Law: Themes and Perspectives* (1998) at pp 81–106.

law has never treated the idea of ownership as an absolute entitlement, and the reasons for this flow from factors which are not only historical, but which form a fundamental part of the system of property rules in the modern law. In the first place, unlike the civil law codes, the English law of property is based on a premise that ownership can be fragmented amongst a number of persons. Ownership is not absolute; rather it is fragmented amongst a number of competing users.[10] The concept of the trust has been the primary vehicle that has allowed fragmentation of ownership. Fragmentation of ownership has allowed things to be utilised in a manner that more closely meets the economic and social needs of a private property system. Commentating on comparative forms of ownership, J.W. Jones was able to say that, in construing the idea of ownership, English common law 'took into account not only power but obligation and made abstract logic yield to social relationship and to the realties of the physical world.'[11] It is for this reason that English lawyers have never had to search for a unified idea of ownership. In this respect, Otto Kahn Freund also once commented that English law had made it 'unnecessary and impossible for it to search for a definition of property in the continental sense'.[12]

The second explanation for the reason that ownership is not absolute and cannot be restricted to a single idea relates to the manner in which the law resolves ownership disputes. As will become apparent later on, the idea of ownership in law is more relative than absolute. Ownership is not a fixed and guaranteed entitlement in respect of a thing: where ownership has been ascribed to a person, it does not mean that the ownership is guaranteed indefinitely. Of course, ownership may be lost to the state by way of a compulsory purchase or to a creditor in the satisfaction of a judgment debt. However, there are circumstances where ownership may be lost through some form of discontinuance or dispossession. Where the owner fails to exercise his right of ownership – either by failure to retain possession or failure to regain possession in the event of a wrongful dispossession – that ownership can be lost to another by the effluxion of time. Moreover, proprietary disputes are resolved by the courts in a manner that looks to the relative claims of one in respect of another. The basis of this is that remedies in some cases seek to protect possession rather than abstract ownership. This in turn requires the court to establish who has a better possession rather than who is the absolute owner of the thing in question.[13] This is the principle of relativity of title that

---

[10] The idea of fragmentation of ownership is examined in Chapter 7.

[11] *Op cit*, at p 87.

[12] K. Renner, *The Institutions of Private Law and Their Social Functions* (O. Kahn Freund (ed) 1949) at p 23.

[13] The majority of the disputes arise in the context of finding lost or abandoned objects; the case law is considered in Chapter 8 in the context of acquisition of proprietary rights.

underpins the law of ownership, possession and title. The principle of relativity of title is based on sound legal, social and economic foundations.[14] In this respect one judge recently commented that 'the English law of ownership and possession, unlike that of Roman law, is not a system of identifying absolute entitlement, but of priority of entitlement.'[15] This is in contrast with the Roman idea of ownership, which did not recognise a principle of relativity of title, that is, the idea that a person could be an owner against some persons and not others.

It may be impossible to reduce the nature of ownership to a single idea, and this may explain the relatively little theoretical analysis of it, at least when compared to the concept of possession. However, this does not mean that the concept cannot be analysed at all in any fruitful manner that may aid the understanding of property law. One commentator writes, 'the fact that ownership, although one of the most important concepts known to law, cannot be reduced to one simple central idea ... should not be taken to mean that certain classifications of that inchoate mass of rules may not yield a better grasp of the underlying conception of ownership itself.'[16] In everyday practical property law, we take it for granted that somebody is the owner of a thing. Whether one has ownership or not depends on the rules that prescribe how ownership can be lost or acquired. These rules are taken for granted and most legal disputes relating to ownership are resolved accordingly. But whilst this may be true, an understanding of the jural nature of concepts such as ownership, possession and title are important in order to understand where the law is coming from and what it is striving to protect. We are reminded by one leading jurist that 'the idea of jural relation is as important for legal phenomena as is the idea of gravitation for physical phenomena.'[17]

Definitions

To the ordinary person in the street the idea of ownership may appear to be a simple one. To the layperson it is a concept that distinguishes what is mine from what is yours. The lay idea of ownership is one that is not employed by the legal mind. To the legal mind ownership is regarded as a right in a thing. However, from this point onwards jurists are generally divided in their opinion as to what the right of ownership actually consists of. The questions

---

[14] Some of these are discussed below, but see also Chapter 8 where there is a discussion of the relativity of title in the case of original acquisition of things. Some of the important justifications behind the property rules based on relativity of title are discussed there.

[15] *Per* Auld LJ in *Waverley Borough Council* v *Fletcher* [1996] QB 334 at 345. See Chapter 8 for a detailed analysis of this decision.

[16] D. Lloyd, *The Idea of Law* (1964) at p 323.

[17] A. Kocourek, *Jural Relations* (2nd edn, 1927) at p iii.

which have received different answers are: what is the nature of the right of ownership, and, how does one tell whether a person is owner or not? Before some of the attempted definitions of this difficult concept are explored, it is important to note that there is something in the layperson's idea of ownership which the legal mind should not forget. In dealing with notions of what is mine and what is yours, it is clearly apparent that the idea of ownership only becomes important when there is a society with people therein. There is no need to entertain questions of yours and mine when there is only one person in the world. This is important in the sense that ownership is a concept that has something to say about relationships between people in respect of things rather than simply relationships between persons and things in which ownership is held. In other words, the idea of ownership revolves on the premise that the constituent elements of ownership govern relationships between persons and not necessarily things.

One leading jurist, Salmond, took the view that 'ownership denotes the relation between a person and any right that is vested in him.'[18] Salmond thought that it was improper to talk of ownership of things and that the real matter was ownership of a right in respect of a thing. Ownership simply meant to have, and what a person had was a right vested in him. Salmond's idea of ownership is not only very wide; it is also open to criticism. The wide nature of his idea is reflected in the fact that one did not own things as such but owned rights. In this respect, a person could own varying degrees of rights in land. In respect of land, Salmond's view would mean that a person could own an easement, a mortgage, a tenancy, as well the fee simple estate in land. All these are capable of being rights which are the subject-matter of ownership. Salmond's idea of ownership is certainly attractive from the point of view of real property law which recognises multi-functional rights in land. However, it fails to appreciate that these rights in land are smaller segments or rights that make up the main right of ownership in their totality. Whilst there may be some sense in saying that I own an easement, the truth of the matter is that my easement is something which is carved out of ownership that is vested in another.

Salmond's wide definition of ownership is problematic in a number of ways. In the first place, given that the ownership of a thing such as land or a chattel will inevitably give the owner certain rights in respect of the land or chattel, to describe a person as owning rights to rights is a little strange. For example, the ownership of land in the form of being vested with an estate of fee simple absolute in possession will give the owner certain rights in the form of posses-

---

[18] Salmond, *Jurisprudence* (9th edn, 1937) at p 339. The same view was echoed however in the 12th edn (1966) edited by P. Fitzgerald, who appreciated the problems of adopting this rather wide definition of the concept of ownership (at pp 250–251).

sion, management, use and so forth. To then describe the ownership of such a person as ownership of a right is to say that a person owns a right to rights. The second problem with Salmond's definition is that it overlooks the real relationship formed as a result of having ownership. Ownership is a relationship between persons rather than a relationship between a person and a right or a thing. It is true that the ownership arises by virtue of a proprietary relationship between a person and a thing; however, the substantive nature of ownership is that it creates relations between persons. The relations between persons in general can be described as rights *in rem*. The right of ownership consists of a number of rights in respect of a thing enforceable against a large number of persons. In this respect, Turner writes: '... ownership is a subjective right, and it must be a relation between persons. The law of ownership is not a set of rules fixing what I may or may not do to a thing but a set of rules fixing what other people may or may not prevent me from doing to the thing, and what I may or may not prevent them from doing to the thing.'[19]

Salmond attempted to find the most comprehensive definition, trying to cover all aspects of things and rights. He certainly seems to have wanted to take ownership as covering things as well as rights. The complexity he faced was to overcome the idea that things, in particular land, could sustain more than one right. Should these rights not be capable of ownership as well as the land itself? Later in his work, Salmond gave a more acceptable definition of ownership when he wrote: 'in its full and normal compass corporeal ownership is the ownership of a right to the entirety of the lawful uses of a corporeal thing.'[20] Despite the use of the words 'ownership of a right', the idea that ownership consists of an entirety of lawful uses is some way towards understanding ownership as a concept that consists of a number of rights in a thing enforceable against persons generally.

Other jurists have battled to find an appropriate definition of ownership. Pollock wrote:

> 'ownership may be described as the entirety of the powers of use and disposal allowed by the law ... The owner of a thing is not necessarily the person who at a given time has the whole power of use and disposal, very often there is no such person. We must look for the person having the residue of all such power when we have accounted for every detached and limited portion of it; and he will be the owner even if the immediate power of control and use is elsewhere.'[21]

The idea of ownership for Pollock consists of a multiple set of rights in a thing which together form ownership. When these are vested in one person we can say that he or she is the owner. However, Pollock goes further in

---

[19] J.W.C. Turner, 'Some Reflections on Ownership in English Law' (1941) 19 Can Bar Rev 342 at p 343.

[20] *Op cit* at p 344.

[21] F. Pollock, *A First Book of Jurisprudence: for Students of the Common Law* (2nd edn, 1904), p 175.

saying that even when the rights of ownership are split amongst more than one person – which they will be in many cases – ownership is determined by examining where the residual right of ownership vests. This is a theme that has influenced the contemporary notion of ownership, which will now be examined. Before that, however, Pollock's notion of ownership makes it clear that, unlike Salmond, ownership is a relation between persons born as a result of a right in a thing, corporeal or incorporeal. The right of ownership, as opposed to ownership of a right, consists of many smaller rights which put together form ownership. However, the process of establishing who is the owner turns on finding that person in whom the residual right of control and power is vested in. Ownership gives rise to relations between persons: in particular, the owner and the rest of the world. In this respect, Turner writes that the word ownership '... is used to describe all rights *in rem* relating to a thing that has a money value, whether corporeal or incorporeal.'[22]

Suggested definition: greatest right

Ownership may be described as a proprietary right which arises as a result of a relationship between a person and a thing. Ownership is not just a right; it consists of a bundle of rights and duties between the owner and persons in general. The rights of ownership may be described as consisting of claims, liberties, powers and immunities. These rights of ownership may be given to more than one person at the same time so that the person who started off with all the rights may lose most of the control and power in respect of the thing in question without losing the right of ownership itself. Although the right of ownership may be fragmented, ownership is not destroyed thereby. To establish ownership in the sense of who is the owner, it is important to examine who has the residual or ultimate right in the thing in which ownership was first born. In contemporary law Honoré provides an excellent account of the nature of ownership.[23] Honoré defines ownership as '... the greatest possible interest in a thing which a mature system of law recognizes.'[24] It is quite possible for a person to part with many of the claims, liberties and so forth without losing the right of ownership. This is important in illustrating that the idea of ownership is not just a collection of all the rights of ownership; rather it is the greatest or ultimate right in a thing. Thus, a person may grant another a lease for 999 years, thereby giving most of the fruits of ownership to the tenant; however, ownership is not lost because the ultimate right vests in the person granting the lease since it is he and no one else who is entitled to the land at the end of the lease.

---

22 *Op cit* at p 343.
23 A.M. Honoré, 'Ownership' in A.G. Guest (ed), *Oxford Essays in Jurisprudence* (1961) at p 129.
24 *Ibid.*

The incidents of ownership: benefits and burdens

Honoré's analysis of ownership describes the rights of ownership as the standard incidents of ownership.[25] He explains them as the necessary ingredients of ownership. They refer to the claims, liberties, powers and immunities which a person acquires as a consequence of ownership. However, as noted in Chapter 2, these claims, powers and immunities are correlative to duties, liabilities and disabilities. The essence of ownership in this respect is that it is a concept that comprises benefits and burdens. The benefits and burdens are imposed on the owner and they govern his relations with all other persons in society; it is this aspect that makes ownership a right *in rem*. These incidents of ownership consist of: the right to possession, the right to use, the right to manage, the right to income, the right to capital, the right to security, the incident of transmissibility, and the incidence of absence of term, the prohibition of harmful use, and finally, liability to execution. Some of these incidents of ownership speak for themselves; others are now explored in a little more depth.

Amongst the incidents of ownership explained by Honoré, possession is the most important. Honoré described it as 'the foundation on which the whole superstructure of ownership rests.'[26] The right to possess is a right *in rem* in that it avails against persons generally. There are two aspects to the right to possess: first the right to be put in exclusive control of a thing; and second, the right to remain in control. The latter amounts to a claim that others should not, without permission of the owner, interfere with possession. It is not surprising to see possession as the foundation of ownership given that possession is the root of title. In the common law tradition, not only does the availability of remedies in most cases depend on possession, but also possession, even when wrongful to start off with, can form the basis of generating ownership in another whilst extinguishing it in a person who lacks necessary possession. [27]

The right to security is an important incident of ownership. Reference should be made back to Chapter 3 where legal and political theorists – notably Jeremy Bentham – regarded security in the ownership of things as central to the functioning of a system of private property. Without the right to security, Bentham argued that a system of private property would not function because of the fear of losing what one would control. In this fear, resources would not be utilised to their maximum potential and the greater happiness of the individual and society would not be promoted. So, what does the right to security involve? It involves an expectation on behalf of the owner that he will remain owner indefinitely if he so chooses. This expectation amounts to an immunity from expropriation. Of

---

[25] *Ibid.*
[26] *Ibid*, at p 130.
[27] See Chapter 8.

course, ownership may be taken away from a person who is declared bankrupt: in such a case ownership is liable to execution, that is, it is subject to a liability. However, apart from this, expropriation powers may be vested in the state and other public authorities. For example, a compulsory purchase of land will inevitably interfere with the right of security; however, most private property regimes provide for compensation when such expropriation takes place.

Ownership must have the incidence of transmissibility and an absence of term – both of which can be explored together. The owner must have the power to transfer ownership freely, either during his lifetime or on his death. The use of the word 'freely' is used here to mean without any restriction and interference from any other person as opposed to the state and law. There may be instances where a person is freely capable of transferring property, however the legal system, for rules relating to illegality and public policy, may interfere with the incidence of transmissibility.[28] For example, whilst a person may have freedom of disposition of property, this freedom may be denied when the purported disposition is contrary to the functioning of a purely liberal market. A disposition which has an excessive deal in vesting will generally be disliked by the law because of its effect on inalienating property in the future. The ability to freely transmit ownership to another presupposes that the owner's interest is not limited in time, for example, like that of a tenant under a lease. This is not to say that a tenant cannot transfer or assign a lease; it simply means that where there is no absence of term, a person is regarded as owner.

Finally, the claims and rights which form part of ownership are curtailed by duties. In the exercise of ownership the owner is prohibited from doing that which would cause harm to others; in other words, the benefit of use is subject to the burden of respecting the rights of others. Ownership must be exercised within the prescribed limits of law, so I cannot use my house in a manner which may cause danger to my neighbour. Duties are owed to persons and the state in general.

Forms of ownership

Ownership can manifest itself in a number of forms. The most obvious form of ownership is that vested in one person at a given time. Usually this person is the sole owner and as such is the person entitled to the greatest right in the thing in which he has ownership. However, in practice ownership is usually not vested in one person alone; it is quite possible for ownership to be shared, either concurrently or consecutively, by more than one person. Other forms of ownership include legal and equitable ownership, which is simply ownership capable of existing at two different systems of law.

---

[28] See Chapter 8.

Ownership may be given to two or more persons either concurrently or consecutively. Concurrent ownership is ownership given to more than one person at the same time. It is usually said that there exists a state of co-owner-ship and such co-ownership can take one of two forms: that is, a joint tenancy or a tenancy in common.[29] The difference between a joint tenancy and a ten-ancy in common is relatively simple. A joint tenancy involves ownership of a thing by more than one person without any one of the joint tenants having a defined share in the thing.[30] Collectively the joint tenants are a single owner, each entitled to the whole of the thing as much as the other. Gray describes a joint tenancy as 'an undifferentiated kind of co-ownership in which an entire estate or interest in property – rather than any defined proportion or aliquot share – is vested simultaneously in all the co–owners.'[31] The right of survivor-ship or *ius accrescendi* is a cardinal feature of a joint tenancy and holds that on the death of one joint tenant the remaining joint tenant or tenants become entitled to the whole. There is nothing that a joint tenant can pass onto his next of kin or any other person in a will. The natural consequence of the right of survivorship is that a joint tenancy will eventually, with the passage of time, revert to a situation of sole ownership.[32]

In contrast, a tenancy in common exists where co-owners have an undi-vided share in the subject-matter of ownership. Thus, no tenant in common is entitled to the whole but only to a share. This type of co-ownership is par-ticularly useful in the context of personal property where, as in the case of a sale of goods forming part of a bulk, until such time as the goods are segre-gated and transferred to the buyer, a number of buyers can be treated as tenants in common.[33] No right of survivorship applies in the case of a ten-ancy in common, so that on the death of one tenant in common his share is

---

[29] The use of the words 'tenant' and 'tenancy' in this context has nothing to do with the mean-ing used in the context of landlord and tenant. The word 'tenant' simply means owner in the case of co-ownership of land.

[30] An excellent examination of the nature of a joint tenancy was undertaken in the High Court of Australia by Deane J in *Corrin* v *Patton* (1990) 169 CLR 540.

[31] K. Gray, *Elements of Land Law* (2nd edn, 1993) at p 462, (3rd edn published 2001). See, gen-erally, Chapter 13 of Gray for a comprehensive examination of co-ownership of land. A joint tenancy of land must have the four unities present. First, there must be unity of possession, which means that each joint tenant is as entitled to possession of every part of the land as any other joint tenant. Unity of possession may be destroyed by statutory intervention: for example, the Family Law Act 1996, Pt IV, ss 30–35 allows a court to grant an occupation order denying one joint tenant possession on the grounds of domestic violence. Unity of interest requires that each joint tenant be vested with the same interest as the other. Unity of title requires the joint tenants to derive their interest in the land from the same act or document; and finally, unity of title requires that the interest of each joint tenant vest at the same time.

[32] The position as regards simultaneous deaths of joint tenants is resolved by the application of the rule governing *commorientes* which holds that the younger of the joint tenants is said to have survived the older: see Law of Property Act 1925, s 184.

[33] See, generally, Chapter 9.

capable of passing in accordance with the rules of succession.[34] Whether a joint tenancy or a tenancy in common has been created depends on a number of facts; there are no hard and fast rules. Express declaration of a joint tenancy and tenancy in common is a starting point, for example, where land is given to A and B as joint tenants. In the absence of this, words of severance will operate to grant a tenancy in common rather than a joint tenancy, since severance indicates that a tenant has a share: for example, land to A and B equally or in equal shares. Without any other facts, the common law prefers a joint tenancy rather than a tenancy in common because of the right of survivorship and for the reason that a single title is much more advantageous from a conveyancing dimension than a title which is fragmented.[35] A joint tenancy can be converted in a tenancy into common by a process called severance. Severance is a process by which a share is created by one joint tenant so as to make the co-ownership in the form of an undivided share.[36]

Co-ownership of land is subject to the statutory reforms made by the Law of Property Act 1925 and the Trusts of Land and Appointment of Trustees Act 1996. It is not possible for a detailed examination of all rules and principles relating to co-ownership to be detailed in a book of this nature. However, mention should be made of the following points. The Law of Property Act 1925 had, *inter alia*, the objective of facilitating conveyancing in an age when the exchange value of land had far superseded its use value.[37] In this respect, title to land should be one that can be easily transferred from one owner to another. Before 1925 a tenancy in common and a joint tenancy were both capable of existing in the legal estate in land. The potential problem with a tenancy in common at law was to hamper its effective conveyance to a purchaser because of the existence of a fragmented title. A purchaser of title to land, which consisted in the form of a tenancy in common, would have to investigate the title of each tenant in common before he could acquire a clean title to the land. Given the scope for excessive fragmentation of title within a tenancy in common, investigating such titles was not only cumbersome but also presented the purchaser of a risk that third party interests may bind him. The Law of Property Act 1925 regulates the co-ownership of land through a number of ways. In the first place, the legal title to co-owned land is treated as

---

[34] In the context of land a tenancy in common only requires unity of possession.

[35] The rule applies to both land and personal property: see *Morley v Bird* (1798) 3 Ves 629.

[36] Whether severance has occurred is a matter of evidence. It can occur by statute in the case of land which allows one joint tenant to serve a written notice on the other, Law of Property Act 1925, s 36(2). It can also occur when one joint tenant seeks to give his share to another, or agrees with the other joint tenant that they are tenants in common, or where all joint tenants regard themselves as tenants in common by some mutual conduct: see, generally, *Williams v Hensam* (1861) 1 John & H 546.

[37] See, generally, S. Anderson, 'The 1925 Property Legislation: Setting Contexts' in Bright and Dewar (eds), *Land Law: Themes and Perspectives* (1998) at p 107.

a mere nominal title; in other words, it does not tell anything about the beneficial ownership of the land. The legal owners are merely trustees and the beneficial interests are to be determined by equity. In this respect law and equity work together in establishing the nature of co-owned land. Second, a tenancy in common is not capable of existing in the legal estate in land; the legal title to co-owned land must always be in the form of a joint tenancy.[38] Third, the Trusts of Land and Appointment of Trustees Act 1996 imposes a trust of land in every case of co-ownership of land. The legal owners are trustees conferred with powers and duties in relation to co-owned land. They hold the land for the beneficiaries, of whom they may be some themselves, and the courts can resolve any disputes relating to such land by an application by any interested person.[39]

In contrast to co-ownership, consecutive ownership is ownership split amongst more than one person on a temporal plane. For example, something may be given to A for life (the tenant for life) and thereafter to B (the remainderman). Such consecutive ownership was a very powerful tool in preserving property, predominantly land within the family. Personal property was never subjected to the same degree of consecutive ownership as was land. This was also a reason for the separate rules relating to the consecutive ownership of land, also known as a settlement. Settlements of land played an important role in the eighteenth and nineteenth centuries as means of passing land from one generation to another.[40] In the age of *paterfamilias*, consecutive interests in land could be reconciled with the needs of the social and economic desires of landowners wishing to settle land for future generations. Given the demise of consecutive ownership of land and the changes in the latter part of the twentieth century it is not intended to explore this form of ownership in depth. Successive interests in land were governed primarily in two ways. First, a strict settlement governed by the Settled Land Act 1925 gave the tenant for life the legal title to land whilst at the same making him a trustee for the other beneficiaries in the land. The trust for sale, on the other hand, conveyed property to trustees for the benefit of the tenant for life and remainderman. The two

---

[38] Law of Property Act 1925, s 1(6) & s 34(1). Furthermore, severance of a joint tenancy is not allowed at common law: see s 36(2) of the Act. A tenancy in common is capable of existing in equity if that was what was intended. Thus, where land is conveyed to A & B as tenants in common, the legal title is held by A & B in the form of a joint tenancy; however, given that the legal title is nominal, A & B hold as tenants in common in equity with all the rules relating to tenancies in common applying to them. Of course, the position of a purchaser of such land is that he needs only investigate the legal title that is single in nature. He may be bound by the interests of any equitable owners in accordance with the doctrine of notice and the principles of registration of equitable interests in the form of land charges.

[39] The Trusts of Land and Appointment of Trustees Act 1996, s 14 allows an interested person in the trust of land to apply to the court for an order relating to such land; s 15 of the Act gives the court guidelines to apply in making an order under s 14.

[40] See S. Murphy and S. Roberts, *Understanding Property Law* (1998) at p 82.

separate forms of regulating consecutive ownership in land were thought to be unsatisfactory by the Law Commission.[41] Successive interests in land after the Trusts of Land and Appointment of Trustees Act 1996 are governed by a trust of land and no new strict settlements can be created. In so far as personal property is concerned, it has never been subjected to consecutive ownership as is the case with land. However, chattels or a fund can be left for A for life thereafter for B in equity through the medium of a trust. Such consecutive ownership would exist in equity giving both A and B equitable ownership. The right vested in A would entitle him to the income in respect of the fund or lifetime enjoyment of the chattel; B would be entitled to the capital which would vest in possession after A's death.

In Chapter 4 the idea of law and equity was explored. It was established that proprietary rights were recognised in law and equity. The division between law and equity means that ownership can exist in both systems of law. Furthermore, legal and equitable ownership can exist in the same thing at the same time; in other words, there can be duality of ownership in respect of a thing. A person can be a legal owner of a thing whilst another can be an equitable owner. The most dominant way in which duality of ownership arises is in the case of a trust. A trustee is the legal owner of something, however, he holds the thing for the benefit of another and as such the equitable ownership is vested in the beneficiary. The legal ownership of the trustee is merely nominal in that it does not carry with it the incidents of enjoyment; rather, the trustee is obliged to manage the property on behalf of the beneficiary. The beneficiary has all the incidents of enjoyment but has no powers of management. In the case of a trust, legal and equitable ownership arises as a result of fragmentation of ownership. The equitable ownership of the beneficiary is sometimes also referred to as beneficial ownership.

Although the discussion of legal and equitable ownership is commonly centred on the trust concept, it is misleading to think of equitable ownership arising only in the case of a trust where the trustee is the legal owner and the beneficiary equitable owner. Equitable ownership may exist independently of legal ownership in respect of a thing. For example, a beneficiary under a trust may constitute himself as trustee for the benefit of another person. Thus, where a beneficiary has equitable ownership of a fund, he may decide to constitute himself trustee for somebody else. In such a case it may well be that a sub-trust is created; however, both trustee and beneficiary are equitable owners in respect of the sub-trust without a legal ownership vested in either of them.[42]

---

[41] See Law Commission, *Transfer of Land: Trusts of Land* (Law Com No 181, 1989) paras 4.1–4.4.

[42] The idea of a sub-trust is clear enough; however, what is more controversial is the role of the sub-trustee in a sub-trust. On the one hand, he can be treated as trustee of his equitable ownership and thus managing that equitable ownership for the sub-beneficiary. However, on the other hand, where the sub-trustee is not doing anything different from the head trustee, it is questionable whether he should remain as a trustee. See *Grange* v *Wilberforce* (1889) 5 TLR 436 at 437; *Re Lashmar* [1891] 1 Ch 258 at 268; and also Hanbury and Martin, *Modern Equity* at p 84.

Apart from beneficial ownership, equitable ownership also embraces things which equity alone regards as capable of being the subject-matter of property. The most common example is the interest of a legatee under a will or next of kin in the case of intestacy. In the case of a will, the executor appointed in the will is under a fiduciary duty to administer the estate of the deceased. This is done by collecting the assets of the deceased and paying any creditors. The remainder of the estate can then be given to the legatees of the will. In the case of a person dying without a will, the court will appoint an administrator who will act in a similar way to an executor. Unlike a beneficiary under a trust, it is quite clear that a legatee under a will or a beneficiary in the case of intestacy has no interest in the assets of the deceased that happen to be in the hands of the executor or administrator. This rules emanates from *Commissioner of Stamp Duties (Queensland)* v *Livingstone*,[43] where the question was whether succession duty was payable on property situated in Queensland. On the facts, a widow was legatee of her husband's will, which contained provision as to property situated in Queensland; however, the widow was domiciled in New South Wales where the Queensland statute regarding payment of duty did not apply. The Privy Council held that no duty was payable on the property situated in Queensland simply because she had no interest in the property until such time as the executors had given that property to her. At most, she was the owner of an equitable *chose in action* – that is, the right to see that the estate was administered in favour of her – and that equitable *chose in action* was situated in New South Wales.

POSSESSION

Definitional problems

If conceptualising ownership is a difficult task, the concept of possession does not present any more ease to the legal mind. It is, however, a concept that cannot be overlooked in property law. Commenting on the synonym of possession, Pollock and Maitland once wrote that 'in the history of our law there is no idea more cardinal than that of seisin. Even in the law of the present day it plays a part which must be studied by every lawyer; but in the past it was so important that the whole system of our land law was law about seisin and its consequences.'[44] Almost a century later it still remains true that the words of Pollock and Maitland cannot be taken lightly in the study of modern property law. It is almost impossible to understand the modern law of ownership and title without understanding the nature and

---

[43] [1964] 3 All ER 692. See also *Eastbourne Mutual Building Society* v *Hastings Corporation* [1965] 1 WLR 861.
[44] Pollock and Maitland, *History of English Law* (2nd edn, 1968) at p 29.

significance of possession. Holmes attributed possession as a 'conception which is only less important than contract.'[45] The expression 'possession is nine-tenths the law' is something which legal philosophers would have difficulty in rejecting. In the case of personal property, many of the proprietary interests that are capable of existing in chattels depend solely on the notion of possession. For example, the special property of bailees in general[46] and that of pledgees is dependent on possession. Today, possession and ownership usually go hand in hand, since possession is one of the fundamental incidents of ownership. In the early law, as mentioned on previous occasions, the reverse was true in that the courts were not concerned with abstract notions of title and ownership. Instead, possession or *seisin* was indicative of whether a person should remain as owner or should lose his ownership to another who had exercised better possession of a thing.

So, what then is possession? To mankind possession of things is an important aspect of life. Without any possession of things in the world it is questionable whether a person has any liberty or security. It is for this reason that Salmond wrote, 'possession is the most basic relationship between men and things.'[47] It is also for this reason that early laws of property had one objective in mind – that is, the protection of lawful possession. Without such protection, not only would life be impracticable but also it would lead to a state of chaos and constant disorder. To the lay mind possession implies some form of control or detention of a thing. Sometimes the word possession is equated with ownership. Kocourek has described the nature of detention of a thing as involving the following elements:[48] (i) a human being; (ii) a material thing or space which may be used by physical acting; (iii) with the requisite power for the act; (iv) by repeated acts; (v) with contact, or with such approximation of contact as to make the act immediately possible; (vi) without interference of others to prevent the act of use. The idea of possession as involving detention is taken by lawyers to suggest that, unlike ownership, which is essentially a *de jure* relationship between a person and a thing, possession is a *de facto* relationship between a person and a thing. This is no better explained than by Salmond, who wrote, 'whether a person has ownership depends on rules of law; whether a person has possession is a question that could be answered as a matter of fact and without reference to law at all.'[49] Inherent in this idea is that the concept of possession exists before legal society and is therefore independent of, and prior to, the law. However, whilst this may be true to some extent, the definitions of possession suggest that there may be possession that is the result of laws rather than facts alone.

---

[45] Holmes, *The Common Law* (1948) at p 206.

[46] See *Ashby* v *Tolhurst* [1937] 2 KB 242.

[47] Salmond, *Jurisprudence* (12th edn, 1966) at p 265.

[48] A. Kocourek, *Jural Relations* (2nd edn, 1927) at p 361.

[49] *Op cit*, at p 266.

In the definitions of possession, which follow shortly, there is a sharp contrast between possession in fact and possession in law: in other words, factual possession and legal possession.

Suggested definitions and forms of possession

There is no doubt that legal theorists and judges have found it almost impossible to give a complete theory of possession. The cases in which the concept of possession has called for discussion illustrate that judges find it very difficult to reduce the concept into a single idea. In one case, Erle CJ described possession as 'one of the most vague of all vague terms, and shifts its meaning according to the subject-matter to which it is applied – varying very much in its sense, as it is introduced either into civil or into criminal proceedings.'[50] Legal theorists have likewise found the concept difficult to define into a single idea. The concept of possession has been the subject-matter of much theoretical writing[51] and it is debatable whether such excessive theorising has contributed to the further confusion over the concept. For example, Dias attributes some of the difficulties in conceptualising possession to the excessive theorising of the concept.[52] He writes, 'the melancholy record of theorizing on this topic should serve as a warning against an *a priori* approach.'[53] The basic problem with conceptualising possession into a single idea relates to the fact that the concept of possession has application in various sectors of legal control. In each of these sectors the idea of possession must be understood in the context in which the law is operating. Thus, it is generally accepted that the civil notion of possession is not necessarily the same as the criminal notion of the word 'possession'. In *DPP* v *Brooks* Lord Diplock commented that 'these technical doctrines of the civil law about possession are irrelevant to this field of criminal law.'[54]

Possession has been defined in a variety of ways by judges and legal theorists. The law and theoretical writings introduce possessory terms such as possession, actual possession, *de facto* possession, legal possession, constructive

---

[50] *R* v *Smith* (1855) 6 Cox CC 554 at 556. The same view was echoed in *United States of America* v *Dollfus Mieg & Co* [1952] AC 582 by Viscount Jowitt who explained (at 605) that 'English law has never worked out a completely logical and exhaustive definition of possession'.

[51] Amongst the many older works, the most influential have been F. Pollock and R. Wright, *Possession in the Common Law* (1888); J. Salmond, *Jurisprudence* (1902). More recently, see B. Shartel, 'Meanings of Possession' (1932) 16(6) Minnesota Law Review at p 611; R.D.C. Stewart, 'The Difference Between Possession of Land and Chattels' (1933) 11(10) Can Bar Rev at p 651; A.E.S. Tay, 'The Concept of Possession in the Common Law: Foundations for a New Approach' (1964) 4 Melbourne University Law Review at p 476; D.R. Harris, 'The Concept of Possession in English Law' in A.G. Guest (ed), *Oxford Essays in Jurisprudence* (1961).

[52] R.W.M. Dias, *Jurisprudence* (1985) at p 289.

[53] *Ibid.*

[54] [1974] AC 862 at 867.

possession, symbolic possession, the right to possession, and the right of possession. In this sense there is no doubt that there are various meanings of the word 'possession'. Any fruitful understanding of possession and its importance in the modern law must first appreciate that for various reasons there are many notions of possession, and second, attempt to understand such notions separately.[55]

Possession in early law: seisin

In the early law, the concepts of ownership and possession were not clearly divorced. This was clearly evident in the fact that it was impossible to gain recognition of a right to possess which was good against the whole world or to vindicate any right to possess without reference to the concept of possession itself. In the early law possession was explained through the concept of 'seisin', a concept described as lying 'at the root of the historical development of English land law.'[56] The idea behind seisin lay in the actual or *de facto* possession of land, which was determinate of whether a proprietary right in land was granted. There were no abstract ideas of title and right; instead possession decided whether a person had a right to land. As such seisin was not a question of right, but rather a question of fact although fact may then lead to a right through the passage of time. Long sustained possession meant peace and order, and seisin literally denoted quiet and peaceful enjoyment of land.[57] From the fifteenth century onwards seisin became confined to persons who held an estate in freehold and seisin gave a presumption of ownership of land. A person who claimed land as a result of losing it to a wrongful possessor had to show his seisin – in other words his possession – in order to recover it. However, given that seisin was a question of fact, even a person who wrongfully took possession of land could raise a presumption of ownership,[58] which could only be defeated by a better showing of seisin in another person – that is the previous possessor pointing a better seisin.

The concept of seisin was not particular to land; it was used to protect property interests in chattels as well as land.[59] However, it came to be employed predominantly in real property law and through the passage of time came to be

---

[55] See B. Shartel, 'Meanings of Possession' (1932) 16(6) Minnesota Law Review at p 611. Professor Shartel argues that the proper line of inquiry into the meaning of possession should seek to examine the differences between cases of possession and the reasons behind them rather than attempt to reduce the concept into a single idea. He writes (at p 612), 'I want to make the point that there are many meanings of the word possession, that possession can only be usefully defined with reference to the purpose in hand; and that possession may have one meaning with one connection and another meaning in another'.

[56] K. Gray, *Elements of Land Law* (2nd edn, 1993) at p 61, (3rd edn published 2001).

[57] See Pollock and Maitland, *History of English Law* (2nd edn, 1898), Vol II at p 34.

[58] See *Minister of State for the Army* v *Dalziel* (1944) 68 CLR 261 at 276.

[59] Pollock and Maitland, *op cit*, at p 32. See also A.E.S. Tay, 'The Concept of Possession in the Common Law: Foundations for a New Approach', *op cit*, at p 484. For a detailed explanation, see Maitland, 'The Seisin of Chattels' (1885) 1 LQR at p 324.

understood as the origin of title or right in land. This is not to say that actual *de facto* possession did not explain proprietary interests in personal property. Seisin, which explains the roots of property law, does not hold the same degree of importance in real property law that it did in its early days. The means by which ownership in land is transferred to another no longer depends on mere delivery of seisin, or in the early language 'livery of seisin',[60] but rather on a grant that does not require actual entry. The idea of actual possession reflecting seisin does, however, play a role in determining issues such as adverse possession of land. Although notions of ownership and title may have become more abstract, the English law of property continues to recognise that ownership, even where based on clear legal ideas of right and title, is a relative concept. The idea of relativity of title and ownership holds that there is no such thing as absolute title to land – and as such a claim to land, and for that matter other property such as chattels – depends on the non-existence of a better claim to the same thing.

Actual *or* de facto *possession*

In the modern law, *de facto* or actual possession is the closest to the ordinary or lay meaning of the term. It comprises control or detention of a thing by a person. To gain actual possession, Holmes writes that 'a man must stand in a certain physical relation to the object and to rest of the world, and must have a certain intent.'[61] The idea behind actual possession is that a person must have a degree of control, which is exercisable immediately over a thing. Actual possession is not just mere possession in the form of detention in the simple sense of the word – for example, 'in my hands'. It is quite possible to be in actual possession of a thing without the thing physically being in the hands of the possessor. Thus, it is quite possible for a person to be in actual possession of a chattel that is not near to same, provided there is control in fact. This simply means that no other person can negative the control of the chattel. A person may leave home to go to work, but he or she does not thereby abandon all personal items within the house if the doors are locked on exit. In such a case there is both an intention to control and control in fact. In this respect, Tay writes: 'possession, one might say, is the present physical power to use, enjoy or deal with a thing, on one's own behalf and to the exclusion of all others.'[62]

Actual possession consists of two major elements: namely *animus possidendi* and *corpus possessionis*. *Animus possidendi* consists of two things: first, an intention to control the thing; and second, an intention to control

---

[60] In the early law of seisin, a person seised could only transfer such seisin through the common law livery of seisin. This was a ceremony in the presence of witnesses followed by ceremonial acts: see Thorne, 'Livery of Seisin' (1938) 52 LQR at p 345.

[61] Holmes, *The Common Law* (1948) at p 216.

[62] A.E.S. Tay, 'The Concept of Possession in the Common Law: Foundations for a New Approach', *op cit*, at p 490.

the thing to the exclusion of others. *Corpus possessionis* is the power to control the thing to the exclusion of everyone else. These requirements for a successful finding of actual possession can be simply reduced to an intention to control and control in fact. Control in fact and an intention to control are both necessary for actual possession of chattels or land.[63] However, in respect of land, the control necessary to constitute possession differs. It is generally accepted that the control necessary for actual possession of chattels is greater than that of actual possession of land. The reason for this relates to the inherent nature of chattels and land. Take, for example, a watch: the control needed to have actual possession of such a thing is greater simply because of the fact that it can be carried away easily. On the other hand, possession of ten acres of land does not require physical possession at all times; it is, in its inherent nature, immovable and as such incapable of control through physical possession.[64] It is precisely for this reason, and others, that arriving at a single idea of possession is a very difficult task.

Control in fact and an intention to control both feature in civil and criminal disputes. In civil law matters relating to adverse possession of land and title to lost and abandoned objects, the courts must ascertain which person at any given time has actual possession. Possession, as explained later, raises a presumption of ownership and can give rise to possessory title good against everyone except the true owner. In the context of criminal law disputes, control in fact and intention to control often become important in deciding whether a person is in possession, for example, of a controlled substance such as a drug. There are no hard and fast rules; in particular, the intention to control – which essentially is the mental element of actual possession – varies in the context of civil and criminal law disputes. A closer examination of these constituent elements of actual possession is now required.

There are no hard and fast rules that explain when a person has control in fact of a particular object. The general rule here is that the degree of control necessary to acquire actual possession will depend on the nature of the object in question. The question is simply one which asks, what is the greatest

---

[63] R.D.C. Stewart, 'The Difference Between Possession of Land and Chattels', *op cit*, at p 653. In the context of finding lost or abandoned objects and the law of adverse possession of land, the courts use such requirements in deciding to whom ownership should be ascribed: see Chapter 7.

[64] It is for this reason that, in the absence of persuasive evidence to the contrary, the owner of the paper title to land is deemed to remain in possession of land even if he is miles away. K. Gray maintains that such an owner is regarded as maintaining a constructive possession of the land even if he is not in actual possession of the whole: *Elements of Land Law* (2nd edn, 1993) at p 292, (3rd edn published 2001). The use of the word constructive possession here must be distinguished from the meaning that is dealt with under the next section. There constructive possession is defined in a very specific way to describe possession that is said to exist when a person with actual possession acknowledges the superior right of possession of another. That other is deemed to have constructive possession.

degree of control capable of being exercised by the person claiming that he has actual possession? The degree of control necessary for smaller chattels will be greater than for larger ones. For example, in *The Tubantia*[65] the plaintiff salvage company had been doing some work on a wreck lying at the depth of some 100ft in the North Sea. The plaintiffs managed to float the wreck by cutting a hole in one side and recovering some of the cargo. The defendants, a rival salvage company, interrupted the work of the plaintiffs. The plaintiffs sued in trespass arguing that their work had given them sufficient actual possession of the wreck and such possession gave them a right to sue in tort. This was so despite the fact that the work had been carried out in short periods of time due to bad weather. The plaintiffs succeeded in their action on the grounds that their work amounted to sufficient use and occupation of the wreck. Finally, in respect of control in fact, it is important to appreciate that the degree of control needed to acquire possession is greater than that required to remain in possession.[66] For example, Professor Bell explains that a person who goes into a shop leaving his bicycle outside in the street does not lose possession of it.[67] However, a higher degree of control is necessary for things which are not possessed or owned by anyone.

In respect of the intention to control, two things are important: first, knowledge of the existence of the thing or object; and second, an intention to exclude everyone else from possession of the thing or object. The idea of intention to control necessarily imports a mental element in the idea of actual possession.[68] A person may seem from all outward appearances to be in actual possession of something: take, for example, a person sitting in someone else's living room containing various items of personal property such as a television set and so forth. However, if such a person sits there as a guest or at the permission of another he is not is possession of any of the items in the room. It does not matter that he has immediate use of such items and that the true owner may be miles away. In this case, the person is not exercising control with the necessary intention required for actual possession. In the words of Pollock, '... an act which is not done or believed to have been done in the exercise or assertion of dominion will not cause the person doing it to be regarded as the *de facto* exerciser of the powers of use and enjoyment.'[69]

Disputes relating to intention to control have predominantly appeared in the criminal law context. Here criminal liability has turned to the question of whether somebody can be in possession of an item when there may be no knowledge of its existence or where there may be no knowledge of its nature.

---

[65] [1924] P78, [1924] All ER Rep 615.
[66] D.R. Harris, *op cit* (note 51), at p 73.
[67] A.P. Bell, *Modern Law of Personal Property in England and Ireland* (1989), p 35.
[68] See de Meyrick, 'The Mental Element of Possession' (1984) 58 ALJ 202.
[69] Pollock and Wright, *op cit*, at p 13.

In respect of the former, the rule has been, despite the absolute strict nature of some criminal offences, that persons cannot be in possession of something of whose existence they are unaware. Thus, in *Warner v Metropolitan Police Commissioner*,[70] the House of Lords, in deciding whether the Drugs (Prevention of Misuse) Act 1964 imposed an absolute offence in the sense that belief, intention and state of mind of the accused is immaterial or irrelevant, held that the mental element of possession in this context was important. Here the appellant, a floor layer, sold scent as a sideline. On one occasion the appellant went into a café and inquired whether anything had been left for him. The proprietor of the café told him there was something under the counter. The appellant walked away with two boxes, which when opened by the police contained scent in one and amphetamine sulphate tablets in the other. The appellant was arrested by the police for being in possession of a controlled drug contrary to section 1 of the 1964 Act. Lord Reid approved the dicta of Lord Parker CJ in *Lockyer v Gibb*,[71] where he said, '… it is quite clear that a person cannot be said to be in possession of some article which he or she does not realize is, or may be, in her handbag, in her room, or in some other place over which she had control. That, I should have thought, is elementary, if something were slipped into one's basket and one had not the vaguest notion it was there at all, one could not possibly be said to be in possession of it.' [72]

The rule that a person cannot be in possession of something of whose existence he or she is unaware requires some modification. First, the rule does not apply where there is some assent to control by the person claiming possession. This covers the situation where, for example, a person may be away from his home when a postman or a milkman delivers milk. Surely in this case, despite the fact that the person is unaware at what time the milk has been delivered, he is in possession as soon as delivery is made. Second, in cases relating to finding of lost or abandoned things, the rule has always been that a person in possession of land is in possession of all things attached or in the land even if he lacks the necessary knowledge that they are there.[73] The justification for this rule lies on the premise that all that is required is an intention to control the land, which includes those things attached or in the land.

In so far as a person who has knowledge of the existence of something, however, is unaware of its nature, the rule appears to be that such person will be deemed to be in possession of the thing even if he or she is unaware of its

[70] [1968] 2 All ER 356.

[71] [1967] 2 QB 243.

[72] *Ibid*, at 248. See also *R v Woodrow* (1846) 15 M & W 404.

[73] See *South Staffs Water Company v Sharman* [1896] 2 QB 44. This and other cases on the law of finding are explored in more depth in Chapter 8 in the discussion relating to original acquisition of property rights.

contents. Thus, if a person is entrusted to carry a parcel for someone else, the carrier will be in possession despite the fact that he is unaware of the contents. Of course, this rule is subject to the condition that the person deemed to be in possession must be a person who would normally be expected to take charge of the thing that is now deemed as in his possession, even though he is unaware of the nature of the thing. In this respect Professor Bell explains that a carrier will be in possession of things, such as a parcel, even if he is unaware of the nature of the parcel providing that the contents of the parcel fall within the normal class of things the carrier is prepared to take charge of.[74] Thus, in *Moukataff* v *BOAC* it was held that an airline company was in possession of some £20,000 belonging to the plaintiffs when such money was placed in mailbags being carried for the Post Office. It did not matter in this case that the airline company was unaware of the precise contents of the mailbags. It is clear, however, that a person may be in possession of something which he or she would not normally control – for example, a controlled drug – if the facts are sufficient to demonstrate that the person manifested an intention to control, for example, a parcel as well as its contents.[75]

Legal possession or de jure possession

Legal possession, sometimes described as *de jure* possession or possession in law, is quite different from actual possession. Legal possession flows from law as opposed to from the actual apparent power of preventing interference with a thing.[76] A person who is deemed to have legal possession will normally also have actual possession. It is, however, quite possible for a person to have actual possession without possession in law. An owner of a gold watch may instruct his friend to take his watch for repairs at a shop. While the friend is taking the watch for repairs – thus being in actual possession of the watch – he does not acquire legal possession because he does not have the necessary intention to control the watch. The necessary intention must be to exclude the whole world from interference with the watch. This example tells us something about legal possession: it is such possession which is recognised by law and enforceable *in rem*, that is, against the world at large. Legal possession flows from the fact that in modern society legal rules protect possession. Such legal protection of possession is obviously necessary in order to maintain peace and order, which would otherwise not exist if there were no rules protecting possessory claims to things that had been legally appropriated.

---

[74] A.P. Bell, *Modern Law of Personal Property in England and Ireland* (1989), p 38.
[75] *Warner* v *Metropolitan Police Commissioner* [1969] 2 AC 256 at 312.
[76] See Pollock and Wright, *op cit* (note 51), at p 16.

In a simplistic world it may be thought that possession in law is that possession which is exercised by the true owner of a thing. However, nothing could be further from the truth. It is quite possible for a person who, in the ordinary sense of the word would not be regarded as having legal possession, to have such possession in the eyes of the law. In the above example relating to the gold watch, what would be the position if a thief stole the gold watch from the true owner's friend? It is submitted that if the thief took control of the watch and thereby intended to control it to the exclusion of the whole world, he would have possession in law and fact. This principle, as will be shown shortly, stems from the very fact that possession raises a presumption of ownership and the thief could protect his possession, albeit initially wrongful, against everyone except the true owner by the appropriate trespassory remedies. His title to the watch would be relative to that of any other title, that is, in this case to the true owner. The true owner would be left with a right to possess, which is quite distinct from actual and legal possession.[77] This right to possess has been described by Pollock and Wright as a form of constructive possession.[78]

Constructive possession

Another quite distinct form of possession is that known as constructive possession. It has already been noted above that such possession will be vested in a person who has lost both actual and legal possession, but still has a right to possession – for example, a right to recover from a wrongdoer such as a thief. The essence behind constructive possession is the right to take actual possession. A person will be deemed as having constructive possession when he or she has a right to take actual possession. The idea of constructive possession extends to cases where a person in actual and legal possession recognises or acknowledges a superior right in another person. The concept of constructive possession remains, however, rather vague and commentaries on the concept are not always consistent. It is also worth noting here that much of the academic and judicial discussion of constructive possession has arisen in the context of personal property, that is chattels as opposed to land. In some instances constructive possession has been explained as being the same thing as legal possession. For example, Salmond explains constructive possession as arising in 'cases where something less than possession in one person is deemed possession in law, and where conversely the actual possession of some other party is reduced to something less than legal possession.'[79] To this end, the thief appropriating something from the rightful owner would, according to

---

[77] *Ibid*, at p 25.
[78] *Ibid*.
[79] *Op cit*, at p 276.

Salmond, only acquire actual possession, whereas the rightful owner would have legal or constructive possession; the rationale being that the rightful owner has trespassory remedies against the thief.

Salmond's reasoning is not consistent with that of Pollock and Wright,[80] who suggest that constructive possession represents a third type of possession and is thus quite distinct from factual and legal possession.[81] In their work constructive possession has been equated with the right to possess which vests in a true owner even where the subject-matter of possession is vested in another person, albeit that the other person is a wrongful possessor. They write: 'the right to possess, though distinct from possession, is treated as equivalent to possession itself for certain purposes, more important with regard to procedure than to the substance of the law.'[82] Thus, in the case of a thief who steals from a true owner, the thief can acquire possession both in law and fact providing he has control in fact and an intention to control adversely to the whole world. There is no doubt – as will become apparent in the next section – that such thief will have possessory remedies against everyone except the true owner. What remains in the true owner is a constructive possession, which is a right to possession that the thief cannot deny because his title is relative to that of the true owner.

The more recent theorising of constructive possession by Professor Bell sheds further light on the matter and suggests that the approach taken by Pollock and Wright is more appropriate.[83] Professor Bell, however, goes further, and with the examples provided within his work it is sufficiently clear how constructive possession operates as a third distinct type of possession. The basic idea behind constructive possession is the right to take actual possession, which must be vested in a person in order to qualify as being in constructive possession. The most obvious instance in which a person will have a right to take actual possession is where the actual possession of some item is in the hands of someone who recognises the superior right of another person. Thus, in the case of an agent who is entrusted with certain property (for example, goods), such agent will have actual and legal possession of the goods; however, the principal will be deemed as having constructive possession. Professor Bell identifies two main degrees of constructive possession: they are immediate constructive possession and qualified constructive possession.[84]

Immediate constructive possession arises where a person has an immediate, and thus unqualified, right to take actual possession. The simplest example here is that relating to a bailment. A bailment arises when a bailor

---

[80] *Op cit.*
[81] *Op cit*, at p 25.
[82] *Ibid.*
[83] A.P. Bell, *The Modern Law of Personal Property in England and Ireland* (1989), p 53.
[84] *Ibid.*

delivers possession of something, such as goods, to a bailee and the bailee agrees to hold possession for a particular purpose or to apply the goods for a particular purpose to be specified by the bailor.[85] If the bailor has an immediate right to call for the redelivery of possession of the subject-matter of the bailment, the bailee will be a bailee at will – that is, simply holding possession for the bailor's interest. A good example of a bailment at will is a gratuitous borrowing of a chattel from a friend. In such a case, given that the friend has an immediate right to call for the delivery of actual possession, the friend who has lent the chattel (that is, the bailor) has a constructive possession of the chattel. The significance of ascribing constructive possession to a person is that such person has sufficient *locus standi* to sue third parties in tort for trespass to chattels or conversion.[86]

Qualified constructive possession arises when there is no immediate right to possession. The right to possession may be consensually delayed, as, for example, is the case where there is agreement that the bailee is to keep the bailor's goods for a fixed period of time. An example of this is the case of a hire of goods. The immediate right to possession may also be lacking when a person exercises a lien over chattels. In these cases the bailee is not at will; in other words, the bailee is not holding possession for the bailor's interest. Rather, actual and legal possession is held for the bailee's own interest. Such constructive possession represents a very weak form of possession. It differs from immediate constructive possession in that the bailor with qualified constructive possession has no right to sue in tort for trespass.[87]

The significance of possession in property law

At the beginning of this chapter it was emphasised that possession was a more important concept in the common law than ownership. It was also mentioned that the aim of this chapter is to appreciate how the concepts of ownership, possession and title are related. The following discussion revolves around the force of possession in the common law tradition and explains how the concepts of ownership and possession are related to one another. In

---

[85] See, generally, N.E. Palmer, *Bailment* (2nd edn, 1991).

[86] See *United States of America* v *Dollfus Mieg et Cie SA* [1952] AC 582, where true owners to gold bars had not lost possession of such gold bars when they had been entrusted to the Bank of England: see Lord Porter at 611. The net effect of this is that both the bailor and the bailee will have a right to sue third parties in tort to protect their own interests. Constructive possession is wide enough to apply to a person who merely has a possessory title. For example, in *Wilson* v *Lombank* [1963] 1 All ER 740 the plaintiff purchased a car from somebody who had no title to sell. Later on the plaintiff took the car to a garage for repairs, in the course of which it was wrongfully taken by the defendants, who were not the rightful owners of the car. The court held in this case that the plaintiff, despite having a mere possessory title to the car, had an immediate right to possession which was sufficient to allow an action in trespass against the defendants.

[87] *Ward* v *Macauley* (1791) 4 TR 489.

order to begin this discussion, the reader must once again remember the general nature of ownership and possession. Ownership is a *de jure* relationship between a person and a thing. This means that ownership is a question of law and not simply fact. Ownership vests in a person a number of rights in respect of the thing owned. Possession, on the other hand, is a *de facto* relationship between a person and a thing. This means that possession is a question of fact. Normally ownership and possession will go hand in hand. However, a person may have possession in fact of a thing whilst at the same time, and in respect of the same thing, there may be a different owner.

The common law tradition regards ownership as a relative concept as opposed to an absolute one. This simply means that possession is a good title of right to a thing enforceable against anyone who cannot show a better title. Relativity of ownership, sometimes referred to as relativity of title, lies at the heart of property law in the common law tradition. Relativity of ownership originates from the force of possession in the common law.

The very first principle of possession is that it raises a presumption of ownership. A person in actual possession of a thing is presumed to be the owner of the thing, albeit this presumption, like any presumption, can be rebutted. In the lay language this may be summarised by saying that 'possession is nine-tenths the law'. However, there are sound legal justifications behind the presumption. First, possession in fact is *prima facie* evidence of legal possession and the possessor has all the legal remedies to protect such possession.[88] Possession is said to be the root of title in that it is only through possession that ownership is born or the chain of title begun. Thus, an equally important principle operating here is that a person may be presumed to be the owner of a thing even when that person has no ownership in the thing – for example, when a thing is found or taken without the authority of the true owner. Suppose that B finds a gold watch which in law belongs to A. If B takes possession, B's possession raises a presumption of ownership, which is good against the whole world except the true owner, who has a better title to it. The true owner can of course rebut the presumption of ownership; however, until such time B will be deemed to have a possessory title to the gold watch. It is the concept of possessory title that now calls for discussion.

Closely related to the idea that possession raises a presumption of ownership is that possession gives rise to possessory title. This is a title that is good against everyone except the true owner.[89] Lord Campbell once explained the rule by commenting that 'against a wrongdoer possession is title'.[90] The origins for the rule of possessory title lie in the fact that English law never developed a sophisticated

---

[88] F. Pollock and R. Wright, *Possession in the Common Law* (1888), p. 20.
[89] *The Winkfield* [1902] P 42.
[90] *Jeffries v Great Western Railway Company* (1856) 5 E & B 802 at 805.

system of rules for the vindication of ownership rights. Instead, the right to ownership largely depended on the right to possession and it was possession that was accorded remedies. In the words of Pollock and Wright, 'the common law never had any adequate process in the case of land, or any process at all in the case of goods, for the vindication of ownership pure and simple. So feeble and precarious was property without possession, or rather without possessory remedies, in the eyes of medieval lawyers, that possession largely usurped not only the substance but the name of property...'.[91] The nature of possessory title is examined below under the heading of 'Title'.

It is important to appreciate that many of the remedies that seek to protect property interests in both land and chattels depend on possession rather than on absolute notions of ownership. Property interests in land and chattels are protected by what are known as property torts.[92] In the case of land an action for trespass to land requires that the plaintiff had possession or a right to immediate possession. In the normal course of things the possessor will be the owner; however, it is quite clear that a squatter will have sufficient standing to sue in trespass.[93] This is because the squatter has possession in fact and law when he has control in fact and intends to control.[94] In the case of chattels there are two torts which seek to protect property interests, namely trespass to goods and the tort of conversion.[95] The success of both of these torts depends on whether the plaintiff has possession or an immediate right to possession. Trespass to goods is a wrongful physical interference with them. The tort of conversion amounts to a dealing with goods in a manner inconsistent with the right of the true owner.[96] It is sometimes thought that, unlike the trespass to goods, the tort of conversion is a truly proprietary remedy in that it protects ownership rather than mere possession. However, it is quite clear that a person in actual possession, such as a bailee of goods, can sue for conversion.[97] What follows is that a person who has neither possession nor an immediate right to possession cannot sue for conversion.[98] Thus, an owner who has neither possession nor an imme-

---

[91] *Op cit*, at p 5.

[92] See, generally, B.S. Markesinis & S.F. Deakin, *Tort Law* (4th edn, 1998), Chap 5.

[93] *Ocean Estates Ltd* v *Pinder* [1969] 2 AC 19.

[94] See Chapter 8 for a discussion on the squatter's right and adverse possession of land.

[95] The modern law is governed by the Torts (Interference with Goods) Act 1977 which uses the collective term 'wrongful interference with goods' to cover trespass, and conversion. A plaintiff will also have the right to sue for negligence if chattels are damaged in this way.

[96] *Lancashire & Yorkshire Railway Co* v *MacNicoll* (1918) 88 LJKB 901.

[97] *Burton* v *Hughes* (1842) 2 Bing 173.

[98] *Gordon* v *Harper* (1796) 7 TR 9. An example of an owner who lacks possession is a landlord who lets out his land to a tenant with furnishings. The landlord, despite being owner, has no right to possession or any immediate right to possession so long as the tenancy continues. Other examples include a lien where the lienee is exercising the lien and the lienor therefore has no immediate right to possession. Such an owner has, however, a right to bring an action for damage caused to his reversionary interest in the chattel: see *Mears* v *London and South Western Railway Co* (1862) 22 CB(NS) 850.

diate right to possession cannot sue for conversion. Finally, where damage is caused to a chattel through the negligence of another person, the plaintiff must show that he had either ownership in the chattel or a possessory title.[99]

Possession plays an important role in the transfer and creation of property interests in personal property. Legal ownership generally cannot be transferred in a chattel until such time as delivery of possession is made.[100] With regard to possessory security interests in chattels, possession is all-important. Both a lien and a pledge require delivery of possession in order for the interests to be effective.[101]

TITLE

The idea of title in property law is sometimes simply equated with ownership, legal right or legal ownership. If A has ownership then it follows that he has title to whatever forms the subject-matter of his ownership. For example, if A holds a fee simple estate in land, A is said to be vested with a freehold title in the land. However, the idea of title in law is much wider than this. The classical analysis of title demonstrates that title is the set of facts upon which a claim to some legal right, liberty or power, or legal interest is based.[102] Thus, it is quite possible to talk of a person having title to a freehold estate in land or title to an easement. However, given that title is the set of facts upon which a claim to a legal right or interest is founded, title can exist even when there is no pre-existing legal interest or right vested in a person who claims he has title. In other words, the facts themselves may lead to a legal right or interest enforceable against others. These facts, that is title, may be enforceable against X but not necessarily against Y. The reason for this is that title is generally a relative concept and must be measured relative to other facts, which may lead to a different conclusion in law.

Title has been defined and contrasted with interest by Professor Goode. He writes: 'interest is to be distinguished from title. A person's interest in an asset denotes the quantum of rights over it which he enjoys against other persons,

---

[99] *Leigh and Sullivan Ltd* v *Aliakmon Shipping Company Limited* [1986] 1 AC 785 at 809, *per* Lord Brandon.

[100] See Chapter 8. However, a contract for the sale of goods may pass ownership in a chattel before delivery of possession: see Sale of Goods Act 1979, s 18, rule 1.

[101] See, generally, M. Bridge, *Personal Property Law* (2nd edn, 1996).

[102] See, for example, Salmond, *op cit*, who writes (at p 331) that '... title is the *de facto* antecedent, of which the right is the *de jure* consequent. If the law confers a right upon a man which it does not confer upon another, the reason is that certain facts are true of him which are not true of the other, and these facts are the title of the right'. It is important to appreciate that the use of the word 'facts' here is not used to denote mere physical facts. Rather the inquiry is into the legal facts pertaining to a person standing in relation to some object or asset. In other words, the question can be put, what is the legal significance of an individual claiming an interest in a thing? In this respect A. Pottage writes: '... title is an abstract quality, which depends upon an interpretation of rights rather than the identification of physical facts': see 'Evidencing Ownership' in Bright and Dewar (eds), *Land Law: Themes and Perspectives* (1998) at p 131.

though not necessarily against all other persons. His title measures the strength of the interest he enjoys in relation to others.'[103] Lawson and Rudden write: 'title is a shorthand term used to denote the facts which, if proved, will enable a plaintiff to recover possession or a defendant to retain possession of a thing.'[104] It follows from these definitions that two or more persons may have independent legal interests in the same thing. For example, both a true owner of an asset and a person with mere possession with the intention to control can have absolute legal interests in the asset. This legal interest is enforceable against third parties by both the true owner and a possessor. Whilst they both have identical legal interests, they have titles that are different in nature. The true owner has a much stronger title than a mere possessor of the chattel. A true owner has an indefeasible title whereas the possessor has a mere relative title. The strength of the true owner's title is greater because it cannot be defeated by anyone so long as the true owner has an intention to control the asset. The title of the possessor is liable to be defeated by the true owner, and thus, whilst he has a legal interest, his title is a relative one.

Nature of titles: absolute and relative

Title to a proprietary interest can be either absolute or relative. In the common law tradition titles are more relative than absolute. An absolute title in property law is one which is indefeasible. A person alleging an absolute title is basically putting forward a set of facts which demonstrate that there is in fact only one title – that is, his title – and that all other titles in respect of the same object are non-existent or simply bad. An absolute title is one which is indefeasible in the sense that there is no one else who can point to a better title in respect of the same object in which a proprietary interest is held. Since the essence of an absolute title is that there is simply nobody else with a better title to the same thing, an absolute title will arise only if there are sufficient facts which lead to this conclusion. There are three classical instances in which a person may prove an absolute title.[105] The simplest way to acquire an absolute title is to create something out of nothing. In this case there can be no other title to the thing other than the one that belongs to the creator. The creation of a book is a good example: here the creator would protect his absolute title by a copyright, which would give him exclusive rights in the book. Another way of acquiring an absolute title is by manufacture. In the absence of further evidence, a person who manufactures something is the first owner and the only owner. Another example of an absolute title is a registered title. A registered title amounts to a guarantee from a certain body, such as the state, that the person registered as owner is the owner and that his

---

[103] R. Goode, *Commercial Law* (1982) at p 52.
[104] F.H. Lawson and B. Rudden, *The Law of Property* (2nd edn, 1982) at p 44.
[105] See F.H. Lawson and B. Rudden, *The Law of Property* (2nd edn, 1982) at p 44.

title is better than any other title. An example of a registered title is to be found in the case of land where the state guarantees the title to a particular piece of land. The idea and nature of registered title is considered below. However, it is important to appreciate that a registered title to land can be defeated, that is changed, by a person who claims adverse possession of land. In this sense it is questionable whether such a title is really absolute.

Titles in property law are seldom absolute; rather, they are relative. The idea of title being relative – sometimes simply referred to as relativity of title – is a particularly common feature of the common law tradition. A relative title, unlike an absolute title, is one that can be defeated by a person showing that he or she has a better title to the thing in question. The idea of relativity of title originates from the nature of possession in law. Possession in law has the effect of making ownership a relative concept as opposed to an absolute one. Possession raises a presumption of ownership and in the absence of further inquiry a person with possession is deemed to be the owner. The idea of relativity of title can be best explained by the following example. If A has a valuable painting which is lost but found by B, whilst A is the true owner in law, B's possession, as we have seen above, is sufficient to give him a possessory title to the painting. If C wrongfully interferes with the possession which B has, B can sue C for trespass to goods or the tort of conversion. B has a relative title to the painting, albeit that A's former possession gave him an absolute title. As against C, B has a title which is good, and C cannot point to the defect in B's title to deny B's right to sue C. The defect in B's title, or, in other words, the fact that a third party (that is A) has a better title than B, is often referred to as the *ius tertii* principle.[106] One commentator has explained the idea behind relativity of title in the following way:[107] 'In the result, when looking at personal property, lawyers are interested in the quality of a given title. This is not an abstract inquiry, but is something to be judged by reference to its beginnings in time relative to that of others.'[108]

An important concept in the understanding of relativity of title is limitation of actions. If one treats title as a relative notion, then we have the rather strange result that there can theoretically be two owners in respect of the same thing. For example, in the case of the painting above, there is no reason why A should not be allowed to sue C for wrongful interference with the painting. However, if C has already paid B then why should A sue C? There is a danger of what Murphy and Roberts describe as a 'multiplicity of actions'.[109] In an ideal world it would be better for there to be one owner

---

[106] This principle has, however, been criticised in that it allows a wrongdoer to benefit from his wrongdoing. The rule has been undermined by the Torts (Interference with Goods) Act 1977, which allows a defendant in certain circumstances to plead *ius tertii*.

[107] R.G. Hammond, *Personal Property: Commentary and Materials* (1992) at p 147.

[108] *Ibid*. Hammond refers only to personal property; however, there is no doubt that the same principle applies in the case of land as evidenced by the rules of adverse possession to land. See Chapter 8.

[109] W.T. Murphy and S. Roberts, *Understanding Property Law* (3rd edn, 1998) at p 64.

rather than two. The most obvious way to get rid of one owner is for the true owner to exercise his rights and recover possession from the person who has a mere possessory title. If the true owner does not exercise his rights of ownership, then the law must get rid of him in an arbitrary way. The way in which the law does this is through limitation of actions. After the expiration of a certain time period, the rights of the true owner are completely extinguished and a good title vests in the person who merely had a possessory title. The Limitation Act 1980 imposes a six-year limitation period in the case of personal property and a twelve-year period in the case of land. After the expiration of these time periods access to litigation is denied so that the true owner loses any title that he may have had.[110]

Forms of title: registered, documentary and possessory

In their nature, titles can be absolute or relative; the form that titles take also varies. The issue can simply be put by asking, what type of facts can a person put forward as evidence to show the strength of the legal interest he or she holds in respect of a thing? In the case of chattels there are generally no elaborate documents that act as documents of title. The title to my car, my television and so forth is simply based on my continued and better possession than any other person.[111] In contrast to these personal chattels, the title to my house will not be based on the simple notion of possession. In the modern law, title to land will be proved in one of two ways: title may be in the form of an unregistered title (that is, purely documentary) or it may be in the form of a registered title. An unregistered title to land consists of a collection of documents, which in their totality prove that a person is the owner of a piece of land. Thus, a purchaser of a title to land which is unregistered must satisfy himself, through perusal of the documents, that the vendor has the interest in the land which is sought to be conveyed to the purchaser. In order to abstract a good root of title, the vendor must be able to find a chain of ownership that stretches over a period of 15 years and leads to the proposed purchaser.

The idea behind a registered title to land is that there is no need to abstract documents purporting to show ownership. Instead, all the information relating to the ownership, and other matters such as charges and interests, is to be found on a central register maintained by the state through the Land Registry.

---

[110] The application of the Limitation Act 1980 to title is not a straightforward task in law: the question is, when will time begin to run against the true owner? These matters are discussed in Chapter 8, which looks at the rules of finding and adverse possession, which are based on relativity of title.

[111] Chattels may have documentary title in certain situations, most notably when a carrier is carrying chattels on behalf of a shipper. The carrier will issue the shipper with a document called a bill of lading, which acts as a document of title to the goods on board the vessel. Delivery of the bill of lading is sufficient to deliver the ownership in the chattels on board a vessel.

A vendor of land can show his ownership in the land by pointing to the fact that he is the registered proprietor of the land in so far as the register is concerned. The significance of the register is that it acts as conclusive evidence as to the proprietor of the land. In other words, the title to the land is guaranteed by the state. An increasing amount of land in England and Wales is subject to registered title and indeed registration is now compulsory for those titles which for some reason remain unregistered.[112] The Land Registry has its headquarters in London; however, there are more than twenty district land registries which deal with the day-to-day business of registered land.

A form of title that features in both real property and personal property law is called a possessory title.[113] It is intended to confine the discussion here to personal property; however, the same principles apply to land. Given the relative force of possession in law, a person may have a possessory title good against everyone except the true owner of a thing. The basis for this is that possession raises a presumption of ownership. As against the person in possession it matters not that there is a person who has a better title than him. The person in possession can enforce his ownership in the thing against everyone except the true owner. The rule relating to possessory title to chattels stems from the decision in *The Winkfield*,[114] where the plaintiff Postmaster General, for the purposes of the claim, was assumed to have possession of mail on a ship. The ship had sunk through the fault of another vessel and the Postmaster General sued to recover the loss from the owners. In allowing the claim, Collins MR held that in the absence of the true owners of the mail possession counted as title.[115]

It has been stated that any person in possession of goods can rely on possessory title, irrespective of the capacity in which he holds them.[116] In the case of a person who acquires possession of goods belonging to another through an innocent act such as finding, there is little doubt that such a finder should acquire possessory title. Moreover, no problems arise in the case of possession of goods in the hands of a bailee, as in the case of *The Winkfield*.[117] What is problematic, however, is the case of a wrongful and dishonest taking of possession from a true owner. For example, can a thief have possessory title to the goods that he has stolen? In *Parker v British Airways Board*[118]

---

[112] For an excellent account, see P. Sparkes, *A New Land Law* (1999), Chapter 1.

[113] Possessory title features in real property law in relation to claims to adverse possession of land where a squatter merely has a possessory title until such time he becomes the registered proprietor of the land in accordance with the principles of registered title. Possessory title features more dominantly in personal property law in relation to chattels.

[114] [1902] P 42.

[115] *Ibid*, at 60.

[116] A.P. Bell, *op cit* (note 83), at p 78.

[117] In this situation the bailee remains accountable to the bailor for the monies received in litigation less the amount that truly reflects the interests of the bailee: see N. Palmer, *Bailment* (2nd edn, 1992) at p 335.

[118] [1982] 1 All ER 834.

Donaldson LJ was of the opinion that if dishonest takers were denied any rights against intermeddlers it would open up the gates for constant taking and denial of possession.[119] It is therefore clear that possessory title will even operate in favour of a dishonest taker.

A final note about possessory title to chattels is that, whilst it was noted above that possession raises a presumption of ownership and against a wrongdoer possession is title, the *ius tertii* rule will apply under the Torts (Interference with Goods) Act 1977. Section 8 allows a defandant to show that a third party has a better right than the plaintiff in respect of the interest claimed by the plaintiff. The third party can then be asked to be joined in the proceedings; failure to do so by the third party may result in a deprivation of right to sue the defendant in the future. The objective here is to allow the court to settle competing claims in one set of proceedings and to avoid double liability of the wrongdoer.

Equitable title

No discussion on title would be complete without an understanding of equitable title. In Chapter 4 it was observed how equitable interests exist alongside legal interests in property. The idea of equitable ownership is a common feature of property law and such ownership is evidenced by equitable title just as legal ownership is evidenced by legal title. Unlike legal title, however, equitable title is a much more absolute concept. Possession does not play a significant role in equitable title because equitable interests are not based on possession; rather they are based on an equitable right, which is said to be *in personam*. The significance of equitable ownership lies not on possession but rather on the fact that such a right will be enforced by equity. All that the equitable owner has is a *chose in action* enforceable against everyone except a bona fide purchaser of the legal title for value without notice. There is no idea of relativity of title in relation to equitable ownership in the same sense as applies to legal ownership and title.

Equitable ownership can be acquired in a number of ways. The most obvious is where there is a declaration of trust giving the beneficiary equitable interest and title in the subject-matter of the trust. Other means of acquisition include a defective transfer of legal ownership. Where some formality has not been complied with, equity will nevertheless hold that a person has acquired the ownership, albeit in equity, on the grounds that equity sees that done which ought to be done. For example, a contract to convey land, provided it

---

[119] *Ibid*, at 837; see, however, *Solomon v Metropolitan Police Commissioner* [1982] Crim LR 606, where the plaintiff who had used stolen money to purchase a car was denied recovery of the car from the police on the grounds of *ex turpi causa non oritur actio*.

complies with the formalities for the creation of contracts for sale of land,[120] will vest equitable ownership in the purchaser even though the conveyance of the title has not taken place. In some cases equitable ownership will be acquired if that is the only thing which the transferee has to give – as, for example, in the case of a transfer of a beneficial interest by a beneficiary. In all these instances, equitable ownership will vest in the equitable owner an equitable title to the subject-matter of equitable ownership. Given that equitable ownership usually does not involve possession, the need for documentary evidence of title seems imperative in these cases to prove such title.

---

[120] See Chapter 9.

7

FRAGMENTATION OF OWNERSHIP

THE IDEA OF FRAGMENTATION OF OWNERSHIP

In the previous chapter it was observed that ownership is the greatest or ultimate right that a person can have in a thing. Furthermore, it was noted that ownership consisted of a number of incidents. The standard incidents of ownership consist of both benefits and burdens, or rights and duties, which are vested in the person who has ownership. The common incidents of ownership include the right to possession, the right to manage, the right to capital and the right to income. Fragmentation of ownership, as the words imply, entails the splitting up of the incidents of ownership and vesting them in more than one person. The idea of splitting ownership and vesting the constituent elements of it in different persons has been a particularly notable feature in English law and other jurisdictions founded on the common law tradition. There are a number of reasons for this. Unlike Roman law, English law has not treated ownership as an absolute relationship between the owner and a thing. The Roman law idea of *dominium* revolved around the fact that the owner was vested with all the incidents of ownership, so that he alone could exercise the incidents of enjoyment and management. In English law, the development of the trust contributed to a large extent in allowing management and enjoyment functions of ownership to be distributed amongst different persons for different social and economic objectives. The trust occupies a central position in the law of fragmentation of ownership and will be considered more closely later in the chapter.

Another factor that has facilitated fragmentation of ownership is the nature of certain types of resources. The nature of land has allowed it to be put to different yet compatible uses at the same time by different users. Land is virtually indestructible and it can be enjoyed for a variety of purposes. An owner of land can carve out of his full ownership smaller segments of that ownership and vest them in different users. Unlike land, however, goods and other personal property did not, from a historical point of view, feature significantly in matters of fragmentation.[1] Goods are generally less permanent than land and more movable, so as to make them less susceptible to simultaneous property interests. This factor goes a long way in explaining the relatively fewer property interests that exist in personal property as compared to land. However, things have long changed and nowadays ownership in personal property can in many ways be fragmented in the same way as it can in land. Indeed, in the modern law of property, fragmentation of ownership of personal property is much more common and often more important than in the case of land. The relative economic significance of land has been displaced by large trust funds. The modern law of trusts generally recognises the fact that the trust operates predominantly in a commercial setting rather than land and family.[2] The idea that management and enjoyment functions can be split is very common in trusts such as pension funds and other large investments where trustees manage assets for beneficiaries.

THE VARIED CONTEXTS OF FRAGMENTATION OF OWNERSHIP

The idea that ownership can be split and its fragmented elements distributed amongst a number of persons can occur in varying contexts. Often property lawyers refer to terms such as horizontal and vertical fragmentation of ownership; sometimes terms such as consecutive and concurrent ownership are used to explain situations where fragmentation of ownership has occurred. Further still, concepts such as trusts and powers of appointment feature predominantly in discussions on fragmentation of ownership. These matters must be explored in more detail. However, for the time being, on a broad level of discussion all property interests apart from ownership are the product of fragmentation of ownership. If one takes ownership as the greatest right that a person can acquire in a thing, any other rights that exist in the same thing must flow from the right of ownership itself. For example, a lease flows from the freehold ownership in land; the freehold owner gives away most of his incidents of ownership to the leaseholder. Most importantly, the right to possession is vested in the tenant; the freehold owner simply retains the right to capital, which, as seen in the previous chapter, entitles him alone to alienate the ownership in the land. A mortgage, which gives the mortgagee a charge on the mortgagor's land,

---

[1] See F.H. Lawson and B. Rudden, *The Law of Property* (2nd edn, 1982) at pp 76–77.
[2] See G. Moffat, *Trust Law: Text & Materials* (3rd edn, 1999) at pp 33–36.

has the effect of vesting in the mortgagee the power of disposition of the land in the event of default of payment by the mortgagor. This power of sale, which is one of the normal incidents of ownership, is simply vested in the mortgagee. Indeed, a mortgage in the case of land involves the demise of a term of years in the land.[3] Many of the limited property interests in personal property likewise are derived from fragmented ownership. For example, a bailment is dependent on the transfer of possession from the bailor to the bailee. In this sense, a bailment is not too far from the ideology of a lease. It involves the transfer of possession of goods for a particular purpose such as hire or loan, possession to be returned to the bailor when the purpose of the bailment has been met.

Like leases and mortgages, ancillary proprietary interests in land such as easements and restrictive covenants are derived from an ownership interest. Easements and restrictive covenants involve the enjoyment incidents of ownership to be transferred to others. An easement, such as a right of way over somebody else's land, is only possible where the owner of land allows this enjoyment incident of ownership to be shared by another. Likewise, a restrictive covenant, which is an agreement by a landowner not to do certain things on his land, entitles the person seeking to enforce the restrictive covenant to exercise some limited ownership powers belonging to the landowner subject to the restrictive covenant.[4] For example, a landowner has, by virtue of his ownership in the land, freedom in the manner in which he chooses to enjoy his land. He may not wish to erect any further buildings on the land. The essence of a restrictive covenant is that the landowner covenants away this freedom or right to another person. Easements and restrictive covenants, unlike leases and mortgages, are annexed to some larger property in other land. Such interests do not exist *in gross*; they require the existence of ownership of other land to be benefited by the interest in question.

TRUSTS

The idea of a trust

It is appropriate to begin discussion on fragmentation of ownership with a consideration of the trust concept. Not only is the trust, in its own right, a means by which the management and enjoyment functions of ownership can be split amongst different persons to achieve social and economic objectives, it is a concept which goes a long way in providing the means of fragmentation of ownership in other contexts.[5] It is not surprising, therefore, that Maitland

---

[3] Law of Property Act 1925, ss 85–86, see Chapter 4.

[4] Restrictive covenants are examined in Chapter 10 in the discussion relating to personal and proprietary rights in land.

[5] For example, and as seen in the last chapter, consecutive and sometimes concurrent interests in real and personal property require the existence of the trust to facilitate such holding of interests.

once wrote: '[O]f all the exploits of Equity the largest and most important is the invention and development of the Trust. It is an institute of great elasticity and generality; as elastic, as general as contract. This perhaps forms the most distinctive achievement of English Lawyers. It seems to us almost essential to civilization, and yet there is nothing quite like it in foreign law.'[6]

The basic idea behind the trust lies in the fact that the management and enjoyment functions of ownership are split between different persons. The role of management is vested in a person called a trustee whilst the enjoyment of the thing subject to the trust is vested in persons called beneficiaries. The fragmentation of management and enjoyment is only possible where the legal title to the property is vested in trustees. However, because the trustees have agreed to hold and manage the legal title for the benefit of beneficiaries, their conscience binds them in equity so as to give the beneficiaries an equitable interest in the property subject to the trust. The net effect of fragmenting management and enjoyment is that there is a consequential fragmentation of title. The trustees hold the legal title, which is a nominal title, while the beneficiary holds the equitable title full of beneficial rewards from the property. The trust in this sense can be seen as a product of equity. One leading treatise on the law of trusts defines the trust:

> 'an equitable obligation, binding on a person (who is called a trustee) to deal with property over which he has control (which is called the trust property), for the benefit of persons (who are called beneficiaries), of whom he may himself be one, and any one of who may enforce the obligation. Any act or neglect on the part of the trustee which is not authorized or excused by the terms of the trust instrument, or by law, is called a breach of trust.'[7]

Historical foundations

In Chapter 4 reference was made to the origins of the modern trust. There it was seen how the trust, in the form of a use, was employed to encounter the problems of freedom of alienation and payment of taxes in the system of feudalism.[8] The system of tenure operated in a way in which no person, apart from the Crown, was absolute owner of land. Instead the ownership of land was fragmented vertically so that the King granted land to powerful lords who could in return grant further segments of land to tenants. A tenant, of course, could grant certain land vested in him to other tenants. If he did this, he had a dual role to play in connection with the land, for he would not only be an overlord to his tenant, but he himself would be a tenant accountable to

---

[6] F.W. Maitland, *Equity: A Course of Lectures* (J. Brunyate (ed), 1936) at p 23.
[7] Underhill and Hayton, *The Law Relating to Trusts and Trustees* (14th edn, 1987) at p 3.
[8] See, generally J.L. Barton, 'The Medieval Use' (1966) 82 LQR 562.

an overlord higher up in the feudal ladder. Within this feudal system of tenure, the death of a tenant entitled the heir of the tenant to take possession or *seisin* of the land – however, not without first paying feudal dues to the overlord. The employment of the use allowed land to be transferred to trustees[9] during the lifetime of the tenant upon use of the tenant and after his death to members of his family, which could include the heir. The advantage of this arrangement lay in the fact that on the death of the tenant, the trustees would simply hold the land for the persons entitled after the tenant. Since there was no acquisition on the death of the tenant, the overlord had no apparent claim to dues. The land simply belonged to the trustees who at all times remained in possession. Equitable intervention, however, meant that the conscience of the trustees would bind them to the use.

The second advantage of the trust lay in the fact that it permitted greater freedom to the tenant in devising his property to persons other than just the heir. The common law was strict in requiring that land be vested in the heir of the tenant. Where the tenant died without an heir, the overlord became entitled to the land by way of escheat.[10] Transfer to trustees, however, allowed land to be enjoyed by those designated in the terms of the use rather than on the strict principles of the common law. Upon recognition of the potential scope of the use in undermining the system of feudal dues and the consequential emptying of the Crown pocket, the Statute of Uses 1535[11] was introduced, which had the effect of undermining certain uses. The basic aim of the legislation was to deny the beneficiary equitable rights in the land. Rather, where the use was employed, the intended beneficiary acquired a legal title to the land and was thus subject to feudal dues in the event of the death of the tenant. In 1540 the Statute of Wills was also passed in recognition that the landowning aristocracy rejected the strict common law rule requiring land to be acquired by the heir. The statute permitted greater freedom in the disposition of property after the death of the tenant; however, such dispositions would be subject to the same feudal taxes that existed before the statute.

Trust and law reform

Although the Statute of Uses 1535 did not completely extinguish the use concept, it cannot be overstated that the use played a fundamental role in reforming law in medieval England. The undermining of the feudal system, which was out of touch with the needs of landowning citizens, and the recog-

---

[9] This basically involved delivery of possession in the presence of witnesses followed by ceremonial acts: see Thorne, 'Livery of Seisin' (1938) 52 LQR 345.

[10] See Megarry and Wade, *The Law of Real Property* (6th edn, 2000) at p 17.

[11] Described as the 'most important single statute in the history of the trust's development' by G. Moffat, *Trust Law: Text and Materials* (3rd edn, 1999) at p 29.

nition of the need for free alienation of land, could not have been achieved without the use.[12] Uses continued to be allowed in cases where they involved the imposition of active duties on the trustees. Where, for example, a tenant put land upon use when he was absent from the land, the trustee's role was essential in collecting rents and paying debts due on the land. In this case the use was entirely genuine and not designed to avoid feudal dues. It was this type of use that paved the way for the development of the modern trust. Furthermore, uses employed in connection with leasehold land did not come within the ambit of the Statute of Uses.

The role of trust in paving the way for law reform was not just seen in the context of feudalism. In the context of married women, it brought about legislation recognising the fact that married women could own property in their own right.[13] Before the Married Women's Property Act 1882, a wife could enjoy separate property in a number of ways. First, equity recognised that a wife could enjoy a separate estate under a trust created in her favour. Provided that there was good reason for the creation of the trust – as, for example, where her husband was a wastrel – the Court of Chancery would enforce the wife's separate estate in equity.[14] Second, marriage settlements, which were essentially a contract between husband and wife recognised and enforced in equity, allowed the wife to claim property as hers which she had acquired after marriage and which trustees of the marriage settlement held for her.

Express trusts

The modern trust can be used in a wide variety of contexts to achieve different social and economic objectives. The modern trust can take a variety of forms depending on the context in which it is employed. Traditional classification of trusts has distinguished between express and imputed trusts and bare and active trusts.[15] Express trusts are those trusts created by a deliberate act of a person called a settlor, or in the case of a trust created in a will, by a testator. Express trusts can be subdivided into private and public or charitable trusts. A private trust is one that seeks to provide for private persons such as family members, friends or other class of beneficiaries closely connected with the settlor. For example, a father of a child may transfer £2000 on trust to trustees to hold for his child until the child attains the age of 21 years.

---

[12] See A.W. Scott, 'The Trust as an Instrument of Law Reform' (1922) 31 Yale LJ 457.

[13] Married Women's Property Act 1882; see Chapter 5, where the property relations of married women were discussed.

[14] See G.S. Alexander, 'The Transformation of Trusts as a Legal Category, 1800–1914' (1987) 5 Law and History Review at p 320.

[15] A complete discussion of these various trusts is outside the scope of this book; however, generalisations can be made to aid the understanding of the trust concept.

However, social behaviour dictates that a person may wish to provide for persons who are in need in terms of poverty or education. Where provision is made for purposes that are generally beneficial to the community, such provisions take effect behind a public or charitable trust. Given the importance of charitable trusts – in terms of their purposes, that they seek to bring benefit, and the monies involved – these types of trust are controlled and enforced by the Attorney General and Charity Commissioners.[16]

Express trusts can be further divided into fixed and discretionary trusts. A fixed trust is one where the beneficial interest of the beneficiaries is fixed. For example, a settlor may transfer £20,000 on trust for his three children equally. In such a case, the trust is fixed, the beneficiaries are entitled to one-third of the money and the trustees have no discretion in the manner in which the money is distributed to the children. In contrast, a discretionary trust is one where the trustees are given a discretion in the manner in which the trust property is distributed. In such a trust, the trustees are under a duty to distribute; however, how they distribute and to whom is left to their discretion. A discretionary trust is very similar to the concept of a power of appointment, which is discussed in the next section.

The distinction between bare and active trusts relates to the duties which are imposed upon the trustee. Where the trustee has only minimal duties – for example, he merely holds the trust property for the beneficiary – the trust is said to be a bare trust. The beneficiaries have paramount control over the trust property which is in the hands of the trustee. On the other hand, an active trust is one where the trustee is under a duty to manage the trust property for the benefit of the beneficiaries. In an active trust the trustee does not merely hold the legal title; instead he is under a duty to manage the trust property in the best interests of the beneficiaries. Thus, if the trust consists of a fund, the trustee must invest the trust fund. The trustee owes fiduciary duties to the beneficiaries and is accountable for failure to manage the trust property effectively.

Imputed trusts

Trusts are not always created by a deliberate act on the part of a person; instead the law in certain circumstances may impute a trust. In other words, title to property may become fragmented by trusts which are imputed by law. Imputed trusts can take one of two forms: they can either be resulting trusts or constructive trusts. The fundamental distinction between resulting and constructive trusts lies in the fact that resulting trusts are implied by law whereas constructive trusts are imposed by law. Mention must also be made

---

[16] See, generally, *Tudor on Charities* (8th edn, 1995).

here to trusts which are imposed by statute: although they are a form of imputed trust, they stand as a freestanding category. They are imposed by statute in certain circumstances: for example of land, whenever land becomes co-owned, a statutory trust in the form of a trust is imposed by statute.[17]

Resulting trusts are said to be implied by law. Unlike express trusts, they are not founded on the express intentions of the person creating the trust. The House of Lords in *Westdeutsche v Islington London Borough Council*[18] has recently redefined the basis upon which equity implies resulting trusts. In the case, Lord Browne-Wilkinson explained:

'under existing law a resulting trust arises in two sets of circumstances: (a) where A makes a voluntary payment to B or pays (wholly or partly) for the purchase of property which is vested either in B alone or in joint names of A and B, there is a presumption that A did not intend to make a gift to B; the money or property is held on trust for A (if he is the sole provider of the money) or in the case of a joint purchase by A and B in shares proportionate to their contributions ... (b) where A transfers property to B on express trusts, but the trusts declared do not exhaust the whole beneficial interest. Both types of trust are traditionally regarded as examples of trusts giving effect to the common intention of the parties.'[19]

Traditional trust classification has categorised circumstance (a) as a situation where the implied resulting trust is referred to as a presumed resulting trust. Circumstance (b) is a situation where the implied resulting trust is referred to as an automatic resulting trust. Lord Browne-Wilkinson, however, does not distinguish between presumed and automatic resulting trusts; instead, he argues that circumstances (a) and (b) are simply examples of trusts giving effect to the common and presumed intention of the parties.[20] Although resulting trusts are divided into the two categories of presumed and automatic, the underlying theme in both trusts is the same. At the heart of the matter is the fact that where a person does not dispose of his property effectively – that is,

---

[17] Trusts of Land and Appointment of Trustees Act 1996, s 1.

[18] [1996] AC 699.

[19] *Ibid*, at 708.

[20] *Ibid*. This has, however, been a source of controversy since it departs from the traditional classification of Megarry J in *Re White v Vandervell's Trustees Ltd* (*Vandervell's Trust No 2*) [1974] 3 WLR 256, where automatic and presumed resulting trusts were clearly distinguished as being different. For further discussion, see G. Moffat, *Trust Law: Text and Materials* (3rd edn, 1999) at p 150 and also R. Pearce and J. Stevens, *The Law of Trusts and Equitable Obligations* (2nd edn, 1998) at p 226. The source of the controversy relates to the fact that automatic resulting trusts are not necessarily based on the presumed or common intentions of the parties in circumstances which give rise to the trust. Thus, where a person seeks to divest himself of his beneficial interest in property, there is no real common or presumed intention that property should result back to his estate. If the beneficial interest remains unexhausted, it results back to the transferor as an automatic consequence, rather than on the implied intentions of the transferor.

through gift or bargain – that undisposed property remains his as it does not belong to anyone else. It is a fundamental rule of property law that rights in things should not be simply abandoned but must belong to a person.

The basis of a presumed resulting trust lies in the presumed intention of a person transferring property. In other words, in certain types of property transfers, equity presumes that property transferred by a person is intended to be subject to a trust rather than, for example, to be given outright. The most common example of a situation which may give rise to a resulting trust is where A purchases property and has it conveyed in the name of B. Where A has provided all the purchase money, the presumption is that B holds the legal title on a resulting trust for A.[21] It is important to stress that this is only a presumption, which, like any other presumption, can be rebutted by evidence suggesting that the transfer in the name of B was intended to take effect as a gift. The basis upon which equity makes a presumption of a resulting trust is that 'equity assumes bargains and not gifts'.[22] Furthermore, the underlying rationale seems to be that a person does not, in the absence of clear evidence to the contrary, voluntarily give away money or other property to another. An automatic resulting trust arises where property is transferred upon trust to another, however, for some reason or other, the beneficial interest in the property remains unexhausted. The most typical situation where this might happen is when A transfers property on trust, but, for some reason, does not identify the beneficiary of the trust. The only logical result here is that the property results back to the person creating the trust. The only intention, if there is an intention, is that it is the transferor's property and not anyone else's, such as the trustee.[23] The basis of an automatic resulting trust lies in the maxim that 'equity abhors a beneficial vacuum'. Just like the common law, which holds that property rights should be vested in persons rather than just abandoned,[24] equity requires that proprietary rights be vested in persons.

Whereas resulting trusts are implied by law, constructive trusts are said to be imposed by law. Constructive trusts are not necessarily based in the presumed or common intention of parties in a property transaction.[25] Finding a coherent and unifying definition of a constructive trust is almost an impossi-

---

[21] See, for example, *Dyer v Dyer* (1788) 2 Cox Eq Cas 92 at 93; 30 ER 42 at 43; and *Burns v Burns* [1984] Ch 317.

[22] *Goodfriend v Goodfriend* (1972) 22 DLR (3d) 699 at 703, *per* Spence J, quoted in K. Gray, *Elements of Land Law* (2nd edn, 1993) at p 386, (3rd edn published 2001).

[23] See, for example, *Re White v Vandervell's Trustees Ltd (Vandervell's Trust No 2)* [1974] 3 WLR 256.

[24] See Chapters 6 and 8.

[25] Common intention may, however, be important in some contexts – as for example, constructive trusts, which are imposed in the co-ownership of land: see *Lloyds Bank v Rosset* [1991] 1 AC 107.

ble task. In the course of its history the constructive trust has operated in so many different contexts that it is impossible to extract any principle which unifies the circumstances in which the trust is imposed.[26] It is suggested that the appropriate way to understand the constructive trust is to examine it in the various contexts in which it operates. A further complexity lies in the fact that not all common law based jurisdictions have analysed the constructive trust in the same manner. The constructive trust has been analysed in two quite different ways. In some countries, and quite clearly in England, the constructive trust has been analysed as an 'institutional' constructive trust; whilst in some countries, most notably Canada,[27] the constructive trust has been analysed as a 'remedial' constructive trust. The distinction between an institutional and a remedial constructive trust is far reaching. The former is imposed as a result of certain facts which make it unconscionable for one person who has legal title to property to deny the beneficial ownership therein in another. It is the facts which give rise to the constructive trust. On the other hand, a remedial trust is not necessarily based on the unconscionable conduct of a person who acquires the legal title to property; rather the trust is imposed to reverse an unjust enrichment. The constructive trust operates as a remedy rather than by recognising pre-existing property rights. The remedial constructive trust is imposed by the court in order to effect a restitution of property. The remedial constructive trust is a much more powerful property concept than an institutional constructive trust. It does not recognise pre-existing property rights, however; once imposed by the courts, it has the effect of substantially altering pre-existing property rights.[28] It is for this reason and others that the remedial constructive trust has yet to find a safe home in English law.[29]

English law takes the view that a constructive trust should only be imposed in the occurrence of certain events that make it unconscionable for the legal owner of property to deny the beneficial interest therein to another. In *Westdeutsche* v *Islington London Borough Council*,[30] Lord Browne-Wilkinson, in an attempt to provide some generalisation about the constructive trust, commented that such a trust is imposed on a person by 'reason of his unconscionable conduct.'[31] His Lordship went on to explain that the constructive trust 'arises by operation of law as from the date of the circumstances which give rise to it: the function of the court is to merely

---

[26] See, generally, Oakley, *Constructive Trustees* (3rd edn, 1997).

[27] See D. Waters, *The Law of Trusts in Canada* (2nd edn, 1984) at pp 379–380.

[28] As, for example, in the case of the insolvency or bankruptcy of a person. Where such a constructive trust is imposed, it can grant equitable rights of property in some so as to gain priority in insolvency proceedings, whilst at the same time denying others the right to the same property.

[29] See P. Birks, *The Frontiers of Liability* (1994), Vol 2, pp 163–223.

[30] [1996] AC 669.

[31] *Ibid*, at 705.

declare that such a trust has arisen in the past.'[32] Given the numerous and different contexts in which the constructive trust has found itself operating, it would be impossible to provide an account of all these contexts in this text.[33] However, some examples can be given where the constructive trust is imposed by reason of the unconscionable conduct of a person. Historically, constructive trusts were imposed on persons standing in a fiduciary relationship who had made profits as a result of the fiduciary relationship.[34] The purpose of the constructive trust was to prevent the fiduciary taking the profit that he had made as a result of an abuse of his position. Thus, in the seminal case of *Keech* v *Sandford*,[35] trustees of a lease who had renewed the lease for themselves were held to hold the lease for the beneficiaries of the trust.[36]

In more recent times the constructive trust has been imposed: to prevent a person benefiting from his crime; to find liability in the case where a stranger intermeddles with a trust either through dishonestly assisting in a breach of trust or knowingly receiving trust property;[37] to prevent a landowner from denying a claimant an interest in land where it would be inequitable to do so;[38] and where a vendor enters into a specifically enforceable contract for the sale of land.[39] More recent still, and perhaps controversial up until the 1990s, the constructive trust became a means by which disputes relating to the cohabitation of land can be resolved. Whilst title to co-owned land may become fragmented by the express declarations of the co-owners of land, it

---

[32] *Ibid*, at 714.

[33] See mainstream trust textbooks, such as Hanbury and Martin, *Modern Equity* (15th edn, 1997), Chap 12.

[34] *Bray* v *Ford* [1896] AC 44, and more recently, *Boardman* v *Phipps* [1967] 2 AC 67.

[35] (1726) Sel Cas Ch 61.

[36] Although the constructive trust is generally imposed where a person has acted unconscionably, in the case of profits made by a fiduciary it may not be possible to point to any unconscionable behaviour despite the imposition of the constructive trust. This stems from the strict principle of equity that no fiduciary is allowed to make a profit, irrespective of honesty and good faith: see *Bray* v *Ford* [1896] AC 44 at 51. The policy of equity here is to take a deterrence approach rather than examine each case on its facts, since it would be very difficult from an evidential point of view to question the fiduciary's motives and whether he acted in good faith. In *Guinness plc* v *Saunders* [1990] AC 663 the House of Lords held that a director of a company who had received an unauthorised payment of some £5.2 million was liable to account for it to the company. This liability to account was imposed irrespective of the director's honesty and good faith – the director had allowed his duty and his interest to conflict and this was sufficient to impose the constructive trust. It is precisely these varying contexts and the different policy considerations within them that have made it difficult to provide a comprehensive definition of a constructive trust.

[37] *Barnes* v *Addy* (1874) 9 Ch App 244; *Royal Brunei Airlines Sdn Bhd* v *Tan* [1995] 2 AC 378 and *Re Montagu's Settlement Trusts* [1987] Ch 264.

[38] See *Binions* v *Evans* [1972] Ch 359; see Chapter 10.

[39] *Lsyaght* v *Edwards* (1876) 2 Ch D 499; the equitable maxim, which holds that equity sees that as done which ought to be done, treats the purchaser of land as equitable owner as soon as the contract is entered into. The remedy of specific performance makes it inequitable for the vendor to deny the transfer of the land to the purchaser.

often happens in practice that title to land may be vested in one person whilst the interests of other cohabitees may be silent on the legal title. There may be a number of reasons why the interests of other cohabitees of land may be undisclosed on the legal title.[40] Where it is a husband and wife, it may just so happen that the husband, who is the sole provider, takes both the legal title and mortgage in his own name. Where it is an unmarried couple, the land may have been purchased before the relationship began, but then a partner moves in with the legal title holder and makes some contribution towards the land, either directly through payment of the purchase price or indirectly by looking after the house. Disputes which occur much later on after the purchase of land or the time at which cohabitation took place are often extremely difficult for the courts to resolve, the main questions being, on what principles do such cohabitees acquire an interest in land, and, how is such interest to be quantified? The constructive trust has been used in this context to allow cohabitees to acquire interests in land when they have acted to their detriment in reliance of a common intention that they will acquire an interest in the property.[41]

Although the institutional constructive trust is firmly an accepted property concept in English law, the courts have generally not liked the remedial trust. There are many reasons for this reluctance. In the first place, it represents a very broad proposition of law. The idea that it is imposed to reverse an unjust enrichment has traditionally been regarded as being too vague. Lord Denning attempted to introduce something along the lines of a remedial constructive trust in the 1970s and it is his statement in one case that illustrates the broad nature of such a trust. In *Hussey* v *Palmer*,[42] Lord Denning commented that a constructive trust 'is a trust imposed by law whenever justice and good conscience require it. It is a liberal process, founded on large principles of equity … It is an equitable remedy by which the court can enable an aggrieved party to obtain restitution'.[43] A second obstacle to recognising the remedial constructive trust has been the uncertainty as to the cause of action which gives rise to its imposition. An institutional constructive trust requires a breach of a recognised legal duty – for example, a breach of fiduciary duty. Until recently it has been unclear in the minds of English lawyers as to what is the basis for imposing a remedial constructive trust. The idea that it is a remedy without a cause of action troubles the legal mind and introduces uncertainty into law. It is submitted that these concerns and obstacles

---

[40] For an excellent account of these social factors and the role of constructive trusts in family co-owned land, see A.J.H. Morris, 'Equity's Reaction to Modern Domestic Relationships' in Oakley (ed), *Trends in Contemporary Trust Law* (1996).

[41] *Lloyds Bank* v *Rosset* [1991] 1 AC 107.

[42] [1972] 1 WLR 1286.

[43] *Ibid*, at 1289.

surrounding the remedial trust in English law may no longer be valid in the twenty-first century. English law has now recognised that there exists an independent law of restitution founded on the principle of unjust enrichment.[44] Where a defendant has been unjustly enriched at the expense of the plaintiff, a remedial constructive trust may be one of the remedies to effect restitution. It may well be very soon that the remedial constructive trusts finds a home in English law as a means by which restitution can be made in cases of unjust enrichment. In *Westdeutsche* v *Islington London Borough Council*,[45] Lord Browne-Wilkinson suggested that the remedial constructive trust, if introduced into English law, would provide a suitable restitutionary remedy.[46]

The significance of trusts in modern property law

There is no doubt that the trust plays an important role in property law. Both express and implied trusts can be used in a wide number of circumstances to achieve different legal, social and economic objectives. Given the flexibility of the modern trust to operate in a wide number of circumstances, mention of a few of those circumstances can be made. In modern practice, express trusts can be employed in family as well as commercial settings. In the context of the family, a parent may wish to provide a future gift for his or her child. Money can be transferred to trustees to hold for the child until he or she attains a specified age or meets any other condition specified in the instrument purporting to create the trust. Another example is where a parent may wish to provide for his or her children in the future in light of circumstances not yet arisen. Money can be given to trustees on trust, either at their discretion or subject to other factors, and to be payable to children who may be in more need of money than others. Also within the family context, express trusts can be used as a means by which the incidence of tax can be reduced. Indeed, in the modern law issues of trusts and taxation are intertwined. Liability to income tax, capital gains tax and inheritance tax can be reduced by the careful imposition of trusts to family wealth.[47] It is inevitable that a person with a high income will pay a much higher rate of income tax; however, if some of that income can be distributed to other members of the family who have only a modest income or no income at all, substantial tax

---

[44] See *Lipkin Gorman* v *Karpnale Ltd* [1991] 2 AC 548, where the principle of unjust enrichment was recognised as the foundation of claims in restitution. More recently, see the landmark decision of the House of Lords in *Banque Financière de la Cité* v *Parc (Battersea) Ltd* [1999] 1 AC 221.

[45] [1996] AC 669.

[46] *Ibid*, at 716.

[47] For an excellent account of the relationship between taxation, trusts and property, see G. Moffat, *Trust Law: Text and Materials* (3rd edn, 1999), Chap 3.

savings can be made. Another example of a trust in the family context is where property is given to an infant beneficiary. An infant beneficiary is incapable of managing property on his or her own behalf. A trustee may be appointed to deal with the property until the beneficiary attains majority.[48]

Although express trusts historically featured dominantly in family matters where property was preserved for members of the family, in modern times the express trust plays an important role in financial and commercial matters. Rather than just providing for family members in the form of a future gift or a settlement of property, a person can make an investment of money through the use of a unit trust. A unit trust is a form of investment which allows the investor to spread the risk over a number of investments. Basically, a managing company, acting as a trustee, invests money belonging to investors in a portfolio of securities such as shares. A unit trust is a particularly useful form of investment for a small investor. The reason for this is that on one's own it is impossible to obtain the same degree of risk minimisation than is available by pooling in funds with other investors and buying a unit of investment in the larger pool, which is managed by the unit trust company. Along similar lines as the unit trust there is the pension trust. Private pension schemes have become very popular in recent times as a means for providing financial provision on retirement. The basic structure of such schemes is that they operate under a trust alongside the law of contract. The trust nature of the scheme revolves around the fact that trustees invest money which is contributed by both the employer and employee during the course of an employee's occupation. The contractual nature of the scheme revolves around the fact that the employee's rights are founded upon the contract creating the entitlement to pension. It is the contract that guarantees the payment of retirement pension on final salary rather than the contributions made. Given the importance of pensions to those who contribute to a pension scheme and the fact that these schemes essentially lie in the control of private individuals, there is much scope for abuse of such schemes. Such abuse was apparent in the Maxwell saga in the early 1990s when pension monies, which were essentially in the control of Maxwell companies, were wrongfully appropriated and dissipated. In modern times such pensions are governed by the law of trusts alongside the Pensions Act 1995 which seeks to provide regulation of such schemes to prevent abuse.

Imputed trusts are as important in property matters as express trusts. Imputed trusts play an important role in both commercial and family matters. In the context of the family, imputed trusts have become a very

---

[48] In the case of land, a conveyance to a minor has the automatic effect that the land is held upon trust by the transferor for the minor: see s 2(6) of the Trusts of Land and Appointment of Trustees Act 1996, which applies to conveyances of land after 1996.

important means by which disputes relating to the ownership of land can be resolved.[49] So far mention has been made of implied trusts in the form of implied and constructive trusts; however one form of imputed trust is that imposed by statute. In the context of the co-ownership of land, the Trusts of Land and Appointment of Trustees Act 1996 imposes a trust of land in every case of the co-ownership of land. Such a trust plays an important function in spelling out the rights and duties of the co-owners of land and how disputes relating to co-ownership of land can be resolved. However, families often fail to express their intentions as to the ownership of family property such as land in a formal way, and imputed trusts are the only means by which such intentions can be implied. Furthermore, where the relationship between the parties is one not founded on marriage, unlike in divorce proceedings, recourse to property law is the only way that such disputes can be resolved. Thus, as we have already seen above, where a cohabitee has no legal title to land, yet contributes directly to the purchase price of the land, such cohabitee may acquire an interest under a resulting trust.

In the context of commercial matters, imputed trusts play an important role in effecting restitution of profits and money gains made by the abuse of fiduciary obligations by fiduciaries. An example is the imposition of the constructive trust on a person who makes a profit by the abuse of fiduciary obligations owed to others. For example, in *Attorney-General for Hong Kong* v *Reid*,[50] Reid, who was the Director of Public Prosecutions in Hong Kong, had accepted bribes in the course of his employment. The bribe money was then used to purchase freehold properties in New Zealand. The Privy Council held that the freehold properties, which were purchased by Reid, were held by him on constructive trust for the Crown. The bribes had been made by the abuse of his fiduciary relationship with the Crown.

POWERS OF APPOINTMENT

Powers of appointment, like trusts, are a means by which fragmentation of ownership can be achieved. Powers of appointment have some similar features to a trust; however, the obligation created in a power is fundamentally different from that created in a trust. A trust imposes an imperative duty on trustees to manage the trust property on behalf of beneficiaries and give the beneficial interest in the trust property to the beneficiaries when they are entitled to it. A power of appointment, on the other hand, is a discretionary concept and does not impose imperative obligations on the holder of the

---

[49] See J. Dewar, 'Land, Law and the Family' in Bright and Dewar (eds), *Land Law: Themes and Perspectives* (1998) at pp 327–355.
[50] [1994] 1 All ER 1.

power to distribute. In order to make sense of this distinction between powers of appointment and trusts, it is important to understand the concept of a power of appointment.

The concept of a power features in a number of contexts in law.[51] Powers are often heard of as being conferred upon public authorities or officials. Sometimes powers are said to be common law powers – for example, a power vested in a person to convey a legal estate in land not belonging to him. A good example is a power of attorney, under which one person may be authorised to do certain things in respect of another person's property – for example, convey the legal title to land. Further still, powers may be conferred by statute. A good property law example of a power conferred by statute is that which is given to a mortgagee of land, who has the power to sell land in the event of default by a mortgagor of land.[52] In the field of trusts, managerial and dispositive powers are conferred upon trustees. A managerial power entitles the trustees to do something in respect of managing the trust property – for example, delegating the duty to another person. A dispositive power entitles a trustee to dispose of trust property wholly or in part to the beneficiary. For example, a beneficiary may not wish to put the whole trust to an end, but may want some money for education. Trustees are usually given powers of maintenance and advancement which allow payment of money from the trust fund to the beneficiaries. In all these examples, an authority is conferred upon a person to do something. A power has been described as 'an individual personal capacity of the donee of the power to do something.'[53] The exercise of a power has the effect of changing the legal relationship between persons or of persons in respect of things. Thomas writes that 'a power signifies an ability to do or effect something or to act upon a person or thing.'[54]

In this chapter powers of appointment are the focus of attention. Powers of appointment, like trusts, allow management and enjoyment functions of property to be fragmented. The basic idea behind a power of appointment was explained by Lord Jessel MR in one case, where he commented that a power of appointment 'is a power of disposition given to a person over property not his own by someone who directs the mode in which that power shall be exercised by a particular instrument.'[55] The person creating the power is referred to as the donor of the power; the person who is given the power is called a donee of the power. The persons who may benefit from the power if exercised are called objects of the power. In this respect, a power of appointment has many of the features of a trust relationship. The function of a power is to

---

[51] See G. Thomas, *Thomas on Powers* (1998).
[52] Law of Property Act 1925, s 101.
[53] *Re Armstrong* (1886) 17 QBD 521 *per* Fry LJ at 531.
[54] *Op cit*, at p 1.
[55] *Freme* v *Clement* (1881) Ch D 499 at 504.

allow the donee of the power to exercise the power in respect of property belonging to the donor in favour of objects. The purpose behind a power is that it allows another to determine who should get the donor's property at some future time, perhaps when the donor is no longer alive, and in circumstances which are not known at the present time. The flexibility of the power in this sense lies in the ability to dispose of property in circumstances not yet known; however, unlike a trust, which is imperative, donees of a power are under no duty to distribute the property. If the future circumstances do not lead to a distribution of the donor's property by the donee, the donor's property will, depending on the type of power in question, be given to that person who is entitled in default of appointment; default of appointment meaning that the donee has failed to appoint and the donor has specified in the instrument creating the power that, if no appointment is made, he wants the property to go to another person. When there is no gift over in default of appointment the property goes to the donor's estate by way of a resulting trust. The idea and function behind a power of appointment can be seen in the case of *Re Weekes' Settlement.*[56] Mrs Slade granted a life interest in her estate to her husband, Mr Slade, so that Mr Slade was entitled to use the estate during his lifetime. Mrs Slade did not specify who was to enjoy the reversionary interest in her estate after her husband's death; however, she conferred a power of appointment on Mr Slade in favour of her surviving children. The advantage of the power was that it did not give any of the children an absolute entitlement to their mother's estate on their father's death; however, the father could appoint any one of the children.

Like trusts, powers of appointment can be classified in various ways. In relation to the class of objects of the power, powers have been classified as general powers, special powers and hybrid powers. A general power is usually defined as a power which entitles the donee to appoint the property to anyone in the world including itself. It is questionable whether a general power is really a case of fragmented ownership, given the fact that the donee can, if he or she decides, appoint him or herself as the object of the power; such a power is tantamount to absolute ownership in the donee. A special power, on the other hand, is a power which can only be exercised in favour of a defined class of objects – for example, children, as in the case of *Re Weekes' Settlement*. A hybrid power of appointment arises where the donor stipulates that the donee can make an appointment to anyone in the world except a specified class of persons. Usually such a power will arise where the donor does not want a specific member or members of the family to get any benefit but anyone else can.[57]

---

[56] [1987] 1 Ch 289.
[57] *Re Byron's Settlement* [1891] 3 Ch 474.

Powers can further be classified into bare and fiduciary powers depending on the nature of the donee. Where the donee is given a power in his capacity as a fiduciary, the power is referred to as a fiduciary power. Where the donee does not stand in a fiduciary relationship to the objects of the trust, the trust is a called a bare trust. The distinction between a bare and fiduciary power lies in the duties which are imposed on the donee of the power. In the case of a bare power, the donee is under no duty to exercise the power and need not even consider exercising the power. It he does decide to exercise the power, he is under a duty not to exercise it excessively or fraudulently. For example, a donee of a bare power cannot exercise the power for purposes which are inconsistent with the instrument creating the power.[58] A fiduciary power is one which is given to a donee in a fiduciary capacity. The most obvious example of a fiduciary power is one given to a trustee in the case of a trust. A modern example of a fiduciary power is one given to trustees of a pension fund to decide who is entitled to surplus funds once the entitlement of the pension beneficiaries has been met.[59] The power in such pension schemes often allows the surplus to be paid to the pensioners in the form of increased entitlements. Failure to exercise the power results in the surplus funds going into the hands of the company. Given the fiduciary nature of the power, donees of the power are under a duty to consider whether they should exercise the power, the range of potential objects of the power, and the appropriateness of individual appointments.[60] Although a fiduciary power like any other power is discretionary, so the court cannot compel the donee to exercise the power, in some circumstances the court may intervene and exercise the power if there is a conflict between the interests of the donee and the interests of the potential objects of the power.[61]

VERTICAL AND HORIZONTAL FRAGMENTATION IN THE MODERN LAW

Ownership may be fragmented vertically or horizontally. Vertical fragmentation involves the splitting up of ownership from top to bottom. Full-blooded ownership starts at the top, with smaller segments of that ownership being

---

[58] *Vatcher v Paull* [1915] AC 372.
[59] *Mettoy Pension Trustees Ltd v Evans* [1990] 1 WLR 1587.
[60] *Re Hay's Settlement Trusts* [1982] 1 WLR 202.
[61] In *Mettoy Pension Trustees Ltd v Evans* [1990] 1 WLR 1587, a company had a power of appointment over surplus funds in a pension scheme in favour of the pensioners. If the company failed to exercise the power it would be entitled to the money. The company had gone into liquidation and the power was now vested in the liquidators. Warner J held that the liquidators were unable to exercise the power because of the conflict of interests that arose from the fact that they owed duties both to creditors and the pensioners under the power. Warner J explained that the court would exercise the power itself in this circumstance.

carved out and vested in persons below. Vertical fragmentation can be understood better by analogy with a ladder, total ownership being vested in a person at the top of the ladder and smaller aspects of that ownership in persons on various rungs of the ladder. As one moves down the ladder, the smaller the ownership interest becoming vested in a person. Vertical fragmentation was a key feature in landowning arrangements in feudal times. The ultimate ownership of land in feudal times was vested in the Crown; however, as seen in Chapter 4, the Crown could grant land to tenants in return for services of various kinds. The land granted to a tenant was usually for a period of time such as the life of the tenant or simply in fee simple. A tenant could also grant smaller interests out of his interest and thus become a lord to a different tenant. For example, the Crown may grant to A in fee simple; A could grant the same land to B for life. In this respect, ownership became fragmented on a vertical plane; the ultimate right of ownership being vested in the Crown and then relative ownership rights in mesne lords and tenants. It is not intended here to discuss tenure in depth, simply because tenure does not feature in the modern law as it did in feudal law. The only modern form of tenure which involves lord and tenant is that of a lease. Although a lease is not the product of feudal law, it involves vertical fragmentation in the form of the ultimate right of ownership vested in the freehold owner and the lesser right in the tenant. A lease is capable of being further fragmented through the creation of a sub-lease so that a ladder effect can be created. It is also worth mentioning that, since theoretically all land belongs to the Crown, every freehold owner of land is really a tenant of the Crown.

Another aspect of vertical fragmentation of ownership is the consecutive or successive ownership of a thing. A person may wish to provide for a series of persons in succession. For example, a person who has land and other valuable assets may want such assets to remain within the family for years to come and to be enjoyed by successive generations. One way of achieving this goal is by creating a series of interests in persons to be enjoyed successively, but without giving any individual person an absolute entitlement to the assets in question. For example, A may start off with total ownership in his assets, which could include land and other things such as a fund; however, in his will or during his lifetime, A can make provision to the effect that his property is to be enjoyed by his son B for life and thereafter to the oldest son of B absolutely. In this example ownership has been fragmented in a similar way to that in the case of tenure. B has a time in the land, which is his life, and, thereafter, the remaining time is vested in B's oldest son. A further aspect of fragmentation here is that income and capital are fragmented, as are the powers of management and enjoyment. B does not have any rights to the capital, and even when B sells land, the rights in the proceeds of sale belong to B's oldest child, whilst B has the right to receive income during his lifetime. Management and enjoyment are fragmented to the extent that, whilst B's oldest son has an interest in the property by way of remainder, he has no right to manage the property during B's lifetime. B may manage the property on behalf of himself and his oldest son as trustee or by independent trustees.

Where property is given in succession it is often said that a person has created a settlement. For example, where property is given to B for life and thereafter to C absolutely, both B and C are beneficiaries under the settlement. B is called a life tenant and his primary claim to the settled property is the income it produces, and in the case of land enjoyment and possession of the land. C is not entitled to any present interest in the settled property, but must await B's death before claiming rights to the settled property. C is often referred to as a remainderman. Both B and C have vested interests in the settled property: B's interest is said to be vested in possession and C's interest is said to be vested in interest. The idea that an interest under a settlement is vested means that there are no contingencies to be met before the particular interest vests. B has an immediate right of possession, and C must await B's death before claiming the property; however, C has an immediate right to future enjoyment of the property. This basic structure of a settlement can be modified in many ways. First, the number of beneficiaries can be more than two – for example, property can be given to B for life, thereafter to C for life and then to D absolutely. Furthermore, certain conditions may be imposed in the settlement which direct the types of person who may be eligible for the settled property. For example, property may be settled for B for life; however, if B is to marry X then the property is to go to C absolutely. In this case B has a determinable interest in the property subject to the settlement; marriage to X has the effect of determining B's interest and giving effect to C's vested interest which now becomes in possession. Further still, property may be given by A to B for life, thereafter for the first of A's grandchildren who qualify as a solicitor. In this example, whilst B has a vested interest in possession, the property after B's death will not vest automatically in a person; rather it depends on the condition that A must have a grandchild who qualifies as a solicitor. The interest of the remainder is contingent on the first qualifying as a solicitor.[62] The use of carefully drafted conditions allows the person creating the settlement to determine who should benefit from the family wealth.[63]

Settlements were once a very important tool, employed in the eighteenth and nineteenth centuries by wealthy landowners to preserve and keep family

---

[62] Contingent interests are subject to the perpetuity rules which strike out certain interests that have an excessive delay in vesting. For example, it is impossible to know if any of A's grandchildren wish to qualify as solicitors. Land and other property cannot simply be kept indefinitely awaiting the contingency to be met: see Chapter 8.

[63] On conditions generally, see Megarry and Wade, *The Law of Real Property* (6th edn, 2000) at pp 291–296.

wealth within the dynasty.[64] As part of his eldest son's marriage, the head of the family would create a settlement designed to keep family property strictly within the family. Land could be devised to the head of the family and his son in terms of limited life interests and remainder given to the first grand-child. Such settlements were called strict settlements and gave the life tenant a nominal legal title over the settled property whilst trustees of the settlement were appointed to exercise general supervision. Strict settlements do not play a significant role in the modern law of property; they belong to an era which no longer exists. The idea of *paterfamilias* and retention of property in the family dynasty no longer dictates property relations. The Trusts of Land and Appointment of Trustees Act 1996 prohibits the creation of new strict settle-ments and where such a settlement is envisaged it takes effect behind a trust of land.[65] It serves no purpose here to examine strict settlements in any fur-ther depth. One leading real property commentator writes:

> 'the strict settlement in its present form is a moribund institution ... The device of the settlement evolved as a form of landholding designed primarily to satisfy the property-related aspirations of a distinctive social elite ... The modern demise of the strict settlement ... owes much to the social changes which have occurred during the last two centuries. Our own society has ceased to be regu-lated to the same degree by status and gender.'[66]

In more recent times, the incidence of horizontal fragmentation has over-taken that of vertical fragmentation. Horizontal fragmentation of ownership involves the splitting up of ownership on a horizontal plane. Rather than a ladder effect where only one person has the right of enjoyment at any given time, horizontal fragmentation involves the enjoyment of ownership being given to two or more persons at the same time. Concurrent ownership of a thing is an example of horizontal fragmentation. In modern society, land is not tied up in the same manner as it was in the eighteenth and nineteenth centuries. Instead, independency and equality between the sexes has meant that society is no longer regulated by status and gender.[67] In modern society, people do not rely for their wellbeing on dynastic wealth; rather, factors such as equality between the sexes, equality in employment and equality in mat-ters relating to property have influenced property relationships in the modern law. Rather than consecutive ownership, concurrent ownership plays a more dominant role. With the aid of mortgage finance, it is more typical of fami-lies to enter into real property relationships jointly at the same time. In the

---

[64] See B. English and J. Saville, *Strict Settlements* (1983).

[65] Trusts of Land and Appointment of Trustees Act 1996, s 2; settlements created before this leg-islation continue to be governed by the Settled Land Act 1925.

[66] K. Gray, *Elements of Land Law* (2nd edn, 1993) at pp 608–610, (3rd edn published 2001).

[67] See, generally, M.A. Glendon, *The New Family and New Property* (1981).

previous chapter, it was observed how the law distinguished between two forms of co-ownership: namely, a tenancy in common and a joint tenancy. Such co-ownership takes place behind a trust of land governed by the Trusts of Land and Appointment of Trustees Act 1996.

Both real and personal property can be subjected to co-ownership. The primary difference between the co-ownership of real and personal property lies in the fact that in the case of real property, co-ownership must take place behind a trust. For example, it is quite feasible for two or more persons to be joint owners of a car or a horse without any recourse to a trust. However, in the case of land, every co-ownership must exist behind a trust of land. Prior to the enactment of the Trusts of Land and Appointment of Trustees Act 1996, a trust for sale arose in every case of co-ownership. The imposition of the trust for sale had the effect that land was held by trustees with a paramount duty to sell the land. The trust for sale was not designed to regulate the modern relationship of co-owners who bought land as a place for the family to live in. Rather, the function of the trust for sale was to sell land and distribute the proceeds amongst the beneficiaries of the trust. This device was particularly useful in the context of a will, where a person may wish land to be sold and the proceeds of sale distributed. Since the trustees were under a duty to sell, the equitable maxim that 'equity regards that as done which ought to be done' had the effect that the interests of co-owners under a trust for sale lay in the proceeds of sale rather than the land itself. This was the basis of the doctrine of conversion.

The application of the trust for sale to modern day co-ownership of land had resulted in some rather bizarre results. The idea that one co-owner, say the wife, had no interest in the land but only in the capital was difficult to justify in an age of residential security.[68] The trust of land reflects the modern social reality of co-ownership of land, in particular that land is purchased as a means of residence and emphasis is placed on its use or security value rather than its exchange value. The key features of the trust of land involve the removal of the overriding duty to sell co-owned land, the abolition of the doctrine of conversion, and jurisdiction given to the courts to resolve co-ownership disputes.

---

[68] See *Transfer of Land: Trusts of Land* (Law Com No 181, 1989), paras 8–118.

8

ACQUISITION OF PROPRIETARY RIGHTS: ORIGINAL ACQUISITION

ACQUISITION IN PROPERTY LAW

In Chapter 4 it was observed how the English legal system classifies proprietary rights. In an attempt to classify property rights it was observed that the classification of such rights takes place primarily through three main methods: first, by examining the nature of the object in which such rights are sustained; second, by examining the sphere of enforceability of the proprietary right in question; and finally, by examining the function performed by the proprietary right in question. From that chapter it was clear that property law recognises a rather complex and wide range of proprietary rights. No less complex are the rules relating to the manner in which such proprietary rights become vested in individuals. This chapter and Chapter 9 examine those concepts that deal with the question of acquisition of proprietary rights. The emphasis is not so much on the substantive rules relating to how such rights are acquired; such discussion can be found in mainstream texts on real and personal property law. Rather, the discussion centres on concepts used by property lawyers in dealing with issues of acquisition of rights. The concepts which come to mind are those such as original acquisition, derivative acquisition, formalities, deeds, sale, assignment and delivery.

There are two broad types of acquisition in property law: namely, original acquisition and derivative acquisition. The most common way of acquiring a proprietary right is through a derivative action, that is, a transfer from one person to another. An example of this is the vesting of a legal estate in land in another person through a conveyance. However, in contemporary property law, original acquisition rules remain an important area of property law. Original acquisition, as we shall soon see, occurs in one of two ways: first, where a person takes first possession of unowned resources thereby acquiring first ownership therein: second, where a person takes control of lost or abandoned resources in circumstances that extinguish the title of the former owner. This chapter looks at original acquisition of property rights, whilst Chapter 9 looks at derivative acquisition of property rights.

ORIGINAL ACQUISITION

The most basic way of acquiring a proprietary right such as that of ownership is by taking first possession of some object that has no owner. It will be recalled from Chapter 3 that first possession formed the basis for justification for the recognition of private property rights. The idea that first possession can grant ownership in unowned resources in a person is often reflected in the property law maxim that 'possession is the root of title'. Most legal systems recognise that it is only through first occupation that a system of private property begins and the chain of ownership is created. In the case of many objects of property, although most notably land, the rule of first possession moves society away from common property and towards enforceable private property rights. In this respect, given the fact that most resources over time will and do become parcelled into private ownership, how important is original acquisition as a means of acquiring property rights in external objects in contemporary property law? The underlying assumption appears to be that such a mode of acquisition requires the existence of unowned resources. Despite its primitive origins, original acquisition remains a significant means by which the right of ownership can be acquired. What has in fact changed are the conditions under which original acquisition rules operate. In primitive society such modes of acquisition operated to resolve disputes resulting from the scarcity value arising from the claims of individuals to common property. Such rules had as their function the provision of a system of allocation of resources which in turn could attain peace and order.[1]

In contemporary property law, original acquisition rules operate under quite different circumstances and also seek to meet different objectives. Justifications for original acquisition rules today are not necessarily to preserve peace and order; instead such rules seek to promote more specific legal, social and economic objectives. So, what are the circumstances under which original acquisition rules operate? It has already been seen in Chapter 3 that claims to land through native title continue to trouble the courts.[2] Such claims are based on original acquisition, which is sought to be recognised as binding on the radical title acquired by the Crown through colonisation.

---

[1] See Chapter 2.
[2] For example, *Mabo v Queensland (No 2)* (1992) 66 ALJR 408.

More frequent, however, are claims to objects that have been lost or abandoned, and the law is equally problematic here. In Chapter 6 it was observed that, in the common law tradition, ownership is regarded as a relative concept. The consequence of this is that the system of property rules does not guarantee ownership indefinitely and without check. By this it is meant that another person exercising a better possession of the object or thing in question can extinguish the right of ownership vested in an individual. This is often justified by simply saying that, in English law, the concept of title is relative. Furthermore, a related matter is that the effectiveness of obtaining a remedy in property law often turns to the question of who has a better possession rather than to the abstract concept of ownership. A person who finds and takes control of a lost or abandoned object can enforce his right of ownership to it against everyone except the true owner. Moreover, he can also defeat the rights of the true owner and obtain a full-blooded ownership right to the object in question.[3] Two of the most obvious examples of original acquisition are claims to lost and abandoned objects and claims to land through the principles of adverse possession.

LOST PROPERTY AND ADVERSE POSSESSION: LEGAL, SOCIAL AND ECONOMIC JUSTIFICATIONS

The principal legal justification for allowing a finder of a lost or abandoned object to acquire a proprietary interest therein turns primarily to the fact of possession. Possession in most common law traditions forms the basis upon which remedies are given. If I find a gold watch in the street and someone other than the true owner appropriates the watch from me, I can go to court and recover the full value of the watch from that wrongdoer.[4] It makes no difference that the person who has lost the watch has a better title than I do. The wrongdoer cannot point to defects in my title, since my possession and consequently my possessory title is better than his. However, it is not simply the fact of possession on its own that justifies the acquisition of ownership by finding. If the true owner does not exert his right to ownership of the lost object within six years of it being lost or abandoned,[5] the finder of the watch has a full right of ownership which is now good against everyone including the original owner. The original owner's title is simply extinguished. In this respect, there are two legal justifications for allowing the right of the true owner to be extinguished. Murphy and Roberts in their text explain that

---

[3] In Chapter 6 it was observed that such original acquisition rules work in conjunction with the Limitation Act 1980, which prescribes the statutory limitation periods which need to elapse before a right of ownership is statute barred and consequently extinguished.

[4] In this specific example the finder of the watch has a right to sue in tort for trespass to chattels.

[5] Limitation Act 1980, s 2.

there is, first, the problem of the multiplicity of actions, and, second, the possibility that a wrongdoer risks paying the full value of the thing to successive claimants.[6] Take the example of the watch which is found by A. If another person, B, appropriates the watch and sells it, A, as a result of A's former possession, can bring an action against B and recover the full value of the watch. There is, however, nothing to stop the original owner (let us say C) from also suing B, for the full value of the watch.[7] In this respect, the rule that allows the right of the true owner to be extinguished through limitation of action is based on sound legal premises. In order to reduce the scope for multiplicity of actions against B, it is better to have one person who is allowed to sue B rather than two. Arbitrarily extinguishing the rights of the true owner is one way of avoiding multiplicity of actions.

The economic justifications for allowing rules for original acquisition through finding lost and abandoned objects are equally important. One potential problem with lost and abandoned property is the devotion of too many resources in finding the true owner. The value of such resources expended may well exceed the value of the lost object in question.[8] The result is that a rule which allows ownership to remain indefinitely vested in the owner irrespective of losing the object or abandoning it, is uneconomical. However, the danger with a rule of 'finders keepers' is that too many resources may be expended in searching for lost and abandoned objects. Moreover, Cooter and Ulen point out that the problem with a rule of 'finders keepers' is that there may be an incentive to steal other people's property and then claim, if confronted, that it was found.[9] The effect of the limitation statutes is to enable property to be allocated to some valued use. Such statutes provide for 'an orderly procedure in which the finder of a valuable item attempts to locate the original owner before claiming the item. The point is to ensure that only cost-effective efforts are made to locate owners in a process that removes uncertainty over title.'[10]

In so far as real property is concerned, despite the more elaborate means of transfer of title to land, original acquisition through the principles of adverse possession has legal, social and economic justifications. The basic idea behind adverse possession is the vesting of a full-blooded legal right of ownership in a person who has taken wrongful possession of land belonging to another. The Limitation Act[11] extinguishes the former title of the true

---

[6] Murphy and Roberts, *Understanding Property Law* (1994), p 53.

[7] His action will be based on the tort of conversion since he will not have the requisite actual possession that is needed for a successful claim for damages for the tort of trespass to chattels.

[8] See A.W. Dnes, *The Economics of Law* (1996) at p 28.

[9] Cooter and Ulen, *Law and Economics* (1988), p 157.

[10] A.W. Dnes, *op cit*, at p 28.

[11] s 15(1).

owner after 12 years of adverse possession by another. The primary legal justifications for allowing rules of adverse possession are essentially the same as
those for lost property considered above. However, the common law tradition in respect of ownership in land often turns more to the question of fact
than right; in particular, the fact of sustained possession.[12] One leading real
property commentator writes: 'the pre-eminent position accorded to *de facto*
possession in English law ensures that there is no such thing as absolute title
to land. All title is ultimately relative: the title of the present possessor will
customarily be upheld unless and until a better claim is advanced on behalf
of somebody else.'[13]

As well as legal justifications for original acquisition through adverse possession of land, there are important social and economic justifications for the
rules. Certainty of title is one of the important social objectives behind rules
of adverse possession.[14] If claims to land based on long possession, however,
are nevertheless allowed to be defeated by others showing that they were
owner some time in the past, it is inevitable that title to land becomes uncer-
tain. Such titles are not conducive to a liberal market engaged in exchange
and bargain. The basic premise must be that long unchallenged possession of
land should not be disturbed. Of course, some sort of wrongful possession of
land should be disallowed; however, the Limitation Act operates in an arbitrary way in providing a cut-off point when the true owner cannot challenge
the title of another possessor of the land to which the original title pertained.
The resulting uncertainty over title has impact not only on the person who
has been in possession of land, but also third parties such as purchasers and
mortgagees who may have interests in the land. In other words, title in real
property law must be seen as operating in a multitude of transactions concerning the same piece of land. Uncertainty over title is undesirable because
the effects are not only far reaching but they also affect more than one transaction. It is only on reliance of title that some of these transactions are
entered into; therefore subsequent uncertainty is a bad thing.

With regard to the economic justifications for adverse possession, law and
economic commentators identify two main justifications.[15] The most obvious
economic justification is the transfer of a resource to a much more productive user. The rules prevent land being left idle for long periods of time by

---

[12] This is not something which is new; it originates from the concept of seisin-possession. This
concept is at the roots of real property law and emphasises that proprietary rights in land are
based on physical possession rather than on abstract title. The concept of seisin-possession was
examined in Chapter 6. For a more detailed account of the concept of seisin, see A.W.B.
Simpson, *An Introduction to the History of English Land Law* (1961).
[13] K. Gray, *Elements of Land Law* (1987) at p 64.
[14] See M. Dockray, 'Why Do We Need Adverse Possession?' [1985] Conveyancer 272.
[15] See Cooter and Ulen, *op cit*, pp 154–155.

specifying rules under which a productive user, even though wrongful in taking the land, can take title from the unproductive original owner. The second justification is that administration costs involved in establishing rightful ownership are reduced. Moreover, the costs of land transactions are generally lowered since the risk of ownership being challenged in such transactions in the future is minimal. These social and economic justifications for adverse possession fit perfectly well into the justificatory theories of private property discussed in Chapter 3. In the background of Bentham's utilitarian justification for laws, adverse possession rules ensure that resources are used so as to benefit society on a much greater basis. Even leading conveyancers explain that 'people who use land and invest their labour in it are benefiting society more than those real owners who neglect it to the extent of ignoring it for twelve years or more. And the law, it is suggested, should value the attachment that comes from working on the land.'[16]

LOST PROPERTY: SOME BASIC PRINCIPLES

Original acquisition rules relating to finding of lost and abandoned objects is not only a fast growing area of the law but also one that is very technical. Explaining the complexity of the law as far back in time as 1888, Pollock and Wright explained that very small differences in fact could have significant effects in so far as the outcome of a case.[17] It is doubtful whether much has changed at the beginning of the twenty-first century; indeed, many of the recent authorities have contributed to forming a law on finding which, according to one commentator, is 'full of twists and knots, set with the occasional gem.'[18] The growth of the law is due to the increasing metal detecting activity that is taking place on open common land.[19] The caselaw itself goes as far back as 1722, and more recently statutory intervention has taken place in the form of the Treasure Act 1996 which seeks to broaden the definition of treasure trove and clarify when title to found objects will vest in the Crown.

The basic principle is that a finder who takes possession of a lost or abandoned object acquires a proprietary right that is good against the whole world except the true owner.[20] In *Armory v Delamirie*[21] the plaintiff, a chimney-sweeper's boy, found a jewel and took it to the defendant goldsmith.

---

[16] Ruoff and Roper, *On the Law and Practice of Registered Conveyancing* (1979) at p 178.

[17] Pollock and Wright, *Possession in the Common Law* (1888), p 40.

[18] C. Macmillan, 'Finders Keepers, Losers Weepers – But Who are the Losers?' (1995) 58 MLR 101, at p 101.

[19] In 1994 there were over 10,000 members of the National Council for Metal Detecting in the UK: see 'Peer Aims to Save Heritage from Metal Detectors', *The Times*, 2 Nov 1994.

[20] This rule is subject to treasure trove, which is discussed later.

[21] *Armory v Delamirie* (1722) 1 Strange 505.

In order to find out what the jewel was, the plaintiff handed over the jewel to the defendant's apprentice. The apprentice removed the stones and handed back the empty socket to the plaintiff. The plaintiff, when offered three half-pence by the defendant, insisted on return of the jewel in the state in which it was handed to the defendant. On the refusal by the defendant to return the jewel, the plaintiff sued in trespass. Chief Justice Pratt held that the finder of a jewel, although he does not acquire an absolute right of ownership, has property that will enable him to keep it against all but the rightful owner. Moreover, in the absence of the defendant returning the jewel to the plaintiff, the jury should award damages to the value of the jewel.

The true owner of a lost object can claim the object from the finder within the limitation period of six years.[22] Thus, in *Moffatt v Kazana*[23] an owner of a bungalow had hidden a box containing money in the loft, the value of the money being some £2000. The bungalow was sold to the defendant some ten years later, the owner of the bungalow unaware that he had put the box in the loft. When the new owners of the bungalow commenced building work they found the box containing the money and sought to claim it as theirs on the basis that it was sold along with the bungalow. Wrangham J held that the personal representatives of the former owner of the bungalow could claim the box and its contents from the defendants. The box was not sold together with the land.

The more problematic cases on finding revolve around the finding of lost and abandoned objects on land that does not belong to the finder, the real question being whether ownership should be awarded to the finder or the occupier of the land. It is here that the law is most problematic and it is doubtful whether a satisfactory test of deciding to whom ownership should be ascribed exists in the authorities. Indeed, many of the early authorities lend themselves to a number of different views on the matter. At one time it was thought that a satisfactory starting point was to determine whether the thing found was found on the private or public part of the land belonging to the occupier.[24] If an object was found on a private area of the land then the general prevailing view was that the object belonged to the occupier of the land and not the finder. It did not matter that the owner of the land was unaware of the existence of the thing found. What did matter was an inten-

---

[22] Limitation Act 1980, s 2. Time begins to run when the lost object is demanded from the true owner or when there is an inconsistent dealing with the object so as to constitute a conversion – for example, a sale of the goods is a conversion causing time to run.

[23] [1969] 2 QB 152.

[24] The authorities, whilst supporting this view, did not make this entirely clear, instead using the test of whether the thing found was 'attached to or buried' in the land. This rule, as we shall soon see, is one that is not supported by reason.

tion to control the whole of the land.[25] If the object was found on those parts of the land which were open to the public in general then the matter was to be resolved by asking, as between the finder and the occupier, who had exercised a better control of the lost or abandoned object?[26]

The authorities, whilst supporting this proposition, do not do so convincingly and as a result a number of possible alternative theories have been advanced by both judges and academics.[27] In *Bridges v Hawksworth*[28] bank notes had been accidentally dropped in the public part of a shop and the shopkeeper was unaware of the existence of these notes. A customer picked up the notes and handed them to the shopkeeper with the instructions that if no one would reclaim them he would come back and take them for himself. Patterson J held that the finder was entitled to the bank notes, which were never in the custody of the shopkeeper. The actual basis upon which the decision in *Bridges v Hawksworth*[29] is reached is somewhat obscure. Goodhart writes that this decision does not support the view that the primary test is one between private and public areas of the land belonging to the occupier.[30] Nevertheless, the subsequent authorities support and suggest that the test is primarily one between private and public land.

In *South Staffs Water Company v Sharman*,[31] two gold rings had been found by contractors engaged to clean out a pool on land occupied by the plaintiffs. The rings were found lying embedded in the mud at the bottom of the pool. It was held that the plaintiffs had a better title to the rings than the finders. In coming to this decision, Lord Russell of Killowen paid specific reference to two authorities, one judicial and the other academic. In so far as concerning the judicial authority, Lord Russell relied extensively on *Bridges v Hawksworth*[32] and distinguished the present case in that the gold rings had been found on land which was private and belonged to the plaintiffs. In *Bridges v Hawksworth*,[33] Lord Russell explained, the notes were found in the 'public' part of the shop, whereas in the present case the objects were found on private land which belonged to the plaintiffs. The second authority used by Lord Russell was the academic argument put forward by Pollock and

---

[25] This rule, however, is subject to two limitations. First, if the occupier is not the owner of the land then he takes subject to the superior rights of the owner: see *Elwes v Brigg Gas Co* (1886) 33 Ch D 562. Second, the right to findings is subject to the rights of the Crown to treasure-trove; this is explored later.

[26] See, for example, *Parker v British Airways Board* [1982] QB 1004.

[27] See A.L. Goodhart, 'Three Cases on Possession' (1927) CLR p 195.

[28] (1851) 21 LJQB 75, [1843–60] All ER Rep 122.

[29] *Ibid.*

[30] *Op cit*, at 198.

[31] [1896] 2 QB 44; see also *Elwes v Brigg Gas Company* (1886) 33 Ch D 562; *City of London Corporation v Appleyard* [1963] 1 WLR 982.

[32] *Supra.*

[33] *Supra.*

Wright in their seminal work, *Essays on Possession in the Common Law*.[34] They write that 'possession of land carries with it in general, by our law, possession of everything which is attached to or under that land, and, in the absence of a better title elsewhere, the right to possess it also. And it makes no difference that the possessor is not aware of the thing's existence.'[35] This aspect of Lord Russell's judgment in *South Staffs Water Company* v *Sharman* is, however, often taken by some to suggest that the real test of deciding whether a lost thing belongs to the finder or the occupier of land is simply to ask whether the thing is attached to or in the land. If the thing is attached to the land it belongs to the occupier of the land. It is submitted that, with respect to the work of Pollock and Wright, this proposition is incorrect and that the appropriate test should be simply between private and public areas of land as advocated above.

The rationale behind the rule that things attached to or in the land belong to the occupier appears to be based on an assumption that such things form an integral part of the land. As long as there is an intention to control the whole of the land, it matters not that the occupier is unaware of the existence of the thing that is now in dispute. In *Parker* v *British Airways Board*,[36] Donaldson LJ commented that the rationale for the rule was that the thing found attached or in the land

> '... is to be treated as an integral part of the realty as against all but the true owner and so incapable of being lost or that the finder has to do something to the realty in order to get at or detach the chattels and, if he is not thereby to become a trespasser, will have to justify his actions by reference to some form of licence from the occupier. In all likely circumstances that licence will give the occupier a superior right to that of the finder.'[37]

However, as Bell[38] explains, such a proposition is not based on any real sound justification:

> '... even if the public has access to premises, they will not normally be given liberty to remove fixtures or make excavations. The manifest control reserved over such activities must surely satisfy the test for possession applied to things lying on the land. The rule is thus not an arbitrary one based on deemed incorporation into the land...'[39]

Surely if I invite you to my house and you find a ten pound note under the dining table, despite not being attached or in the land, such ten pound note will belong to me on the principle that I intend to control the whole of my

---

[34] (1888).
[35] *Ibid*, at p 41.
[36] [1982] 1 All ER 834.
[37] *Ibid*, at 837.
[38] A.P. Bell, *Modern Law of Personal Property in England and Ireland* (1989), p 44.
[39] *Ibid*.

house. In this respect, it is submitted that the better test is to determine whether the thing is found on a private area of the occupier's land or on an area which is open to the public at large. We now turn to the question of things found on the occupier's land which is open to the public or a certain section of the public.

Where a thing is found on an area of land belonging to the occupier that is open to the public or a class of public, the rule has been that occupation of such land does not always entail possession of things found on such land. In such circumstances the occupier is required to take active steps to ensure that he manifests a sufficient intention to control the lost object in question. Furthermore, where the object found is attached to or in the land, then the occupier of the land has a right superior to that of the finder, regardless of the occupier's lack of knowledge of its existence. In *Parker v British Airways Board*,[40] a passenger at Heathrow Airport found a gold bracelet in the executive lounge. The bracelet was handed to an official of British Airways, who were the occupiers of the lounge. The finder handed the bracelet to the officials with the express instructions that if the owner did not claim it, it should be given back to him. British Airways Board sold the bracelet and kept the proceeds of sale. The Court of Appeal held that the finder was entitled to the bracelet and now the proceeds of sale, since British Airways Board had done nothing to control lost property on their premises. In such cases, where the area is a public area the occupier must manifest an intention to control not only the premises, but also things which may have been lost or abandoned. For example, it would have sufficed if there were a notice to the effect that lost property belonged to British Airways. This rule is consistent with the idea of actual possession examined in Chapter 6.

The rules relating to finding have been the subject-matter of wholesale debate in the Court of Appeal in *Waverley Borough Council v Fletcher*.[41] The case attempts to clarify the uncertainty in the rules discussed above. It also addresses the complex problem of things found on land belonging to local authorities, but which they do not occupy. Whilst the decision on the facts of the case may be satisfactory, it is doubtful whether the rules relating to finding are any more clear than before. On the facts of the case, Mr Fletcher visited a public park in Surrey in pursuit of his hobby, which was metal detecting. The freehold owners of the park were Waverley Borough Council. The Council had prohibited the use of metal detectors on the park; however, vandals had removed the notice to this effect. Mr Fletcher found a medieval brooch buried some nine inches under the surface of the park. The finding of the brooch was reported to the Council, which – after a

---

[40] [1982] 1 All ER 834.
[41] [1996] QB 334.

coroner's report had declared that the brooch was not treasure trove – attempted to recover the brooch from Mr Fletcher. Mr Fletcher claimed to be entitled to the brooch on the principles examined above. In the first place, he was entitled to keep the brooch against everyone except the true owner of the brooch. Second, since the brooch was found on a public area of land, the Council had not, as required by *Parker v British Airways Board*,[42] manifested a sufficient intention to control lost and abandoned objects on the land. The Council counter argued that the rule had always been that things found attached to or in land belonged to the occupier irrespective of the lack of knowledge on behalf of the occupier. This, however, raised the question as to whether the Council could be deemed to be the occupier of the park.

At first instance[43] Mr Fletcher succeeded in establishing a better claim to the brooch than the Council. The trial judge rejected the theory that everything attached to or in the land belonged to the occupier irrespective of the lack of knowledge on his part. In his view, the rule that 'everything attached to or in the land' was not a universal principle but rather was restricted to those things that occurred naturally or those things which had become attached to land and covered over time. The distinction between things found under ground and those above in the case of lost and abandoned objects was not a sensible one.[44] This is, it is submitted, the correct approach. The brooch had never become an integral part of the land such as fixtures; neither had the Council made any attempt to control lost or abandoned objects in the park. The Court of Appeal reversed the decision at first instance and concluded that the Council, as owners and occupiers of the park, had a better right to the brooch since it was found attached to or in their land. The rule emanating from *Waverley Borough Council v Fletcher* is that an owner or occupier of land has a superior right to things attached to or in the land than a finder of such things. The test does not depend on private or public areas of land. Moreover, the Council being a trustee for the general public had a superior right to that of a finder who removed the brooch without licence.

The decision of the Court of Appeal in *Waverley Borough Council v Fletcher* may be justified on its facts; however, it is not clear why the landowner should be more favoured than a finder as concerns things which are attached to or in the land. There were obviously wider concerns in the case about the use of metal detecting activity and the interference with the soil in the park. However, we have already observed that such lost and abandoned things cannot be treated as an integral part of realty. Moreover, the

---

[42] [1982] 1 All ER 834.

[43] High Court of Justice, Queen's Bench Division, 17 Feb 1994, unreported. For a critical account of this decision, see C. MacMillan, 'Finders Keepers, Losers Weepers – But Who are the Losers?' (1995) 58 MLR 101.

[44] See MacMillan, *ibid*, at p 103.

rule is not an arbitrary one based on incorporation into land since, where things are lying on private lands, it is clear that a private owner has a right superior to that of a finder.

The rules relating to finding are subject to the ancient royal prerogative of treasure trove. Where finds are deemed to be treasure they belong to the Crown, who will pay compensation in return for the finding. The purpose of this rule is that such finds should be available to museums. Until the Treasure Act 1996, the law relating to treasure trove was not only outdated but also illogical.[45] The types of objects falling into the category of treasure trove were deemed to be too narrow and there was the problem that treasure trove was restricted to hidden objects as opposed to those lost or abandoned. The consequence of this was that many objects found through metal detecting activity were not caught by the rules on treasure trove. The definition of treasure is now to be found in section 1 of the Act: included are objects which are at least 300 years old with a precious metal[46] content of at least 10 per cent; findings of two coins at least 300 years old with the same degree of precious metal content; and finds of more than ten coins which are at least 300 years old. Section 8(1) of the Act imposes a duty on a finder to report an object which he believes or has reasonable grounds to believe to be treasure. Failure to report such a finding can lead to prosecution.

ADVERSE POSSESSION: BASIC PRINCIPLES

The basic idea behind adverse possession of land is that a person who takes possession of land, albeit wrongful to begin with, acquires a possessory title to the land which, after the expiration of 12 years, is good against the whole world. The title of the paper owner is simply extinguished through the lapse of time. It is often difficult to understand how wrongful possession of land can give birth to a full-blooded ownership right against the whole world. This is especially so in a context where ownership rights are dependent on the existence of elaborate title deeds and a system of registration of such rights.[47] However, once again we see that, even in the face of title deeds to land and registration of such ownership rights, possession retains an all-important function in deciding the relative strength of ownership. In this respect, leading conveyancers openly admit that '... misunderstandings have sometimes arisen from an unwarrantable belief that title deeds are sacrosanct

---

[45] See Marston and Ross, 'Treasure and Portable Antiquities in the 1990s Still Chained to the Ghosts of the Past: The Treasure Act 1996' [1997] Conv 273.

[46] This is defined as gold and silver in s 3(3) of the Treasure Act 1996.

[47] The nature of adverse possession within the system of registration of title has recently been carefully explored by Sedley J in *Central London Commercial Estates Ltd v Kato Kagaku Co Ltd* [1998] 4 All ER 948.

documents, whereas the truth is that neither a conveyance nor a land certificate retains its value if the landowner is so indifferent as to lose physical control of his land.'[48]

The basic rules relating to acquisition of ownership in land through adverse possession are found in the Limitation Act 1980 and caselaw.[49] The Limitation Act 1980 contains three important statutory principles relating to adverse possession. First, no action can be brought by a landowner to recover his land after the expiration of 12 years from the date on which the right of action accrued to him.[50] Second, the right of action to recover land is deemed to have accrued to the landowner when the landowner has either been dispossessed of his land or has discontinued use of his land.[51] Finally, no right of action is deemed to have accrued unless the land is in the possession of some person in whose favour the limitation period can run; and where any such right of action is deemed to have accrued on a certain date and no person is in adverse possession on that date, the right of action is not deemed to have accrued unless and until the land is again taken in adverse possession.[52] These statutory principles can be explained in the following way. Whilst it is clear that no action to recover land after 12 years from the date upon which the right of action accrued to the landowner is allowed, time does not simply run because the land is unoccupied.[53] Time only begins to run when the landowner has been dispossessed of his land or where he has discontinued use of his land and the adverse possessor has taken possession of the land for the limitation period. If there is any break in the adverse possession – for example, where A takes adverse possession from B, but B recovers his land within, say, six years – time stops running. Any new claim based on adverse possession cannot rely on A's six years of adverse possession. However, the Act allows the limitation period to be built up by a series of adverse possessions by different possessors providing that at no time during the aggregate period of 12 years there has been a break in the adverse possession.

Much of the caselaw on adverse possession has centred on the concepts of discontinuance, dispossession and possession by the squatter or wrongful intruder. A claimant to title by adverse possession must show that the landowner has either been dispossessed of his land or that he has discontinued use of his land. The former implies some form of ouster by the intruder – that is, the intruder has forced the landowner out of his land. The latter

---

[48] Ruoff and Roper, *On the Law and Practice of Registered Conveyancing* (1979) at p 531.

[49] For a detailed study of these principles the reader is advised to consult texts on real property law: for example, K. Gray, *Elements of Land Law* (2nd edn, 1993), (3rd edn published 2001).

[50] Limitation Act 1980, s 15(1).

[51] *Ibid*, s 15(6); Sched 1, para 1.

[52] *Ibid*, s 15(6); Sched 1, para 8(1).

[53] *M'Donnell* v *M'Kinty* (1847) 10 ILR 514.

implies that the landowner has simply discontinued use of his land, that is, abandoned the land. In respect of dispossession and discontinuance two things should be made clear from the start. First, dispossession cases are very rare in practice, the majority of the cases deal with discontinuance by the landowner. However, even with respect to discontinuance, the claimant to title by adverse possession has a difficult task in showing that the landowner has discontinued use of his land. Even when the landowner is not in actual possession of the land, he is deemed to have retained constructive possession of the land.[54] Second, the majority of cases on adverse possession in practice illustrate that adverse possession rules operate in a more sophisticated context than appears from the popular use of the words adverse possession. The cases are not those of an aggressive intruder taking possession of land belonging to another. Rather, the most common adverse possession disputes relate to claimants who have either mistakenly or innocently taken possession of land belonging to another. The rules operate to give certainty of title over land which has long remained unchallenged; certainty of title, as we have seen above, seeks to promote wider social and legal objectives.

A wholesale review of the rules relating to adverse possession was undertaken by the Court of Appeal in *Buckingham County Council* v *Moran*.[55] The case addresses the important question of what constitutes adverse possession by the adverse possessor. Moreover, it also addresses the long-standing problem of the effect of a future use by the landowner on adverse possession. In 1955 the plaintiff council purchased a plot of land for the purpose of a road diversion project. The land was left undeveloped until such time as the project could go ahead. In 1967 the predecessor in title of the defendant incorporated the council's plot of land into their adjoining property and sold the whole lot to the defendant. The defendant fenced in the plot with the adjoining property and placed a new lock and gate on the property so that the only access to the plot could be through the defendant's land. In 1985 the plaintiff council brought proceedings to recover the land. The Court of Appeal held that the defendant had, through his acts of enclosing the land with his own land, annexed the plot to the adjoining property. This had the effect of sufficiently dispossessing the plaintiff from possession of the land. It mattered not that the plaintiff had some future use for the plot of land.

In respect of the possession needed by an adverse possessor to claim a successful title by adverse possession, Slade LJ held that the claimant must satisfy four criteria. In the first, it must be shown that the paper owner has lost possession of his land.[56] Second, that the adverse possessor takes factual

---

[54] *Fletcher* v *Storoschuck* (1981) DLR (3d) 59 at 62.
[55] [1990] Ch 623.
[56] *Ie* either a dispossession or discontinuance of land.

possession of the disputed land. The type of possession required here is a special one in that the adverse possessor must show that his possession was open,[57] not by force, and not with the consent of the landowner. The cases on possession do not lay down any hard and fast rules as to what amounts to possession other than that such possession must be exclusive possession. Physical exclusive control can only be determined with reference to the specific facts. Acts which amount to possession in one case may be wholly inappropriate to another case simply because of the nature of the land in question.[58] Third, possession must be adverse. This does not mean that possession should be hostile in any way; rather the 'adverse' aspect of possession relates to the fact that possession must be inconsistent with the paper owner's title. Thus, even where a claimant to land claims adverse possession in circumstances of innocent entry into the paper owner's land, such possession still amounts to adverse possession as it is clearly inconsistent with the paper owner's title. Finally, there must be an intention to possess (*animus possidendi*) by the intruder. There must be strong evidence that points to an intention to possess, such as equivocal acts of excluding the whole world from the disputed land.[59]

The effect of a successful claim to adverse possession of land is that the paper owner's title is completely extinguished. Thus, the adverse possessor does not acquire the former paper owner's title since there is no conveyance thereof.[60] Any rights that the former paper owner enjoyed, such as rights of way over neighbouring land, do not avail themselves to the adverse possessor. In the case of an unregistered title to land the adverse possessor acquires a possessory title to a fee simple in the land as soon as time begins to run against the paper owner. It is often difficult to appreciate how such a fee simple can be granted in the adverse possessor when, at the same time and until 12 years have elapsed, such an estate also vests in the paper owner. However, given the concept of relativity of title examined in Chapter 6, the grant of such a fee simple in the adverse possessor concurrently with the paper owner is feasible. In the case of a registered title, until such time as registration takes place, the adverse possessor does not become the proprietor of the land. Instead the paper owner, who in this case would be the registered proprietor, holds the land on a statutory trust for the adverse possessor.[61] The adverse possessor's rights are regarded as overriding interests.[62] This is a

---

[57] This is so that the landowner has the opportunity of challenging his title against the intruder.
[58] See *Lord Advocate* v *Lord Lovat* (1880) 5 AC 272 at 288, and also *Powell* v *McFarlane* (1977) 38 P&CR 452.
[59] See *Powell* v *McFarlane* (1977) 38 P&CR 452 at 472. See also M. Dockray [1982] Conv 256. Acts which point to an intention to possess include enclosure of the land and change of locks.
[60] See *Tichborne* v *Weir* (1892) 67 LT 735.
[61] Land Registration Act 1980, s 75.
[62] Land Registration Act 1925, s 70(1)(f).

rather strange proposition in light of the fact that the effect of adverse possession is to grant a legal estate in the adverse possessor as opposed to an equitable one.[63] However, this needs to be understood in the context of the practicalities of registered conveyancing. To say that the registered proprietor, until such time as registration takes place, holds on trust for the adverse possessor is a compromise between two competing property principles: first, the principle of relativity of title; and second, the principle of registration of title. In the early days of registration of title, indefeasibility of title was seen as crucial to its success. To allow adverse possession rules to defeat a registered title was inconsistent with the idea and aims of the system of registration of title.[64] However, to allow no claim to adverse possession of land in the case of a registered title would be far too rigid a rule. The use of the trust reflects a compromise between the two rules and a practical way of protecting the rights of the adverse possessor.

Given that land may be subject to more than just the mere right of ownership, how do adverse possession rules operate when the land is subject to a lease? This has been a controversial issue and the answer depends very much on whether the title to the land is unregistered or registered. If an adverse possessor takes possession of land subject to a lease, it is clear that if the limitation period has run its course, the tenant under the lease is statute barred from bringing an action against the squatter.[65] The landlord, however, is not barred from claiming the land after the expiration of the term of the lease. However, where a tenant surrenders his lease despite the fact that an adverse possessor of the land may have possessed land for more than 12 years, the effect of the surrender of the lease to the landlord is to give him an immediate right of possession against the squatter. This is the rule emanating from the controversial House of Lords decision in *Fairweather* v *St Marylebone Property Co Ltd*.[66] It is extremely difficult to find how this decision can be justified; it is inconsistent with the basic axiom of property law that a person cannot give a better title than the one he already has. Therefore, a lessee whose title has been extinguished cannot surrender anything to the landlord.

In the context of a registered title a different and more satisfactory approach has been taken. Where a tenant's title has been extinguished by virtue of the Limitation Act 1980 and the adverse possessor is registered as the leaseholder proprietor, there is nothing that the previous registered

---

[63] In *Central London Commercial Estates Ltd* v *Kato Kagaku Co Ltd* [1998] 4 All ER 948, Sedley J commented (at 953) that it was wrong to view the interest of the squatter as equitable when in fact he had acquired a legal estate in the land by virtue of the adverse possession.

[64] See Ruoff and Roper, *On the Law and Practice of Registered Conveyancing* (5th edn, 1985) at p 531.

[65] See, for example, *Taylor* v *Twinberrow* [1930] 2 KB 16 and, more recently, *Chung Ping Kwan* v *Lam Island Development Co Ltd* [1997] AC 38 (PC).

[66] [1963] AC 510.

leaseholder can surrender to the landlord. Instead, the landlord is subject to the adverse possessor, who now becomes the registered proprietor of the lease for the duration of the lease that was originally granted.[67] Furthermore, if the adverse possessor has not yet applied for registration as proprietor of the lease, the present registered proprietor whose title has become extinguished holds the lease on statutory trust for the adverse possessor. If the registered leaseholder attempts to surrender the lease to the landlord, then, unlike in the case of a registered title, the landlord takes subject to the adverse possessor's right, which is an overriding interest. The landlord would in this case be impressed with the statutory trust which was impressed on the registered proprietor of the lease.[68]

It will be appreciated that establishing a successful claim to adverse possession of land is a very difficult task. It requires a complete rejection of the paper owner's title by the adverse possessor, accompanied by acts on his behalf that amount to ownership of the land. Provided this has been satisfied, the adverse possessor may apply to the Chief Land Registrar under the Land Registration Act 1925 to be registered as first proprietor in the case of an unregistered title; alternatively, to be entered as proprietor in the case of a registered title to the land in question. The more problematic case, however, arises where the paper owner furnishes evidence to show that he had retained the land for some future use; thus, despite not being in occupation of the land, he had never intended to discontinue use of the land. It was at one time thought that no claim to adverse possession could arise where land had been retained for some future use unless the acts of the adverse possessor were wholly inconsistent with the paper owner's future intended use.[69] The rationale behind this was that, unless the acts of the adverse possessor were totally inconsistent with the future use, the adverse possessor was deemed to have been given an implied licence to occupy the land. Given that the grant of a licence (that is, consent) to occupy the land is inconsistent with the idea of adverse possession, there could be no adverse possession. This rule was abolished in *Buckingham County Council v Moran*,[70] where it was held that such a proposition was far too broad. The rule itself is contrary to the Limitation Act 1980, which attempts to put an end to litigation.

---

[67] *Spectrum Investments Co v Holmes* [1981] 1 WLR 221.
[68] *Central London Commercial Estates Ltd v Kato Kagaku Co Ltd* [1998] 4 All ER 948; see C. Harpum, 'Estates in the Clouds – The Squatter, the Lease and the Car Park' (1999) 115 LQR 187.
[69] See *Leigh v Jack* (1879) 5 ExD 264.
[70] [1990] Ch 623.

9

ACQUISITION OF PROPRIETARY RIGHTS: DERIVATIVE ACQUISITION

DERIVATIVE ACQUISITION

The idea behind derivative acquisition is that a proprietary right is transferred from one person to another. Indeed, the most common way of acquiring a proprietary right is through a transfer from one to another. Such transfers can be gratuitous (that is, in the form of gift), or they may be consensual (for example, taking place under a contract for sale). Moreover, such transfers can take place during the lifetime of the transferor, in which case it is often said that such transfers are *inter vivos*. Alternatively, transfer of a proprietary right can take effect on the death of the transferor; in such a case the transfer is said to be testamentary. Testamentary transfers require writing and the execution of a properly drafted will. Although the basic idea behind derivative acquisition is clear enough – that is, the transfer of a right from one person to another – derivative acquisition can be effected in one of two ways.

The first way of effecting a derivative acquisition is when a person transfers a pre-existing proprietary right to another. For example, the owner of a house can voluntarily transfer ownership in the house to another through the appropriate means of transfer of ownership in land. The appropriate method of transfer will be determined by the nature of the object in question.[1] It is also worth noting here that a transfer can occur involuntarily – for example, the law may impose a transfer where the holder of the property right is declared bankrupt. The second type of derivative acquisition occurs when one person expresses the intention to create a proprietary right in another person. In such cases, a person having a right in an object creates another

---

[1] In the case of land, where a transfer is in the form of a gift, such a transfer will require the use of a deed to effect the transfer of ownership. Where a transfer is pursuant to a sale, it will require the use of a contract, exchange of contracts, a conveyance by deed completed with registration.

right in the same object and vests that right in a different person. The right created is usually one which is lesser or ancillary to the right held by the creator of the right. Numerous examples of such derivative acquisition can be given. If A is the owner of land, he will be vested with a freehold estate which will purport to give him ownership in that house. Without transferring ownership in that house to another, A can grant in another person, B, a lease, an easement or the benefit of a restrictive covenant. Such a grant cannot properly be described as a transfer of a right in the sense that A is not transferring his lease to B; rather, A is creating different rights in B. This is different from the case where one tenant transfers his right under a lease to another. It is an example of the first means of derivative acquisition, that is, a simple transfer of a pre-existing right to another. Other examples of creating a right in another is where a person declares himself trustee for another. If such a trust if properly declared, the person who has declared such a trust has created a beneficial right in another person called a beneficiary. Given that property rights are recognised both in the common law and in equity, derivative acquisitions of property rights can occur in both contexts.

Whether derivative acquisitions are effected by a transfer or a creation of a right, such acquisitions are, in the majority of cases, hedged with formality requirements. Transfers and creation of proprietary rights take place for a number of reasons; some transfers are simply in the form of gifts whilst others represent sales. It will be seen later that the purpose behind formality rules varies from one type of transaction to another. There is no other area of private law which is encumbered with so many formal requirements; textbooks on the law of contract devote relatively little time to the question of formality simply because contract law has relatively fewer formality requirements. Almost every aspect of property law, although much more marked in the context of real property, is hampered with formality requirements. It is this aspect of property law that often contributes to the technicality of the law. This chapter examines the function of formality rules in property law. It will be observed that formalities perform a wide range of functions in law, not least because transfers of proprietary rights differ in their purposes. Some transfers represent gifts, others represent bargains, and as such the formality required in each case seeks to achieve a different objective. Generally, the formalities required for gifts usually seek to effect the donative intent of the person making the gift. With respect to consensual transfers such as bargains, the primary legal goal of formalities is to make those bargains legally binding.[2] This chapter continues with a look at some of the basic principles relating to derivative acquisition in real and personal property. At one time there was very little difference in the rules relating to derivative acquisition of

---

[2] See J. Baron, 'Gifts, Bargains and Form' (1989) 64 Ind LJ 155 at p 156.

interests in land and goods. The conveyance of ownership in land was usually effected through feoffment with livery of seisin. This old fashioned
terminology meant nothing more than a simple gift of an estate in land
accompanied by delivery of possession.[3] Today, whilst transfer of ownership
to goods can be effected by delivery of possession, no such delivery of possession of land can transfer ownership therein.

DERIVATIVE ACQUISITION OF INTERESTS IN LAND

Transfer of interests in land

As regards interests in land, it is necessary to use a deed to transfer the interest.[4] The ownership to my house can only be transferred by the use of a deed.
Likewise, a leasehold interest can only be transferred through the use of a
deed. Historically, a deed constituted a document which was signed, sealed
and delivered. Today, however, the need for sealing has disappeared and it is
sufficient for the document to be merely signed, witnessed and delivered.[5]
The idea of sealing was once thought to be the decisive characteristic of a
deed; however, recent legislation has made it clear that a document will only
be a deed if it is clearly expressed to be so on the face of the document.[6] The
transfer of interests in land, unless by virtue of a gift, will usually be preceded
by a contract. For example, where I intend to sell my house to another, or I
intend to assign my lease to another, a contract is entered into before there is
a conveyance of the freehold title to my house, or the term of years that is
vested in me. Such contracts are governed by the Law of Property
(Miscellaneous Provisions) Act 1989. This Act requires all contracts for the
disposition of interests in land to be in writing, contain all the terms and conditions expressly agreed to and signed by both parties. Failure to comply
with such formality renders the contract void. Compliance, however, gives
the transferee an equitable interest in the subject-matter of the contract until
completion of the transaction through the use of a deed. The fact that the
contract can grant an equitable estate in the transferee is based upon the
equitable maxim that 'equity sees that as done which ought to be done.'[7]
Where the matter is simply one of form rather than substance, equity will
allow recognition of the property right intended to be transferred on the
basis that equity looks to substance and not form.

---

[3] See J. Williams, *Principles of the Law of Personal Property Intended for the Use of Students in
Conveyancing* (1856) at p 33.
[4] See Law of Property Act 1925, s 52.
[5] Law of Property Act (Miscellaneous Provisions) Act 1989, s 1(1).
[6] *Ibid.*
[7] This matter is discussed later in the chapter under the heading of 'Acquisition of Equitable
Interests'.

In the case of certain interests in land, the use of a deed on its own is insufficient to transfer the proprietary interest. Where the title to the land in question is a registered title, the transfer of a proprietary interest therein is only effective if accompanied by registration.[8] For example, A can only transfer his ownership in land to another if he transfers the interest in a deed and then complies with the registration process.[9] The function of the registration process is to switch ownership from A to the person who has been given title in the deed of conveyance. It was seen in Chapter 6 that the purpose of registration is to replace the separate investigation of title that takes place on every purchase by a title guaranteed by the state. There are two stages to the registration process: first, a transfer in the correct form; and second, registration of the transfer. Registration must be sought within a certain period of time; the statutory period of time is two months in the case of first registration of title.[10] Failure to register carries with it the penalty that the conveyance of the legal estate in land becomes void. The title, which is deemed to have passed under the deed of conveyance, automatically becomes vested in the transferor who now holds the legal title for the transferee under a trust until such time as a fresh disposition of the legal estate and application for registration is made.[11] In other cases, the transfer must be registered and until such registration the transferee merely acquires an equitable estate in the land.[12] Like the transfer of a freehold estate in land, a lease that has more than 21 years to run can only be assigned effectively if followed by registration.[13]

The discussion so far has concentrated on the transfer of ownership of land, that is, the freehold title and also the transfer of a lease with more than 21 years to run. However, the types of proprietary rights capable of existing in land are, of course, much more complex. The title to land may be burdened with a right of way, more commonly known as an easement. Title may also be subject to a covenant restricting the manner in which a landowner may use his land. The question arises as to how such rights become transferred to others? These rights are often described as rights which are ancillary to title, but nevertheless they form an integral part of the title. It would be impractical and indeed nonsensical if such ancillary rights had to be transferred independently of the transfer of title. Such rights 'travel' along with the transfer of the title to land. Both statute and the courts have formulated principles upon which such rights form an integral part of the title to the land.

---

[8] The idea of registration of title was examined in more detail in Chapter 6.

[9] The principles relating to registration of title and dealings with registered title are to be found in the Land Registration Act 1925 and the Land Registration Act 1997.

[10] Land Registration Act 1997, s 123A(2).

[11] *Ibid*, s 123A(5).

[12] See, below, the discussion on acquisition of equitable property rights.

[13] Land Registration Act 1925, s 123(1), as amended by the Land Registration Act 1986, s 2 (1).

In general terms the concept of annexation seeks to ensure that such ancillary rights continue to 'travel' with the title to land in question. It is outside the scope of this book to examine the rules relating to such ancillary rights and transfer thereof; however, some examples can be given to show how the concept works. The title to land may be burdened with a covenant that the landowner may not erect any further buildings on the land.[14] Such a covenant amounts to a restrictive covenant capable of creating a legally recognised burden on land. In order to ensure that such a covenant not only binds the original covenantee, but also successors in title, the covenant will have to be annexed to my land. Annexation basically means that the covenant in question is not merely personal between the covenantor and covenantee; rather, it is particular to the land in question in that it is affixed to it. Like a restrictive covenant, title to land may be burdened with an easement. For example, a neighbouring landowner may have a right of way over land belonging to another in order to get to his own land. Better still, a public authority may have a right of way over land such as the right to put a water pipe through another person's land. Again, special rules have been formulated in order to allow the burden of such an easement to pass with the title to the land. As a general rule such an easement will automatically pass with the title to land as constituting an overriding interest.[15]

Creation of interests in land

Creation of interests in land, like the transfer of such interests, in the majority of cases requires the use of a deed. The deed itself is often executed after a contract for the creation of the interest. Thus, the creation of a lease in land usually involves a two-stage process: the contract for a lease, followed by a deed.[16] There is one exception to this rule and that concerns a lease for a term not exceeding three years. Where a lease is for a term of less than three years and is one which starts forthwith at a best rent reasonably obtainable, then such a lease need not comply with the requirement for a deed.[17]

---

[14] Restrictive covenants are examined in Chapter 10.

[15] Land Registration Act 1925, s 70(1)(a). An overriding interest is a special feature of registered title to land. The basic idea behind an overriding interest is that it is a proprietary right in land which does not depend on registration for its enforceability. Such a right binds a purchaser of a registered title to land irrespective of notice thereof. See *National Provincial Bank Ltd v Hastings Car Mart Ltd* [1964] Ch 9 at 15; see also; R. Smith, *Property Law* (3rd edn, 2000) at p 217.

[16] Law of Property Act 1925, s 52(1).

[17] *Ibid*, ss 52(1), (2)(d) and 54(2). A lease for less than three years can be created orally or simply in writing. It must be noted that whilst the creation of a lease for less than three years may be made orally, the transfer of such a lease must be made in writing as a basic minimum requirement: see the Law of Property Act 1925, s 54(2) which states that 'no interest in land can be created or disposed of except by writing'. The absence of writing applies only to the creation of a short-term lease, not to its transfer or disposal.

Easements such as rights of way are likewise created by deed. In such a case an owner of land can grant an easement by express words to that effect.[18] The most common way of creating a mortgage in land is by way of deed which has the effect of granting a charge in the mortgagee.[19] Again, the deed purporting to grant a charge in the mortgagee is usually preceded by a contract for a mortgage. The creation of interests in land such as leases, mortgages and easements will often require some form of registration, substantive or otherwise, for their validity in registered title to land.

DERIVATIVE ACQUISITION OF INTERESTS IN PERSONAL PROPERTY

Unlike real property, where numerous interests can be created and transferred in the same piece of land, personal property is rather different. The difference stems from the very nature of personal property and historical factors. Personal property, unlike real property, has never been subjected to the doctrine of tenure and estates. Instead, interests in personal property are simply explained on the basis of two concepts: namely, ownership and possession. Possession and ownership are hard to divorce since in the majority of cases possession is not only a prerequisite to having ownership, but also an indicator of ownership.[20] An important type of interest that can be created in personal property is bailment. This requires delivery of possession; how such possession can be delivered is examined below. The rules relating to the transfer of interests in personal property depend primarily on whether the property in question is a chose in possession (for example, a tangible thing), or a chose in action (something intangible such as a debt).

Choses in possession

There are three basic ways in which ownership to chattels can be transferred from one person to another: sale, delivery and deed. The first represents a consensual transfer, whilst delivery and deed are usually, although not always,[21] gratuitous in nature.

---

[18] Easements are a very complex feature of real property law. Although the basic rule is that such easements are created in a deed, the manner in which such easements are created is much more diverse in law and practice. In a majority of cases such rights will arise by implication of law rather than an express grant. A discussion of the rules relating to implied grant of easements is outside the scope of this book; one example, however, can be given. The most common type of implied grant of an easement occurs where such an easement is necessary for the enjoyment of a piece of land. Thus, I may have an easement over another person's land, say my neighbour, simply because I cannot access my land other than by walking over my neighbour's land.

[19] Law of Property Act 1925, s 87.

[20] See Pollock and Wright, *An Essay on Possession in the Common Law* (1888) at p 4.

[21] For example, a transfer to vest ownership in a trustee is not gratuitous but one pursuant to the terms of the trust. The trustee's function is to manage the property on behalf of his beneficiary in accordance with the terms of the trust instrument.

Sale

A sale of a chattel is sufficient to transfer the legal ownership therein to the purchaser. The change of ownership is accomplished by the contract of sale and there is no separate need for delivery of the chattel.[22] The rules relating to the sale of goods form a large part of the common law. It is fair to say that such rules form a special branch of property law, operating usually in a commercial setting. The modern rules began with the Sale of Goods Act 1893 and were then consolidated in what now is the major sale of goods legislation, the Sale of Goods Act 1979.[23] The property rules as to passing of ownership depend primarily on whether the goods which are the subject-matter of the contract of sale are specific goods or unascertained goods. The Sale of Goods Act 1979 distinguishes between specific goods and unascertained goods. Specific goods are described as those goods which are 'identified and agreed upon at the time a contract of sale is made'.[24] Thus, the sale of a car to another person constitutes the sale of a specific good. In commercial practice, however, it may be the case that a seller of goods may not have the goods yet to be delivered under the contract simply because they have not yet been manufactured. It may also be the case that the goods form part of a bulk: for example, 300 gallons of crude oil lying in a tank containing 500 gallons. In such cases, the goods forming the subject-matter of the sale cannot properly be described as specific; they are more accurately described as unascertained. Unlike the sale of the car, unascertained goods are not identified and agreed upon at the time the contract is made. It is not known which 300 gallons of crude oil the purchaser will get out of the 500 lying in the tank. Unascertained goods are usually goods described by quality and quantity, but not identified at the time of the contract. The typical type of unascertained goods that cause problems in sale of goods contracts are goods that form part of a bulk.

Where a contract for the sale of goods involves specific goods, the basic rule is that ownership passes to the purchaser when the parties to the contract of sale intend it to pass.[25] Usually it is not the case that express words are used to identify when property is to pass to the purchaser. In order to ascertain the intentions of the parties to the contract, the Sale of Goods Act requires one to look at the terms of the contract, the conduct of the parties and the circumstances of the case.[26] Given that this usually involves a

---

[22] It must be noted, however, that the sale of a chattel involves both a contract and a conveyance.

[23] The Sale of Goods (Amendment) Act 1995 has recently amended the Sale of Goods Act 1979 (hereafter SGA 1979). The principal amendment is examined below.

[24] SGA 1979, s 61.

[25] *Ibid*, s 17(1).

[26] *Ibid*, s 17(2).

difficult task, the Act lays down a series of rebuttable presumptions that apply in different situations.[27] The most important rule relating to specific goods is that where the contract is one that is unconditional in nature – that is, nothing further has to be done to the goods – the ownership in the goods passes to the purchaser as soon as the contract is made.[28] Section 18 of the Act continues to examine a number of common situations relating to specific goods: for example, contracts for sale where the specific goods have to be put into a deliverable state, have to be priced or are contracted on an approval basis. The section lays down the appropriate presumption as to when ownership passes in the goods.

If the contract of sale involves goods that are unascertained, no ownership in such goods can pass until the goods are ascertained.[29] Thus, a contract of sale of 200 gallons of oil forming part of a tank containing 500 gallons does not pass any ownership to the purchaser until that time the oil has become ascertained.[30] Likewise, in the sale of goods yet to be manufactured (in other words, future goods), no property passes until such goods have been ascertained. If no ownership can pass in unascertained goods until such time as the goods have become ascertained, the question is when do goods become ascertained? The idea behind ascertainment of goods is the identification of the particular goods to be used for the performance of the contract of sale between the purchaser and seller. In the example of the sale of 200 gallons of oil out of a tank of 500 gallons, ascertainment occurs when the 200 gallons of oil has been put separately in a different tank.[31] The presumptive rule as to when ownership passes in unascertained goods is found in section 18, rule 5, which states that ownership passes to the purchaser when such goods in a deliverable state are unconditionally appropriated to the contract. The concept of unconditional appropriation has attracted considerable attention by the courts. The accepted view is that unconditional appropriation occurs when the seller performs his last act in performance of the contract.[32] This is a very strict requirement; unconditional appropriation does not occur simply if the seller has put the goods to one side. If the seller is obliged to ship the

---

[27] SGA 1979, s 18.

[28] SGA 1979, s 18, rule 1. This represents a clear-cut exception to the common law rule that, in the absence of a deed, legal ownership in chattels only passes when delivery has been made and not when the parties intend it to pass. See A.P. Bell, *Modern Law of Personal Property in England and Ireland* (1989) at p 323.

[29] SGA 1979, s 16.

[30] This is subject to the amendment made by the Sale of Goods (Amendment) Act 1995, which does not prevent property passing in tenants in common with other purchasers. This is explored below.

[31] It appears that ascertainment can occur when a specific bulk has been reduced to the contract quantity: see *Wait and James* v *Midland Bank* (1926) 31 Com Cas 172.

[32] See *Carlos Federspiel & Co* v *Charles Twigg & Co* [1957] 1 Lloyd's Rep 240.

goods to the buyer, unconditional appropriation will not occur until such shipment has taken place, even though the goods have been completely separated from other goods.

The main problem with unascertained goods, particularly those such as bulk goods, is the position of a purchaser who has paid for goods but has not yet taken delivery because they have been unascertained. Until the Sale of Goods (Amendment) Act 1995,[33] a purchaser of such goods faced two main problems. In the first place, given that no property would have passed to such a purchaser of goods, in the event of the insolvency of the seller, such a purchaser lacked priority over the general creditors of the seller. Second, the purchaser of such goods would lack the necessary *locus standi* to sue third parties (for example, carriers of goods) in tort for damage to the goods. The 1995 Act overcomes this problem by allowing a purchaser of unascertained goods to acquire an undivided interest in the bulk provided that a number of conditions are satisfied.[34] First, the bulk must itself be identified; second, the purchaser must have contracted for the purchase of a specific amount of the bulk; and finally, payment must have been made under the contract.

Deeds and delivery

A sale of a chattel represents one means by which legal ownership can be transferred from one person to another. It is the contract of sale that accomplishes the transfer of the legal ownership and not the separate delivery of the chattel itself. In the absence of a sale, the legal ownership in a chattel can be transferred by way of a gift. A gift represents a gratuitous transfer of ownership as opposed to a consensual transfer. There are two basic ways in which a gift can be made. The first and most obvious way is by delivery of the chattel to the donee of the gift. The delivery of the chattel is required to give the donee the possessory title in the chattel so delivered. In the absence of delivery of the chattel, a gift can be effected by deed. Where neither of these criteria has been satisfied, then no matter what the intentions of the donor of the gift, the gift is said to be incomplete. Sometimes it is simply said that there is an imperfect gift. In such circumstances, the donee of an imperfect or incomplete gift has little in the way of remedies. Consideration provided by the donee of the gift may be sufficient to turn the gift into a contract accompanied with common law and equitable remedies for breach of contract. In the absence of consideration it becomes very difficult to enforce the gift.[35]

---

[33] This Act was passed in response to the recommendations of the Law Commission (Law Com No 215, 1993).

[34] See new ss 20A and 20B of the Sale of Goods Act 1979.

[35] There are very limited circumstances in which a failed gift will be rescued. Two such circumstances are: first, where the rule in *Strong* v *Bird* (1874) LR 18 Eq 315 applies; and, second, where the principle of *donatio mortis causa* applies. Both of these are considered below. Rescue may also be available under the fast-growing doctrine of proprietary estoppel, which is examined more appropriately in Chapter 10.

Where the donor of a gift manifests a donative intent in a deed, such a deed is sufficient to transfer the legal ownership in a chattel to the donee. Under the Law of Property (Miscellaneous Provisions) Act 1989 a deed is a document expressed to be a deed, signed, witnessed and delivered. In the absence of a deed, legal ownership in a chattel can be transferred by delivery. Indeed, this is the most common and preferred method of making a gift. The common law rule was first explained in *Irons v Smallpiece*,[36] where a father expressed a donative intent to give his two colts to his son, but retained possession of them until his death. It was held that this was an imperfect gift and that the colts remained part of the father's estate.[37] It appears that there are two basic requirements for an effective gift to take place: first, a donative intention to give by the donor of the gift;[38] and second, delivery of the subject-matter of the gift to the donor. It is essential that both of these requirements be satisfied. Thus, in *Re Cole*,[39] a husband took his wife to their new home and told her that 'it's all yours'. The wife was unable to challenge the husband's trustees in bankruptcy over their claims to the contents of the house, simply because there had been no delivery of the contents of the house to the wife.

If legal ownership can be transferred by delivery of the chattel, what is meant by delivery? The basic idea behind delivery is the transfer of possession from the donor to the donee of the gift. The question is, what types of possession are sufficient to make an effective delivery of a chattel? The courts have accepted that actual and constructive possession are both sufficient to effect a delivery of a chattel. Where a person hands over the chattel to another, this is sufficient to effect a delivery of the chattel and the donee of the gift will be in actual possession. Thus, in *Thomas v Times Book Co*,[40] an author of a play who had mislaid the manuscript told the donee that if he found the manuscript he could keep it. The donee successfully found the manuscript and it was held that the gift was complete in the donee.

Giving a person actual possession is relatively straightforward; it simply requires handing over possession, and we may refer to this simply as amounting to actual delivery. It also appears that constructive delivery will suffice to

---

[36] (1819) 2 B & Ald 551.

[37] See also *Cochrane v Moore* (1890) 25 QBD 57, and *Re Cole* [1964] Ch 175.

[38] The requirement of a donative intent to make a gift is imperative in order to differentiate a gift from other cases of transfer of possession by a third party, such as under a bailment.

[39] [1964] Ch 175; cf *Pascoe v Turner* [1979] 2 All ER 945 where similar facts prevailed. In this case the plaintiff had been living with the defendant and when their relationship ended he told her that the house and everything in it was hers. The Court of Appeal held that the contents of the house were hers. Unlike in *Re Cole*, the defendant retained sole possession of the house and the contents therein. The case, however, can be explained on the principle of proprietary estoppel, which has the effect of granting positive proprietary rights: see Chapter 10.

[40] [1966] 2 All ER 241.

effect a gift. The idea of constructive possession was considered in Chapter 6 as amounting to a situation where one person in actual possession of chattels so holds that possession on behalf of another. That other person is said to be in constructive possession of the chattels. The classic example is where an agent is in actual possession of chattels on behalf of his principal. The principal is said to have constructive possession in that he has the power to control what happens to such chattels. Furthermore, the agent recognises the superior right of the principal to possession of the chattels in question and will return them immediately if requested to do so. Thus, the most basic example of effecting a constructive delivery of chattels is where chattels are entrusted to an agent such as a carrier. Whilst the carrier may have actual possession of the chattels, the fact that he recognises the superior right of his principal to such chattels is sufficient to effect constructive delivery to the principal.

The concept of constructive delivery is, however, much wider. If the principal wants his agent to take the chattels in his possession by way of gift, then he need not require the agent to deliver the chattels back to the principal only to have them redelivered to the agent. He can simply allow the agent to take the chattels by way of gift and thereby revoke any constructive possession of such chattels. Seen in this way, it can be said that the principal has effected a constructive delivery of the chattels. For example, A tells B to take A's television and deliver it to an address in London. The handing over of the television to B amounts to giving B actual possession of the television. A, however, still retains constructive possession of the television up and until the point of delivery to the address in London. If, during the transit to London, A informs B that no delivery to London should take place, but instead, he or she should take the television for him or herself absolutely, a gift has been effected. In such a case A has made a constructive delivery to B. It will be seen from such an example that the idea behind constructive delivery is that there is no change in physical possession. In *Pascoe* v *Turner*,[41] the plaintiff made a gift of the contents of his house to the defendant. The defendant had been living in the house belonging to the plaintiff for some time, the plaintiff having moved elsewhere. The court found that the defendant had been made a complete gift of the contents so that the defendant now became a donee of the contents and was not required to recognise any superior rights of the plaintiff, who simply lost his constructive possession in the contents.

Another common way in which a constructive delivery of chattels can be made is where a bailor of goods instructs the bailee to hold the goods for another person. This can arise where the bailor does not wish to disturb the bailment but rather changes the bailor in that relationship. The process by which by this occurs is called 'attornment'.[42]

---

[41] [1979] 1 WLR 431.

[42] The process of attornment requires the bailee to acknowledge that he now holds for the donee rather than the original bailor of the chattels. Such acknowledgment must be made to the donee.

Finally, actual delivery of chattels is often impracticable where the chattels are incapable of physical delivery at the time the donative intent is expressed. In such cases the question is whether symbolic delivery is permissible to effect a gift. For example, I have in my possession a furniture set comprising 20 bulky pieces. I hand over one chair out of such furniture and tell you that the furniture is yours. Has delivery been made of all 20 pieces of the furniture set? There is authority to suggest that the handing over of a symbol representing a larger bulk will be sufficient to effect delivery. In *Lock v Heath*[43] a husband delivered to his wife a chair expressing the words that 'I give you all the goods mentioned in the inventory'. The court held that such a delivery of the chair was sufficient to transfer all the furniture listed in the inventory. There appears, therefore, to be no objection to handing over a key to a deposit box to effect delivery of the contents of that box. It is important, however, that the handing over of the symbol representing something else allows the donee to gain complete, undisturbed access to the thing represented by the symbol.[44]

Where there has been no effective delivery of the chattel to the donee of the gift, the gift is said to be incomplete. In such a case there is very little the donee of the gift can do at common law or in equity. In the absence of consideration the donee lacks a contractual remedy and in equity the maxim 'equity will not perfect an imperfect gift' will also deny any such relief. Mention, however, must be made of the rule in *Strong v Bird*,[45] which allows a failed gift of personal property to be rescued in special circumstances. The rule applies in circumstances where a donor during his lifetime manifests a donative intent to the donee, but never makes effective delivery of the subject-matter of the gift to the donee. Providing such a donative intent continues until his death, then provided he has not abandoned the subject-matter of the gift, the gift becomes complete when the donee is appointed as administrator or executor of the donor's estate. In such circumstances the donee of the gift may take the subject-matter of the gift, since it does not form part of the donor's estate. In *Strong v Bird* the facts concerned an attempt to release a debt owed by a stepmother to her stepson. The stepmother had lent her stepson some £1100 and it was agreed that such monies loaned would be repaid by her stepson by a reduction in the rent the mother paid to him whilst living with him in his house. After paying reduced rent for two quarters the mother continued to pay full rent. It was held that the appointment of the stepson as sole executor of the mother's estate was sufficient to release the debt. The rule is based on two main grounds: first, that the vesting of the property in the donee in his capacity as executor or administrator is sufficient

---

[43] (1892) 8 TLR 295; see also *Kemp v Falk* (1882) 7 App Cas 753.
[44] See *Wrightson v McArthur & Hutchinson (1919) Ltd* [1921] 2 KB 807.
[45] (1874) LR 18 Eq 315.

to complete the imperfect gift; and, second, the presumed intention of the donor was to release the debt. For the rule to operate it is important to show that the donor attempted to make an immediate *inter vivos* gift and that he continued to have that intention until his death.

Intangible property: choses in action

The derivative acquisition of intangible property, also known as choses in action, is a much more difficult area of the law than that of tangible property.[46] The difficulty stems from the fact that the common law courts were unable to accommodate intangibles in the same way as tangible property. The reason for this was attributable to the very fact that such property did not dominate the courts until relatively later on in history. It was not until the middle of the nineteenth century that intangible property came to play a more significant role in property matters. The failure of the common law to deal with intangible property resulted in the intervention of equity to iron out the deficiencies of the common law. The intervention of equity led to legislation covering the transfer of intangible property. The result has been that the present rules relating to the transfer of intangible property are a combination of equitable principles and statute.

There are also other reasons why the common law failed to provide a comprehensive system of rules relating to transfer of choses in action. A classic example of a chose in action is a debt; other examples include patents, copyright and shares. The example of a debt perhaps best explains why the common law found it difficult to accommodate transfers of choses in action. A debt is a personal obligation owed by a debtor to a creditor and, as such, it was difficult to see why the debtor need pay to anyone other than the original creditor. Any attempt to transfer the debt to another was seen as contrary to the very nature of the relationship set up by the debt. Furthermore, as Bell explains in his text, transfer of the benefit of a debt was seen as maintenance and thus contrary to public policy.[47]

The rules relating to transfer of choses in action depend primarily on whether the chose in action is a pure intangible or a documentary intangible.[48] Examples of pure intangibles include debts, patents and copyright, whilst examples of documentary intangibles include bills of exchange, promissory notes and share certificates.

---

[46] For a detailed analysis of the rules relating to intangible property see A.P. Bell, *Modern Law of Personal Property in England and Ireland* (1989) at pp 361–404, and M. Bridge, *Personal Property Law* (2nd edn, 1996) at pp 119–140.

[47] *Op cit*, at p 361. The rule continues to apply in some cases even today – for example, the assignment of a cause of action in tort will not be allowed since it will be tantamount to maintenance: see *Trendtex Trading Corporation* v *Credit Suisse* [1982] AC 679.

[48] This division is put forward by R.M. Goode, *Commercial Law* (2nd edn, 1995) Chap 2.

Pure intangibles

The rules relating to the transfer of ownership in pure intangibles are found in equity and statute.[49] Equity has played a significant role in dealing with the transfer of choses in action. The statutory provisions do not alter the substantive rules of equity; instead they aim to overcome procedural difficulties involved in the use of the equitable principle. The concept used by the law in dealing with the transfer of a chose in action is 'assignment'. Such a concept covers a situation where the benefit of a chose in action is given to another person. For example, A may be owed £100 by B. A can either gratuitously or for consideration transfer the obligation to pay the debt to another person such as C. The debtor–creditor relationship now exists between A and C, and C can give a full discharge to A for the debt owed.

Equity has long recognised the assignment of a chose in action. At law A may be owed £100 by B and he may wish to assign that debt to C. In equity this can be done by means of an equitable assignment. An equitable assignment does not transfer the right of action at common law from A to C; it merely confers upon the assignee, C, the right to invoke the aid of equity. Thus, in such a case of assignment the assignor has to be joined as a party to the proceedings, primarily because it is to him that the legal obligation to pay is owed. It may be questioned upon which principle equity intervenes to give relief to the assignee of the debt. The answer basically lies in the equitable maxim that 'equity considers that as done which ought to be done'. This means that, since the assignor and the assignee of the debt have agreed that the common law right under the debt should now be the property of the assignee, the assignor must allow an action to be brought in his own name so as to make the transaction effectual.[50] The rule that the assignor must be joined as a party to the proceedings does not apply in cases where the assignment is of a chose in action that is exclusively in the jurisdiction of equity. The best example of this is the assignment of a legacy under a will or the assignment of an interest under a trust.

The manner in which an equitable assignment takes place is relatively straightforward. The assignment need not take any particular form; the only requirement is that the meaning and intention of the assignor is clear.[51] The assignment need not, as a general rule, comply with any need for writing.[52] The assignee must consent to the assignment in order to make it effective;[53]

---

[49] The principal statutory provision is s 136 of the Law of Property Act 1925.

[50] See *Tailby* v *Official Receiver* (1888) 13 App Cas 523.

[51] *Brandt's Sons & Co* v *Dunlop Rubber Co* [1905] AC 454.

[52] An assignment of a pure equitable chose in action (for example, an assignment of an interest under a trust) will have to satisfy the requirement for writing set out in s 53(1)(c) of the Law of Property Act 1925 since assignment means disposition of an equitable interest for the purposes of that section: see *Grey* v *IRC* [1960] AC 1 (later in this chapter).

[53] *Standing* v *Bowring* (1885) 31 Ch D 282.

however, it is clear that the debtor need not be informed of the assignment.[54] Although the assignee need not give any notice to the debtor, it is important that he does so for two main reasons. First, if the debtor makes any payment to the assignor in ignorance of the assignment, the assignee is bound by such payments.[55] Second, notice allows the assignee to gain priority over subsequent assignments and those assignments where no notice has been given to the debtor.[56]

The more controversial aspect of equitable assignment is whether such assignment requires consideration or whether assignment can be gratuitous. The authorities do not provide any clear rules relating to the requirement of consideration. The statutory provision dealing with assignment of a chose in action does not require any consideration.[57] Given that the statutory provision was enacted not to change the substantive law, but rather to deal with procedural problems, it ought to be that the same rule should apply to equitable assignments. The answer to the consideration question seems to depend on the nature of the assignment in question. Equity makes a fundamental distinction between complete and incomplete assignments in the same way as it does for complete and incomplete gifts. It has been seen above that an imperfect gift fails in equity and will only be rescued if the donee of the gift has provided consideration. In the same manner, where an assignment of a chose in action is complete the assignee need not furnish any consideration to effect the assignment.[58] The meaning of complete assignment is that the assignee must be in a position to take action against the debtor without any further acts of the assignor. A complete assignment can be distinguished from an incomplete assignment, which requires further acts to be done by the assignor – for example, a debt which may accrue for work to be done later[59] or a gratuitous agreement to assign which is nothing more than a promise to do something.[60]

The equitable rules relating to the assignment of a chose in action posed one major procedural problem for assignees. The assignment of a legal chose in action required the assignee to invoke proceedings in the court of equity, which then compelled the assignor to initiate proceedings in the common law courts to recover, for example, a debt. In contrast to this, the assignee of a purely equitable chose did not require assistance from the assignor but could initiate proceedings on his own behalf in the court of equity because equity

---

[54] *Ward* v *Duncombe* [1893] AC 369.

[55] *Stocks* v *Dobson* (1853) 4 De GM & G 11.

[56] This stems from the equitable priority rules in personal property enunciated in *Dearle* v *Hall* (1828) 3 Russ 1.

[57] Law of Property Act 1925, s 136.

[58] See, for example, *Holt* v *Heatherfield Trust* [1942] 2 KB 1.

[59] *Brice* v *Bannister* (1878) 3 QBD 569.

[60] *Re McArdle* [1951] 1 Ch 669.

had jurisdiction over the matter. The Judicature Acts of 1873 and 1875 overcame this problem by amalgamating the courts of law and equity into one Supreme Court of Judicature. A plaintiff could initiate proceedings in one court and seek equitable and legal relief depending on the nature of his case. The Judicature Act,[61] and now section 136 of the Law of Property Act 1925, allows the assignee of a chose in action to sue in his own name subject to certain conditions. It must be stressed that the statutory rule on assignment does not change in any way the equitable rules relating to assignment. It lays down the requirements, which, if satisfied, will allow the assignee to sue in his own name. Failure to comply with the statutory principles will deny any right to sue in the assignee's own name, and the assignee will have to rely on the equitable principle discussed above: that is, to compel the assignor to sue the debtor in law. Section 136 of the Act requires that an assignment of a legal chose in action will be effective in law if it is absolute, in writing, and notice of such assignment is given to the debtor.

Whether the assignment of a chose in action is one in equity or one under statute, the general rule is that it takes place subject to equities existing at the time of notice to the debtor. What does this mean? The basic idea, although the rules are very complex indeed, is that the debtor must not be prejudiced by the assignment to the assignee. The debtor, for example, can plead all defences that he could have pleaded against the assignor. In simple terms, the assignee cannot defeat any claims of the debtor which naturally flow from the debt and which would have succeeded against the assignor. A good example of the 'subject to equities' rule is illustrated in *Roxburghe* v *Cox*,[62] where an army officer, Ker, assigned to the Duke of Roxburghe the money he would receive from the sale of his army commission. The money, £3000, was paid on 6 December to the credit of his account with Messrs Cox. On 6 December Ker's account had been overdrawn to the amount of £647. Notice of the assignment was given to Messrs Cox on 19 December. It was held that Messrs Cox could set-off the amount of £647 against the right of the Duke to £3000.

Documentary intangibles

The rules relating to the transfer of documentary intangibles are different from those relating to pure intangibles. Documentary intangibles include negotiable instruments such as bills of exchange, cheques and promissory notes; also included are share certificates and other commercial papers such as bills of lading.[63] The primary thing to note about documentary intangibles

[61] Judicature Act 1873, s 25(6).

[62] (1881) 17 Ch D 520.

[63] A bill of lading is a document used in international sales involving sea transportation. The main function of a bill of lading is that it acts as a receipt for goods shipped, evidence of the contract of carriage between the shipper and carrier, and also as a document of title. In normal circumstances the delivery of the bill of lading gives the transferee of the bill the right to demand goods delivered at a particular port. It is the delivery of the bill by the seller to the buyer which transfers the rights to the ultimate goods that form the subject-matter of the international sale.

is that the transfer of rights therein can only be done through the medium of the document in question. The basic common law principle is that the transfer of rights in a document can only be achieved through delivery of the document accompanied by indorsement thereof. Statutory provisions, which lay out the procedure in which transfer should take place, supplement the common law. For example, in the case of shares in a company, transfer can only take place when such transfer of a share certificate is forwarded to the company's registrar, followed by registration on the company's register.[64]

The best example of a documentary intangible is a bill of exchange. A bill of exchange is also referred to as a negotiable instrument, which means that it is a document which is transferable by delivery and indorsement. There is no need for a separate instrument for assignment of the rights created in the document.[65] A bill of exchange is defined as an 'unconditional order in writing, addressed by one person to another, requiring the person to whom it is addressed to pay on demand ... a sum of money...'.[66] In essence, a bill of exchange represents an instruction by a drawer of the bill to a drawee to pay to the bearer of the bill a certain sum of money. Bills of exchange were and continue to be used in commerce as a means of payment for goods purchased. Commercial practice requires documents instead of cash money in circumstances where it would be both impracticable and dangerous to pay in cash. Thus, what is required is a document that can be easily transferred and one which can allow the transferee of the document to enforce the obligation created in the document in his own name. Ever since the nineteenth century the custom has been that the delivery of the document accompanied by indorsement was sufficient to transfer the rights therein, even without notice to the party liable on the document (for example, the drawee, which was usually a bank). The technical rules relating to the transfer of rights in bills of exchange are found in the Bills of Exchange Act 1882. The rules depend on whether the bill in question is a bearer bill or an order bill. An order bill of exchange is one which specifies the name to whom the drawee must pay. In such case the transfer of the rights in the bill can only happen if delivery is accompanied with indorsement.[67] Indorsement involves signature of the indorser on the back of the bill. A bearer bill is one which does not have a specified person as the bearer. Transfer of the rights in the bill can take place by simple delivery of the document.[68]

---

[64] Stock Transfer Act 1963.

[65] For an excellent introduction to negotiable instruments, see *Richardson's Guide to Negotiable Instruments* (8th edn, 1991).

[66] Bills of Exchange Act 1882, s 3(1).

[67] *Ibid*, s 31(3).

[68] *Ibid*, s 33(2). For a more detailed summary of the rules relating to transfer of bills of exchange, see L. Sealy and R. Hooley, *Texts and Materials in Commercial Law* (1994) at pp 491–500.

DERIVATIVE ACQUISITION OF PROPERTY INTERESTS IN EQUITY

So far the discussion has centred on the derivative acquisition of property rights in law. This is, however, an incomplete picture of the way in which property rights are acquired. In Chapter 4 it was seen that property rights are capable of existing both in law and in equity. The dual system of law and equity allows persons to acquire rights in law and equity. In the same way in which property rights can be both created and transferred in law, they can also be created and transferred in equity. Any attempt to deal with factual problems relating to the acquisition of property rights requires an appreciation of the equitable rules relating to acquisition. The reason for this stems from the very fact that the equitable rules relating to acquisition are not completely divorced from the common law and statutory rules. The difference in many cases is one of form and substance. Whereas common law pays more attention to questions of form, equity looks to the substance and inner intentions of the parties involved in creating and transferring property rights. Where the inner intent can be found and, for matters of substance, the parties have done what they intended to do, then, despite matters of form, equity seeks to give effect to the parties' intentions by recognising that the rights have been created or transferred in equity. Therefore, if property rights fail to be created or transferred at law for reasons relating to form, it is not the end of the matter in solving factual problems. Defective transactions may be recognised in equity, although, of course, the relative strength of equitable rights (as seen in Chapter 4) will be different from legal rights. The matter is no better explained than by two commentators who write (in the context of land) that 'equitable entitlements in land have evolved from equity's historic thematic concerns with substance rather than form, with the inner reality of intent rather than the external manifestations of conduct, and above all with the priority of conscience-driven obligation over strict legal entitlement.'[69]

Creation of equitable property rights

Equitable property rights may be created in a number of ways. The central theme here is equity's historic concerns about unconscionable conduct and the need to look at the substance of property transactions rather than their form. In one case Romilly MR explained that 'courts of equity make a distinction between that which is a matter of substance and that which is a matter of form; and if it finds by insisting on the form, the substance will be defeated, it holds it inequitable to allow a person to insist on form, and

---

[69] K. Gray and S.F. Gray, *Land Law* (1999) at p 169.

thereby defeat the substance.'[70] The equitable maxims originating from the practice and procedure of the Court of Chancery enable property rights to be created in equity in a host of different situations. Some of these maxims have already been mentioned in Chapter 4; however, the following can be mentioned here. In the creation of equitable rights of property, the following maxims play an important role: equity sees that as done which ought to be done; equity looks to the intent rather than the form; equity will not suffer a wrong to be without a remedy; and equity follows the law. Given the flexibility of equity in the creation of property rights, it would be impossible to provide a complete commentary here; however, some of the more important methods of creation are examined to illustrate equitable intervention.

Declaration of trust

It is perhaps most appropriate to use the example of a trust as the means by which an equitable property right can be created. The trust formed the basis of the origins of the early Court of Chancery and it best explains the concerns of equity over matters of conscience and substance. An owner of property can declare a trust in one of two ways: first, he may simply declare that he holds the property as trustee for another; or second, he may transfer the subject-matter of the trust to different trustees to hold for the benefit of the beneficiary. If a trust has been effectively declared, the beneficiary acquires an equitable interest in the subject-matter of the trust property. The trustee merely holds the legal title for the beneficiary. Equity will recognise the interest of the beneficiary on the basis of intention, substance and conscience. Intention plays a paramount role in the enforcement of trusts; equity seeks to give effect to the intentions of the person creating the trust rather than looking at the matter of form and the fact that the owner at law is the trustee. As regards substance, it is the beneficiary that has been given the real enjoyment in the property; equity treats the title of the trustee as being merely nominal. As regards conscience, equity will compel the trustee to hold for the beneficiary on the grounds that it would be unconscionable for him to deny the rights of the beneficiary, which he has clearly accepted as being paramount.[71]

There are generally no formalities required for the creation or declaration of trusts. Equity's main concern relates to intention: a trust will only be recognised as having been declared if there is sufficient intention to declare such a trust. It is quite possible to create a trust of personalty without any

---

[70] *Parkin* v *Thorold* (1852) 16 Beav 59 at 66.
[71] The essence of conscience as being at the heart of the enforcement of a trust has been explained recently by Lord Browne-Wilkinson in *Westdeutsche Landesbank Girozentrale* v *Islington London Borough Council* [1996] 2 All ER 961 at 988.

writing providing that there is a sufficient intention to create a trust.[72] In so far as trusts of land are concerned, they must be evidenced in writing. Section 53(1)(b) of the Law of Property Act 1925 provides that: 'A declaration of trust respecting any interest therein must be manifested and proved by some writing signed by some person who is able to declare such trust or by his will.' This section has its origins in the Statute of Frauds 1677 and performs an evidentiary function, without which it would become very difficult in the event of disputes to establish the intentions of persons creating trusts of land. This section does not require that the trust of land be in writing; instead the requirement is merely evidential, so that the trust has to be manifested in writing. Failure to comply with section 53(1)(b) does not render the attempted declaration of trust as void, but makes it unenforceable. To hold the trust as being void for failure to comply with the section would open the door for trustees to deny the trust in cases where the section had not been complied with and to take the property themselves. Since equity will not allow a statute to be used as an instrument for fraud, other evidence can be admitted to show the existence of the trust.[73]

The intention to create a trust may not be expressly declared; instead the court may declare that a trust has arisen in certain factual situations. In Chapter 7 it was seen that trusts may be imputed by law in various situations. Imputed trusts are found by the courts in respect of the conduct of parties in certain property transactions. Such trusts are created by law and as such do not depend on any formality in so far as their creation is concerned.

Specifically enforceable contracts to convey property

Where parties to a property transaction enter into an agreement to transfer or create a legal property right in another person, the legal property right is only transferred when the contract has been completed. For example, an agreement to transfer the legal ownership in land to another person will only be complete when the ownership has been transferred through a deed of conveyance, or, in the case of a registered title to land, by registration. Until the contract has been completed through compliance with all the necessary legal formalities, the purchaser or other transferee of a legal right does not acquire any legal rights in the subject-matter of the contract. However, the position of a purchaser is rather different in equity. A fundamental maxim of equity is that 'equity sees that as done which ought to be done'. This maxim has its roots in the fact that equity looks to matters of substance rather than form,

---

[72] It is not imperative that the person declaring the trust uses words such as 'trust' but he must do something or use words which are designed to put the trustee under an obligation to recognise the beneficial interest in the subject-matter of the trust property as belonging to the beneficiary: see *Re Kayford Ltd* [1975] 1 WLR 282, *per* Megarry J at 607.

[73] *Rochefoucald v Boustead* [1897] 1 Ch 196.

so that where a contract has been entered into, equity assumes that it will be completed and in the meantime vests in the promisee an equitable interest equivalent to the legal interest which the promisor has promised to transfer or create. The basis of giving the promisee an equitable interest is that equity can compel the performance of contract with the remedy of specific performance. The remedy of specific performance plays an integral part in the recognition that the promisee has an equitable interest in the subject-matter of the contract. The example of an estate contract will illustrate the operation of the principle a little more clearly. A freehold owner of land can only transfer his ownership by sale with the use of a contract and then a deed of conveyance. When the contract is made, and subject to payment of the purchase price, equity intervenes and recognises that the vendor has an equitable estate in the land, which will become merged with the legal estate when the contract has been completed.[74] Given that equity treats that as done which ought to be done, and the fact that land is unique, damages for breach of contract are usually inadequate and the remedy of specific performance is more appropriate and practical in the circumstances. An estate contract is an equitable interest in the land, protected and enforced in the same way as other equitable interests in land.

The operation of the maxim that equity sees that as done which ought to be done, and the availability of the remedy of specific performance, applies in a number of situations where there is an agreement to transfer or create a right in another person. The maxim applies to agreements for the transfer and creation of leasehold interests in land[75] and mortgages of land, as well as easements. Such agreements must, however, comply with the formal requirements of section 2 of the Law of Property (Miscellaneous Provisions) Act 1989. This section requires the agreement to be in writing, signed by both parties and incorporate all the terms agreed. It is only if this section has been complied with that equity can award the remedy of specific performance. Although predominantly operating in the field of real property rights, it has scope for the recognition of equitable interests in personal property where the agreement to convey a personal property interest is capable of being superficially performed.[76]

---

[74] *Lysaght* v *Edwards* (1876) 2 Ch D 499. The recognition of an equitable estate before completion is not limited to contracts to convey, but can extend to gratuitous transfers. For example, in *Mascall* v *Mascall* (1985) 49 P & CR 119 a father executed a voluntary transfer of a house to his son and handed over the land certificate. After the transfer had been sent to the Inland Revenue for stamping, and returned, the father sought a declaration that the transfer was ineffective. The court held that the gift was complete despite the fact that the land certificate had not been sent to the Land Registry. The father had done everything in his power to effect the gift and the fact that registration had not taken place was immaterial in the eyes of equity. Applying the maxim that equity treats that as done which ought to be done, it followed that registration would follow as a matter of form.

[75] *Parker* v *Taswell* (1858) 2 De G & J 559.

[76] See *Oughtred* v *IRC* [1960] AC 206, where an agreement to convey shares in a private company was held to be specifically enforceable.

Defective transfer of legal interests

A rather different situation to an agreement to convey a legal interest in property is that of a defective transfer of a legal interest. Sometimes a transfer remains defective for reasons of substantive registration. For example, in the case of a registered title to land, transfer of legal ownership will only be effective when the transferee is registered as proprietor of the freehold title. Until this is done, the transferor remains the registered proprietor. The same principle applies to other rights in land such as leases, the grant of an easement, and the creation and transfer of a registered charge (mortgage).[77] Dispositions or creation of such rights which remain unregistered do not convey any legal estate or interest to the transferee; instead the transferee takes the estate or interest in equity alone.[78]

Transfer of equitable interests

Equitable proprietary rights are regarded as choses in action on the grounds that they are rights *in personam*. An equitable right is enforced *in personam*, which means that a person vested with an equitable right can enforce the right by asking the court to compel the person against whom the right is enforceable to perform the obligation he has agreed to carry out. In relation to the examples discussed, it can be seen that the person who has been granted an equitable right has the right to enforce it against specific persons. For example, a beneficiary can compel the trustee to carry out the terms of the trust; a person vested with an estate contract can compel the legal owner who has promised to convey the legal title to him to convey such title through specific performance. The fact that equitable rights do not attach to the 'thing' in question, but rather individuals, means that all that an equitable property right holder has is a right of action against a person or a series of persons. The transfer of equitable rights does not involve delivery or deeds; rather it involves a transfer of the right of action.

Transfers of equitable interests are governed by section 53(1)(c) of the Law of Property Act 1925. This section requires that dispositions of equitable interests be in writing and signed by the person disposing of the equitable interest. Failure to comply with this section renders the disposition void.[79] The function behind this section is to prevent hidden oral transactions in

---

[77] Land Registration Act 1925, ss 18, 21, 33 and 34.

[78] Land Registration Act 1925, ss 19, 22 and 101. Such defective dispositions take effect as minor interests in registered land and as such will fail to bind third parties dealing with the legal title if not registered. However, where a transferee under a defective transfer is in actual occupation of the land, the interest is an overriding one under s 70(1)(g) of the Land Registration Act 1925 and will automatically bind third parties dealing with the legal title to the land.

[79] *Vandervell v IRC* [1967] 2 AC 291.

equitable interests. For example, an equitable owner has no legal title to convey to another, and even where he is in possession of land, that possession is not one which is derived from legal ownership. If he wants to transfer his interest to another, there is nothing in the form of title or possession that he can grant in the transferee. In this context, the need for writing to transfer his equitable interest is of paramount importance. The writing acts in a title way; in other words, passing his equitable title to another. For example, in the case of a trust, a beneficiary has nothing by way of possession or title to give to a transferee of the equitable interest in the trust. Compliance with section 53(1)(c), however, leaves no room for doubt as to who is the beneficiary of the trust and to whom the trustees must convey trust property. The caselaw surrounding section 53(1)(c) has been most active in the context of trusts and attempts by beneficiaries under trusts to dispose of their equitable interests for taxation purposes.[80] Such matters are more specific and dealt with more adequately in the traditional texts on trust law.[81]

TESTAMENTARY DISPOSITIONS AND QUASI-TESTAMENTARY DISPOSITIONS

Wills and intestacy

The preceding discussion on derivative transfer and acquisition has examined most of the concepts in the context of *inter vivos* transfers, that is, transfers taking place during the lifetime of the transferor. Derivative transfer and acquisition can, of course, occur when a person leaves property to others after his death. These are referred to as testamentary transfers or dispositions. Testamentary transfers of property can arise in one of two ways. First, where a person dies without having made a will, his property devolves to others by way of statute in the form of the intestacy rules. Second, where a person dies having made a will during his lifetime, the devolution of his property is governed by the will which he has executed.

A person who dies without having made a will is said to have died intestate. The rules governing the devolution of his property are to be found in the Administration of Estates Act 1925.[82] Once the debts and expenses of administering the estate are met, the remaining estate[83] is available for

---

[80] See *Grey* v *IRC* [1960] AC 1; *Vandervell* v *IRC* [1967] 2 AC 291; *Oughtred* v *IRC* [1960] AC 206; *Re Vandervell's Trust No 2* [1974] Ch 269.

[81] See Hanbury and Martin, *Modern Equity* (15th edn, 1997) at pp 78–89.

[82] This Act has been amended by the Intestates' Estates Act 1952, the Family Provision Act 1966, the Family Law Reform Act 1969, the Administration of Justice Act 1977 and the Family Provision (Intestate Succession) Order 1987.

[83] The use of the word 'estate' here is used to describe the total sum of assets and liabilities of the deceased. It is not used in the technical sense of denoting an estate in land.

distribution amongst the relatives of the deceased. The rules relating to beneficial entitlement on intestacy are designed to reflect the wishes of the average testator.[84] The word testator is used to describe a person who makes a will. The intestacy rules attempt to deal with three common situations which may arise after the death of a person: first, where the deceased leaves behind a spouse without children, in which case the spouse takes all; second, where the deceased leaves behind a spouse with children, in which case, where the estate is worth more than £75,000, the property is divided amongst the spouse and the children; finally, where the deceased leaves behind no spouse or children, in which case the estate is given to near relatives.[85]

If property is to be left to designated people after death the transferor needs to make a valid will. A person making a will is described as a testator. The effect of a will is to designate the persons to whom the property of the testator should vest after his death. The will itself does not provide the mechanism of transfer; it merely provides evidence of the testator's intentions. The transfer of the property occurs through the vesting of the property in the personal representatives of the deceased. A will is to be distinguished from an *inter vivos* gift as regards both the time it takes effect and the formalities required. With respect to time, an *inter vivos* gift usually takes effect forthwith, whereas a gift in a will only takes place on the death of the donor. With regard to formalities, *inter vivos* gifts usually require the use of deeds – for example, a gift of land, and then followed by registration. A will, on the other hand, need only meet the requirement of formality laid down in section 9 of the Wills Act 1837.[86] Although a will need not be in any particular legal language or form, section 9 requires a will to be in writing, signed by the testator and witnessed. The essence of a will is that it is only a declaration of the intentions of the testator; it is sometimes simply said that a will is ambulatory in nature. The consequence of this is that a person making a will is perfectly free to deal with his property after making the will and, if he or she should so desire, to transfer the property during his or her lifetime to persons other than those identified in the will. From the viewpoint of the persons entitled in the will, called legatees under the will, they acquire no interest in the property.[87] It is only when the personal representatives of the deceased distribute the property to the intended beneficiaries that they acquire any proprietary rights in the deceased's estate. It may, however, be the case that the liabilities of the deceased's estate are so large that the assets are used to meet those liabilities, in which case many dispositive parts of the will become fruitless.

---

[84] See Mellows, *The Law of Succession* (5th edn, 1993) at p 173.

[85] It is not in the ambit of this book to examine the rules of intestacy in depth; however, an excellent account of these rules can be found in Mellows' text, *op cit*.

[86] As amended by the Administration of Justice Act 1982, s. 17.

[87] *Commissioner of Stamp Duties* v *Livingstone* [1965] AC 694.

Whilst rules relating to intestacy and wills deal with the persons who become entitled to property after the death of a person, the actual manner in which transfer of property to the intended beneficiaries occurs is through personal representatives of the deceased. Property vests in personal representatives of the deceased who are obliged to transfer that part of the estate which is left after payment of debts and expenses to the intended beneficiaries. A personal representative is a term that includes executors and administrators. In making a will the testator will appoint an executor to distribute his property after his death. In the case of a person who has died intestate, a person who is interested in the estate being administered must apply to the court for what is known as 'letters of administration' appointing an administrator. The duties of the administrator are essentially the same as those of executors. All the property of the deceased vests in the personal representatives.[88] It is only after the property has vested in the personal representatives that they are able to transfer it to the intended beneficiaries. All the property of the deceased is held upon a statutory trust for sale,[89] which means that land can be sold to meet the liabilities of the deceased. Where property is left, which is not required for liabilities, the personal representatives can then transfer to the beneficiaries. In the case of land it should be noted that there is no need for a deed to transfer the land to the beneficiaries; all that is required is a written assent.[90]

Donatio mortis causa

A form of quasi-testamentary transfer of property is recognised in law and has been described as a *donatio mortis causa*. It is a gift which has been described by Buckley LJ

> '... to be of an amphibious nature, being a gift which is neither entirely *inter vivos* in nature nor testamentary. It is an act *inter vivos* by which the donee is to have the absolute title to the subject of the gift not at once but if the donor dies. If the donor dies the title becomes absolute and not under but as against his executor. In order to make the gift valid it must be made so as to take effect on the donor's death.'[91]

A *donatio mortis causa* is a gift that is made in contemplation of death; it is a gift subject to a condition precedent. The condition precedent is the death of the donor. Once the donor dies the gift is absolute and the donee of the gift can enforce his or her right to the subject-matter of the gift against everyone,

---

[88] Administration of Estates Act 1925, ss 1(1) and 3(1).
[89] *Ibid,* s 33(1).
[90] *Ibid,* s 36(1).
[91] *Re Beaumont* [1902] 1 Ch 889 at 892.

including the personal representatives of the donor. In order to understand a *donatio mortis causa* we can examine the following scenario. A is lying on his deathbed suffering from a serious illness. A may have made a will during his lifetime although he need not have done so. A is visited by B who looks after A during the course of A's illness. A may give to B a gold watch, a bank deposit account book and a key to a box. A informs B that he is to have these things after his death. If A dies having made a will in which he leaves all of his property to C, is B entitled to any of the things which A gave to him during the time A was alive, or is C entitled to the whole of the estate by virtue of the will? Certainly, one can say that the gold watch belongs to B since all that is needed for transfer of the title to the watch is delivery to B during A's lifetime. More problematic are the deposit account book and the keys to a box. Here there appears to be incomplete delivery of the subject-matter of the gift, and as such C seems to have a better claim to the bank account and the box which is found in A's possessions. Despite this, the principle of *donatio mortis causa* allows B to claim the monies in the bank account along with the box and its contents. The rule operates to perfect an imperfect gift. In this sense one can see the problems of accommodating a *donatio mortis causa* as an *inter vivos* or a testamentary transfer of property. *Donatio mortis causa* provides a very informal way in which property is acquired.

The requirements for establishing a valid *donatio mortis causa* were laid down by Lord Russell CJ in *Cain v Moon*.[92] First, the gift must be made in contemplation of death, although it need not necessarily be in expectation of death. Common examples include a serious illness and embarking upon a hazardous journey.[93] Second, the subject-matter of the gift must be delivered to the donee. In the case of chattels this requires delivery of possession and it is clear that delivery of symbolic possession will suffice.[94] As concerns intangibles such as bank deposit accounts or cheques payable to the donor, it is, given the very circumstances in which the gift is made, difficult to transfer rights in a chose in action. The rule here is that the transfer of the document representing the thing in question will be sufficient to allow the donee to claim the particular chose in action.[95] It is now also clear that delivery of title deeds to the donee is sufficient to effect a *donatio mortis causa* of land.[96] Finally, the gift must have been made conditional upon the donor's death and intended to revert back to him should he recover.

---

[92] [1896] 2 QB 283.
[93] A *donatio mortis causa* remains valid if the donor dies from a cause different from the one originally contemplated: see *Wilkes v Allington* [1931] 2 Ch 104.
[94] For example, delivery of keys to a box: see *Re Wasserberg* [1915] 1 Ch 195.
[95] See *Birch v Treasury Solicitor* [1951] Ch 298, *Darlow v Sparks* [1938] 2 All ER 235 and *Re Mead* (1880) 15 Ch D 651.
[96] *Sen v Headley* [1991] Ch 425.

ACQUISITION AND THE FUNCTION OF FORMALITY RULES

One of the most striking aspects of property law, albeit most notably in the context of real property law, is the compliance with formalities in the creation and transfer of proprietary rights. By formalities it is meant the insistence on compliance with form in order to give legal validity to a particular property right, which is either being transferred or is being created out of a larger proprietary right such as ownership. In this respect one commentator defines formality as '… a requirement that matters of substance must be put in a particular form in order to have a specified legal effect.'[97] The insistence on formalities in property law is said to be in contrast to other areas of the common law, such as contract which has relatively fewer formality requirements.[98]

In the context of real property, creation and transfer of rights in most cases will only be effective provided there is a contract, a deed, which is then followed by registration. For example, a transfer of ownership in land by way of sale requires a contract, a deed and registration. In the context of personal property transfers, a consensual transfer requires a contract of sale. In the absence of a sale, a gratuitous transfer requires a deed where no delivery of the subject-matter of the gift has taken place. The question is, why does property law impose such a heavy insistence on formality? The answer to this question has not, until relatively recently, attracted the same degree of attention as the question of the nature and application of particular formalities rules to a particular type of property transaction.[99]

In attempting to address the question of the function of formality rules in property law it is important to understand the context in which such formality rules have arisen. For example, the traditional justifications for formality rules in the context of real property are said to be based on two principal reasons.[100] In the first place, formalities are said to protect original parties

---

[97] P. Critchley, 'Taking Formalities Seriously' in Bright and Dewar (eds), *Land Law: Themes and Perspectives* (1998) at p 508.

[98] P. Critchley, *ibid*, at p 509. However, this view needs to be taken cautiously since the definition of formality is said to be wide enough to include the substantive requirements for contract formation as formality. Friedmann argues that the rules that acceptance must match the terms of the offer, and the requirement of 'definiteness' may all operate as formalities: see 'Law Rules and the Interpretation of Written Documents' (1964–65) 59 Mw UL Rev 751 at pp 775–776.

[99] P. Critchley, *op cit*, provides an excellent account of the function of formality rules in property law. Critchley's account of the function of formality rules draws upon themes developed by jurists in the United States: see in particular, L. Fuller, 'Consideration and Form' (1941) Col LR 799, J. Perillo, 'The Statute of Frauds in the Light of the Functions and Disfunctions of Form' (1974) 43 Fordham LR 39, and J. Baron, 'Gifts, Bargain and Form' (1988–89) 64 Id LJ 155.

[100] See G. Battersby, 'Informal Transactions in Land, Estoppel and Registration' (1995) 58 MLR 637 at pp 637–638.

making a disposition of ownership or an interest in land. Unlike personal property, real property has the characteristic of durability, land is said to be permanent and thus rights created therein have a degree of permanence and stability.[101] In this respect a property transaction involving land is treated as more important than any other type of property transaction. The insistence on written documents such as contracts and a deed of conveyance protects the original parties from ill-thought transactions that they may regret later on. The second reason for formality rules in real property law is that they protect third parties. An efficient system of conveyancing is dependent on the ability of third parties to establish exactly what they are purchasing, what interests already exist in the land and how that land is restricted in its use in the future. The insistence on writing and registration seeks to promote this end of conveyancing.

Formalities, however, perform a wider set of functions than the specific functions considered above. Moreover, they are not restricted to property transactions involving land, but they also extend to personal property transactions such as those involving delivery and deed. Fuller identifies three main functions performed by legal formalities.[102] The first is described as the evidentiary function. The insistence on writing, attestation and so forth seeks to provide evidence in the event of controversy. The extent for controversy is much more acute in the case of property rights, which have a tendency of lasting for a long period of time. This is most notable in the context of land transactions. The Statute of Frauds 1677 – some of the fundamental principles of which are now to be found in the Law of Property Act 1925 – provides the best example of the evidentiary function of formality rules. Section 7 of the Statute of Frauds 1677[103] requires all trusts of land to be manifested and proved in some writing. From an evidential point of view this section performs three main functions.[104] First, writing and signature seek to safeguard against the possibility that the purported declaration of trust of land was a fabrication. Second, writing and signature seek to provide evidence that the intended property transaction was indeed a trust of land and nothing else. Finally, the aspect of writing provides the trustees, beneficiaries and, in the event of a dispute, the courts with concrete evidence of the terms of the intended trust of land. Other examples of the evidentiary function carried out by formalities include deeds of a gift and wills.

Fuller refers to the second function performed by formalities rules as the 'cautionary' function. Fuller explains that the cautionary function acts as a

---

[101] See Lawson and Rudden, *The Law of Property* (2nd edn, 1982) at pp 22–25.

[102] *Op cit*, at p 800.

[103] See now s 53(1)(b) of the Law of Property Act 1925.

[104] See T.G. Youdan, 'Formalities for Trusts of Land and the Doctrine in *Rochefoucald* v *Boustead*' (1984) 43 CLR 306 at p 315.

check against irrational and inconsiderate action.[105] Where a formality requires the aid of legal advice and assistance – for example, in the process of a conveyance of land – such advice in the context of formalities will ensure that the parties are warned of the consequences of their actions. Another good example of a formality, which performed the cautionary function, was the use of a seal, that is, the affixing of a wax wafer to a legal document. Although the use of a seal is no longer important to give a deed the status of a deed, the requirement of writing and attestation in the contest of wills is a clear example of the cautionary function performed by those formalities.

The final function performed by formality rules has been explained by Fuller as the 'channelling function'. This simply means that formalities have the function of channelling the intentions of parties in a particular transaction towards a particular legal effect. In this respect, historically a seal performed this function very effectively. The imposition of the seal on a document sought to give legal validity to the document in question. Furthermore, in the case of transfer of rights in documentary intangibles such as negotiable instruments, the indorsement of such documents followed by delivery allows rights to be legally transferred to the transferee. The formality of indorsement followed by delivery is a good example of the channelling function since compliance with such formality gives effect to enforceability in the hands of the transferee.

The functions of formality rules discussed above are not exhaustive; more recently other theorists have continued to add to the functions identified by Fuller. Perillo has identified two important functions performed by formality rules.[106] He describes them as the 'clarifying function' and 'publicity function'. Where a formality consists of writing – for example, as in the case of transfer and creation of many interests in land – the formality of writing seeks to influence the nature of the interest being transferred or created. For example, in the contract stage of a sale of land the formality of a written contract requires that all the terms and conditions are reduced in writing.[107] This clearly clarifies what interest is being sold, what its nature is and how it can be dealt with. Such matters are not achieved in mere oral discussions that may have taken place between the parties to the transaction. In respect of the publicity function, this is designed to protect third parties who may come to deal with the property that has been the subject-matter of a transaction. By far the most important formality performing this function is that relating to registration. In the context of land, creation and transfer of interests in land are not complete until registration in the land register. Publicising the creation and transfer of

---

[105] *Op cit*, at p 800.
[106] *Op cit*, at pp 57–60.
[107] Law of Property (Miscellaneous) Provisions Act 1989, s 2.

such rights in the register will protect third parties – for example, a mort-gagee, who will be able to see exactly what title he is giving money by way of mortgage on. Another dimension to this is that, where there is no publicity – for example, where an interest created such as a mortgage has not been regis-tered – a third party (for example, a subsequent mortgagee) need not be concerned that he is bound by the prior unregistered mortgage.

FREEDOM OF DISPOSITION AND PUBLIC POLICY

Like the law of contract, property law works on the premise that there is pri-vate autonomy in property transactions. This simply means that the law views private individuals as having the power to effect changes in their legal relations. The power to effect changes in one's legal relations in respect of things is necessarily a fundamental incident of having property. It will be recalled from Chapter 1, and from Hohfeld's analytical scheme of rights, that one of the consequences of having a property right is that the holder of that right has a power to effect changes in the legal relationship constituted between himself and the thing in which he has a proprietary right. This aspect of private autonomy necessarily imports a sense of freedom of disposi-tion in property law. I am able to transfer my things to anyone I want to, and in any manner I may wish to do so. Indeed, in relation to transfers after my death by virtue of a will, one of the fundamental axioms of testamentary law is freedom of testamentary disposition.[108] The very fact that individuals have private autonomy in the transfer of things and rights therein to others is cru-cial to an efficient system of property distribution. In this respect Moffat writes: '... if in a pure liberal market society the market is to carry out its function of allocation of resources amongst various uses, property must be freely alienable. This seems to require a system of property law designed to sustain freedom of disposition.'[109]

Despite this principle of private autonomy in property law, the state plays a role in 'regulating' transfer of property rights. There is a strong public interest in the private acts of individuals who attempt to dispose of their property to others. It may be questioned as to why there is such a public interest in private acts dealing with acquisition and transfer of property rights. On a theoretical level of analysis, the state interest in private property transactions may be justified by the desire to achieve wider social and eco-nomic goals. Property is an important means of liberty and survival; without any property there is no liberty or security. Property is also a fundamental vehicle through which commerce and economic wellbeing is generated. The

---

[108] See J. Finch, L. Hayes, *et al*, *Wills, Inheritance and Families* (1996) at p 21.
[109] G. Moffat, *Trust Law: Text and Materials* (1994) at p 198.

state therefore has a strong interest in seeing that property is distributed in a manner that maintains liberty and security but at the same time generating economic wellbeing. The level of interest and consequential interference with the private acts of transfer and acquisition depend on the types of distributive justice the state wishes to achieve. In this respect, political theorists have constantly argued in one form or another for state interference in the liberty of individuals to deal with property distribution.[110]

Leaving broader political issues to one side, the law of property does in many ways restrict certain transfers of property. Certain transfers of property rights are said to be void or voidable. The reason given for striking down certain transfers of property is that such transfers are contrary to public policy. Economists have long argued that property should have the characteristics of transferability since it is only through this characteristic that resources can be shifted from a less productive use to a more productive one.[111] However, Moffat explains that within a liberal property system one encounters a basic paradox.[112] Moffat explains this paradox by stating: '… if freedom of disposition conferred upon a person disposing of property means that he or she can regulate the circumstances in which, and the extent to which, the recipients can deal with the property, the recipients do not have freedom of disposition. In this sense unrestricted freedom of disposition cannot logically be permitted and fully maintained'.[113] The classic example of how freedom of disposition may allow an individual to destroy future freedom of disposition is where property is given to another with an excessive delay in vesting of the interest therein. It is quite possible to make a gift to another, or to transfer property to another by other means which do not immediately vest the property in the hands of the transferee but make it subject to a time restriction. For example, an individual can purport to make a gift of land today but in the document purporting to make the gift can state that the donee is not entitled to the land until he attains a specified age or meets some other contingency. In such a case he has made a gift but it is said to be subject to a condition precedent. Such a gift can only exist through the medium of a trust since trustees will have to administer the property until the contingency is met. One thing which is striking from this example is that, if it takes a considerably long time for the contingency to be met, the land subject to the gift is not freely alienable; it is in fact tied up and taken out of circulation.

In order to deal with the problem with excessive delay in vesting (or remoteness of vesting) and inalienability, the common law has long established a rule against remoteness of vesting. The rule is described as the 'rule

---

[110] See R. Nozick, *Anarchy, State and Utopia* (1974) and J. Rawls, *A Theory of Justice* (1972).
[111] See R. Posner, *The Economic Analysis of Law* (1972) at pp 10–13.
[112] *Op cit*, at p 198.
[113] *Ibid*.

against perpetuities'. It found its origins in social and economic conditions quite different from the ones in which it operates today. Historically, the rule was designed to keep future interests in land within reasonable limits where settlors of land attempted to provide for successive generations.[114] The modern rule has been explained in the following manner: 'a limitation of any interest in any property, real or personal, is void if by any possibility it might become vested after the perpetuity period has expired. The perpetuity period consists of a life or lives in being at the time of the gift, together with a further period of 21 years...'.[115]

The basic effect of the perpetuity rule is that property must vest within the perpetuity period, which is a life in being plus 21 years. If property does not so vest within this period the gift is void. The common law rule was modified by statute in the form of the Perpetuities and Accumulations Act 1964, which allows a settlor to incorporate in the document purporting to give effect to a future interest, usually a trust instrument, and a maximum statutory period of 80 years. Related to the perpetuity rule is the 'rule against inalienation'. This rule deals with a similar problem concerning the tying up of resources indefinitely. In the process of distributing property to others a person can make a disposition such as 'fifty thousand pounds to be invested forever for the upkeep of my horses'. This is generally described as a non-charitable perpetual trust. One can see the immediate problem with this: £50,000 is invested indefinitely and, as such, is inalienable. The rule against inalienation states that the duration of such a trust should not exceed more than a life in being plus 21 years.

The perpetuity rules represent one of many types of rules that seek to interfere with freedom of disposition and it is clear that there are sound policy reasons behind the rule. Sometimes freedom of disposition is interfered with simply on the grounds that the intended transfer, whether consensual or gratuitous, has taken place simply to avoid a legal consequence. In this respect, the transfer is seen as one that cannot really be regarded as a natural transfer, but as one which seeks to interfere with the due process of particular sets of legal principles. It is trite law that a creditor can demand payment from his debtor out of the debtor's property. Where the debtor's property is insufficient to pay all his debts, the debtor is insolvent and his creditors will remain unpaid. In the case of an insolvent person, better described as a bankrupt, the legal rules and principles of bankruptcy seek to provide a fair distribution of the bankrupt's property to his creditors. Against this background, a person who is about to start a risky business and foresees financial

---

[114] See A. Simpson, *A History of the Land Law* (2nd edn, 1986). It is not intended here to discuss the rule in the context of land since it has little contemporary significance.

[115] Megarry and Thompson, *Megarry's Manual of the Law of Real Property* (7th edn, 1993) at p 183.

danger is often tempted to put his existing property out of reach of potential creditors. Such property can be transferred to other members of his family or can be settled in other jurisdictions. It is clear that such transfers of property do not represent normal transfers but are ones which are specifically designed to disturb justified legal consequences.

The common law has long recognised that any such attempts to keep property away from creditors should be disallowed.[116] The modern rules are to be found in the Insolvency Act 1986. Section 423 of the Insolvency Act allows the court to set aside transactions at an undervalue when such transactions were specifically entered into for the purpose of putting assets beyond the reach of creditors.[117] Section 339 of the same Act allows the court to set aside transactions at undervalue within certain time limits. It differs from section 423 in two respects. First, section 339 does not require the trustees in bankruptcy to show to the court that the transferor intended to defraud creditors. Second, section 339 works with certain time restrictions, whereas section 423 applies irrespective of when the transfer took place; the only important thing is that there was an intention to defraud. Section 339 has a five-year time limit attached to it. However, within that five-year time limit, the section distinguishes between two vital time periods:[118] first, a two-year period ending with the date of adjudication of bankruptcy of a person, in which case a transaction at undervalue can be set aside irrespective of the solvency of the transferor; second, the remaining period of three years in which, before a transaction can be set aside, it must be shown that the transferor was insolvent.

A final example of how freedom of disposition may be interfered with can be taken from the area of wills and testamentary disposition. It has been seen that for a transfer to take effect after the death of the transferor, such transfer is only effective if the transferor makes a valid will. In the will, the transferor, that is the testator, can give his property to anyone he so wishes. He could give all of it to charity and leave nothing for his dependants such as a spouse and children. In such a case the question arises as to whether such freedom of disposition can be interfered with on the grounds that such family members and dependants have not been provided for? Interference with such freedom of testamentary disposition needs to be justified by some state goal or objective. Some commentators explain that in the context of testamentary transfers, the public interest in how people bequeath their property may be justified from the interests of society as a whole.[119] The orderly transfer of

---

[116] *Re Butterworth, ex p Russell* (1882) 19 ChD 588.

[117] The section requires the court to be satisfied that the transferor intended to defraud his creditors: see *Barclays Bank plc v Eustice* [1995] All ER 511.

[118] Insolvency Act 1986, s 341.

[119] See J. Finch, L. Hayes, *et al, Wills, Inheritance and Families* (1996) at p 22.

property to family and dependants is the means by which family solidarity is achieved. Whether or not the law recognises a general duty on a testator to acknowledge the rights of family members, the law does in certain circumstances allow interference with freedom of disposition when family members and dependants are not provided for.

In order to overcome the problem of family members and dependants who have not been provided for, the Inheritance (Provision for Family and Dependants) Act 1975 was passed. The main purpose of this legislation is to give the court a discretionary power to make an award to a surviving spouse and other dependants on the ground that the disposition of the deceased's estate does not make reasonable financial provision for the applicant. Although the Act originally applied to wills, it now extends to intestacy as well. The basic idea behind this legislation is that an application is allowed to be made by the deceased's spouse, a former spouse, a child of the deceased or any other person who immediately prior to the death of the deceased was being maintained by the deceased.[120] The ground for making an application must be that the deceased's will or the rules of intestacy do not make a reasonable provision for the applicant. The court has a wide discretion in making orders that will seek to provide for such applicants from the deceased's estate. The order may be one requiring the payment of a lump sum or periodic payments from the estate.[121]

---

[120] Inheritance (Provision for Family and Dependants) Act 1975, ss 1(1) and 25(1) and (4).
[121] *Ibid*, s 2.

10

DEMARCATING PROPRIETARY RIGHTS FROM PERSONAL RIGHTS

PROPERTY RIGHTS AND PERSONAL RIGHTS

Property law is essentially concerned with the 'regulation' of proprietary rights. The use of the word regulation covers matters such as acquisition, enforceability, use and transfer of rights in relation to material resources of value. Proprietary rights should, however, be distinguished from personal rights. Personal rights are not rights in a particular thing, rather, they are said to be rights *in personam*, that is, enforceable against a particular person as opposed to a particular thing. The distinction between a proprietary and a personal right is significant since a proprietary right has much wider legal implications in relation to third parties than a purely personal right. Throughout the preceding chapters it has been observed that a proprietary right is a right *in rem*; sometimes property lawyers simply say that a proprietary right is a right in *res*, meaning that it attaches to the thing itself rather than a particular person. A right *in rem* binds the whole world and it matters not that another has interfered with possession of the thing in which the right is held. The right of property continues into the hands of third parties. The same is not true of personal rights; such rights bind particular persons and they are generally governed by the law of contract and tort. Personal rights do not have the quality of endurability since they are governed by principles of privity between the persons in whom the right and duty is vested.

The distinction between a proprietary and a personal right can be better explained with the following examples. First, take the example of A who is vested with the freehold title to land. A has vested in him a proprietary right which cannot be destroyed by anyone else;[1] such a right is enforceable against the whole world. It matters not who has interfered with A's ownership because

---

[1] The state may, of course, have an expropriation power in the form of compulsory purchase.

A can enforce his right of ownership against everyone in the world. A can, of course, grant B a lease out of A's freehold interest. If the lease is properly granted to B, B will likewise have a property right in the land in the form of a term of years. Both A and B have property rights in the land, with A having the ultimate right of ownership and B a lesser right in the form of a term in the land. A can sell his freehold title to C; however, C would be bound by B's property right in the land sold by A. Whatever term is left in the lease, C would be expected to respect the rights of B. In other words, as far as C is concerned, he now becomes B's landlord. Now take the same example, but instead of A granting B a lease in his land, let us assume that he allows B to park his car in A's garage for a fee of £20 per week. Such a permission to enter upon another's land is called a licence. The arrangement between A and B in this second scenario is merely contractual and B has a contractual claim against A. If A refuses to honour the agreement, B can sue A for damages. B has a mere personal right against A; he has no rights in A's land. If A sells his freehold title to C, B has no claim against C if C refuses to allow B to park his car in the same garage.

The above examples relate to interests in land, but the same is true for property interests in personalty. If A purchases a car, A has a right of ownership in the car which is enforceable against the whole world. It matters not who has interfered with A's ownership of the car since A has a right in the car as opposed to a right against a particular person. If B wrongfully interferes with possession of A's car, A can demand the return of the car from B. However, as observed in Chapter 4, it may be impracticable for A's car to be returned to him – for example, where it is destroyed by B. In such a case A has the right to sue B for damages in the tort of conversion.[2] The fact that A may not get his car back when it is destroyed does not alter the proprietary nature of A's right in the car. The proprietary significance of A's ownership in the car lies in the fact that it is enforceable against the world at large. One point to note about proprietary rights in personalty is that, unlike real property law, personal property generally recognises a limited amount of property rights that can be sustained in such property. Most notably, whereas the lease of land to a tenant grants the tenant a proprietary right in the land,[3] no such property right is granted in the lease of a good such as a car or television.

SIGNIFICANCE OF A PROPRIETARY ANALYSIS OF A RIGHT

Analysing a right as proprietary as opposed to personal is significant for a number of reasons. First, as seen in the above examples, a property right has

---

[2] See, generally, Chapter 4.
[3] There are both historical and conceptual reasons for this: for example, the grant of a time in the land is consistent with estate ownership.

the hallmarks of enforceability against third parties. A legal right of property is a right *in rem* and as such binds the whole world. An equitable property right, despite being labelled a right *in personam*, is enforceable against everyone except a bona fide purchaser of the legal title without notice of such right.[4] Personal rights such as those arising through contract are pure rights *in personam*; they bind only the parties to the contract and are governed by the principle of privity of contract. Second, in the context of insolvency, a proprietary right allows the holder of such a right to take priority over other creditors of a debtor in circumstances where the debtor has possession of the owner's property. The same is true where the debtor may have legal title to property but the equitable ownership belongs to another – for example, under a trust. In this respect, Goode writes it is

> 'upon the debtor's insolvency that the distinction between ownership and a personal right to an asset becomes of crucial significance, for it is the basic policy of insolvency law to adopt the non-bankruptcy ordering of rights and thus to respect proprietary rights held by another prior to the debtor's bankruptcy ... Owners and secured creditors can withdraw from the pool the assets they own or over which they have security.'[5]

The third advantage of a proprietary right, and closely related to the first two, lies in the fact that the owner of property has the right to follow or trace his property, and any wealth that is acquired by the use of the property, into the hands of third parties. It is often said that the owner of a proprietary right has a restitutionary claim which is made through the process of tracing.[6] Tracing is recognised both at law and in equity; however, there are fundamental differences between the two.[7] A person is entitled to trace his property at common law provided that his property has not been mixed with any other property.[8] It does not matter whether the plaintiff's property has been substituted for other property. The right to trace in equity is much wider because of the wider range of claims that can be made through the tracing process. For example, it does not matter that the plaintiff's property

---

[4] See Chapter 4.

[5] R.M. Goode, 'Ownership and Obligation in Commercial Transactions' (1987) 103 LQR 433 at p 434.

[6] See A. Burrows and E. McKendrick, *Cases and Materials on the Law of Restitution* (1997) at p 663. The authors write: 'tracing can perhaps be described as the technique by which a person can follow his property into different forms/or different hands. In our view, the essential role of tracing in the law of restitution is that it enables the plaintiff to establish that property retained or received by the defendant is retained or was received at the expense of the plaintiff even though (i) the property is not in the same form as when subtracted from the plaintiff, and/or (ii) the property was received by the defendant from a third party, rather than being subtracted directly from the plaintiff.'

[7] For a comparative discussion, see G. McMeel, *The Modern Law of Restitution* (2000), pp 359–384.

[8] *Taylor v Plummer* (1815) 3 M&S 562.

has been mixed with property belonging to the defendant or other property belonging to third parties.[9] On the other hand, tracing in equity is narrow when viewed as to the types of person who can use the tracing process. A prerequisite to tracing in equity is that the plaintiff be vested with a prior equitable interest and also be subject to a fiduciary relationship.[10] The right to follow equitable property will only fail when the legal title to the same property finds itself in the hands of a bona fide purchaser of the legal title for value and without notice of the equitable interest. Finally, the right of ownership, which is the greatest right a person can have in a thing, carries with it a number of incidents. The most important of these incidents is the right to possession, which is protected by the property torts of trespass and conversion. Personal rights may grant occupation to another – as, for example, in the case of a licence to occupy another person's land; however, such rights do not grant possession.

DEMARCATING PROPERTY RIGHTS FROM PERSONAL RIGHTS

Despite the clear conceptual differences between proprietary rights and personal rights, it is not always a simple process of drawing the boundary between personal rights and property rights on a given set of facts. A given set of facts may initially suggest that a person is vested with a personal right; however, closer examination may reveal that the substance of the right is essentially proprietary. The courts in this country are generally reluctant to elevate personal rights into proprietary ones and there are a number of reasons for this reluctance.[11] These reasons must be understood in the various contexts in which questions have arisen. For example, as will become apparent later, refusing to accord proprietary significance to personal rights in land often relates to the detrimental effect that is said to attach to conveyancing. On the other hand, in commercial contexts the concern relates to the effect on insolvency and the imbalance that can occur in the distribution of a debtor's estate.

It often happens that rights which are personal from their outward appearance are nevertheless treated as if they are proprietary rights. The approach of the law is not to look at mere labels, but rather to consequences. A right is not personal simply because people who create such a right call it a

---

[9] See *Re Hallett's Estate* (1880) 13 Ch D 696.

[10] See *Re Diplock* [1948] Ch 465. More recently, in *Westdeutsche Landesbank Girozentrale* v *Islington Borough Council* [1996] AC 699, the House of Lords has confirmed the strict requirement of these conditions.

[11] See *National Provincial Bank Ltd* v *Ainsworth* [1965] AC 1175: here the House of Lords rejected that a deserted wife had any proprietary right in the matrimonial home which was in the name of her husband. When the husband deserted the wife, she had a mere personal claim against her husband which was not binding on third parties such as a bank.

personal right. The same is true of proprietary rights. A person may so frame a right that it is intended to have a proprietary effect; however, refusal by the law to recognise the proprietary effect may reduce it to a mere personal right. If distinguishing proprietary rights from personal rights is not necessarily dependent on the label used by the persons in creating the right, how does one then distinguish on a given set of facts whether a right is proprietary or personal? In many cases the distinction may be clear – for example, a permission to enter upon another's land is merely personal in contrast to the grant of a fee simple in another, which is proprietary. However, where facts contain aspects that demonstrate characteristics of both, the courts have to balance a number of factors[12] in coming to a conclusion. It is the conclusion that determines whether a particular right is proprietary as opposed to the initial label. Gray, writing in the context of equitable property rights, argues that 'to approach problems of this kind in terms of a property analysis is to turn the process on its head and to begin with a conclusion. Where an equitable interest is protected against third parties, the reality of the matter is that it is not protected in this way because it is property, but rather that it is property precisely because – ultimately through the equitable intervention of the court – it is indeed protected.'[13] In the next two sections the problem of distinguishing personal rights from proprietary rights is undertaken with reference to specific contexts in which questions have arisen.

PROPERTY AND PERSONAL RIGHTS IN REAL PROPERTY

In the context of land there have been many instances where personal rights – or at least, what looked to be personal rights from the outset – have been elevated to the status of property rights. There are various reasons for this process: some relate to historical factors, as in the case of leases and restrictive covenants. In other cases, the courts have construed a right as proprietary because one party has deliberately framed the right as personal so as to avoid the consequences that flow from a proprietary analysis of the right. This is certainly true in cases where a person, in substance, grants in another a lease, yet the right is framed as a licence so as to avoid the statutory protection afforded to a tenant. Further still, and perhaps more problematic, is the use of the contractual licence as a means of providing residential security in modern family living arrangements. In such cases, where the contractual licence is used as a means for long-term residential security in land, the question arises as to whether such a licence in such a context can simply be analysed as conferring

---

[12] These factors include *inter alia* the consequences of reaching one conclusion as opposed to another in respect of the parties who dispute the right in question and the effect of the conclusion in respect of third parties.

[13] K. Gray, *Elements of Land Law* (2nd edn, 1993) at p 924, (3rd edn published 2001).

a personal right. If a contractual licence is to be treated as conferring a property right in the holder of such a licence, the question is when and to what extent? These matters can now be explored in a little more depth.

Leases

A lease is essentially a contract between two parties for the grant of a time in land.[14] Like any other contract a lease contains terms and conditions implied by law or expressly incorporated by the parties to the contract. Typical terms include the payment of rent and the duty to keep in repair the land subject to the lease. By its nature, a lease is an executory contract whereby rights and obligations remain outstanding between the parties during the course of the lease.[15] In this respect, a lease has its roots firmly in the law of contract and confers upon a tenant a personal right enforceable against the landlord. Breach of any terms contained in the lease entitles the innocent party to sue for damages for breach of contract. However, a lease is also a proprietary interest in land. According to section 1 of the Law of Property Act 1925 a lease is one of the only two estates capable of existing in law. The proprietary origins of a lease lie in factors which are historical. Given that the essence of a lease is to grant in another a time in the land – for example, 25 years – such transfer of possession is not too far from the idea of estate ownership and tenure that existed in medieval law.[16] It will be recalled that under the system of tenure and estate all land was held of a lord. Although leases were not originally subject to medieval tenure and estates, it soon became obvious that the remedy of ejectment would be available to a tenant, who could recover land from anyone who had interfered with it during the currency of the tenancy.[17] Given the fact that the tenant's remedy for wrongful interference with his tenancy was no longer limited to damages, but he could seek recovery of the land itself,[18] the right generated under a lease became more akin to a right *in rem* rather than a right *in personam*. The lease is the only true form of tenure that exists in the modern law.

The lease is a classic example of the transformation of a personal right into a proprietary one. In *Hammersmith and Fulham London Borough Council* v *Monk*[19] Lord Browne-Wilkinson explained that a lease as 'a contract between

---

[14] In *Prudential Assurance Company Ltd* v *London Residuary Body* [1992] 2 AC 286 Lord Templeman explained (at 390) that a lease is 'a contract for the exclusive possession and profit of land for some determinate period'.

[15] See *National Carriers Ltd* v *Panalpina (Northern) Ltd* [1981] AC 675 at 705.

[16] See Chapter 4.

[17] See Megarry and Wade, *The Law of Real Property* (6th edn, 2000) at p 1442.

[18] The action was called *quaere ejecit infra terminun*: see also A.W.B. Simpson, *A History of the Land Law* (2nd edn, 1986) at p 71.

[19] [1992] 1 AC 478.

two persons can, by itself give rise to a proprietary interest in one of them ... The contract of tenancy confers upon the tenant a legal estate in the land: such legal estate gives right to rights and duties incapable of being in contract alone.'[20] However, despite the fact that a lease constitutes a proprietary right in land, in recent times there has been much debate as to what principles govern leases. If leases are proprietary, should property law principles alone decide the outcome of leasehold disputes or should contract law govern them?[21] The issue arose in *Hammersmith* where one joint tenant, in relation to a weekly tenancy of a flat, served a notice to quit without the knowledge of the other. If the notice to quit were valid then the tenant who did not have any knowledge of the notice to quit would be left no rights in the property. From a contractual point of view the notice to quit by one tenant would be sufficient to end the tenancy since, for renewal of the tenancy, consent of all joint tenants was required. The fact that one tenant had served a notice to quit was sufficient to show that there was no joint consent for renewal. Viewed from a property angle, the notice to quit would be improper since the unity vested in joint tenants would require mutual participation to end the tenancy. The House of Lords opted for the contractual approach.

The dominance of contract law over property in the governance of leases in the modern law continues. There is a movement away from the historical position that a lease simply involved the grant of an estate in land for the payment of rent, and so long as possession was capable of being vested in the tenant, the lease continued for the duration of the term. Any breach that did not interfere with possession was not sufficient to terminate the lease.[22] The position is rather different now, so that even where possession is not disturbed a lease can be terminated on the general contractual principles of frustration and repudiation.[23] The lease as a proprietary interest lies between the law of contract and the law of property as a species of a right *in personam* but also as a right *in rem*. It can be said that the co-existence of the law of contract and property seeks to make the lease a commercially important tool in modern social and economic conditions. The proprietary aspect of the lease, which essentially lies in its enforceability against third parties, makes it a valuable mode of holding land for a particular purpose. The contractual nature of the lease and the application of contract principles of frustration and repudiation recognise the tenancy as a 'consumer contract'.[24]

---

[20] *Ibid*, at 491.
[21] See S. Bright and G. Gilbert, *Landlord and Tenant Law: the Nature of Tenancies* (1995) at pp 69–102; C. Harpum, 'Leases as Contracts' [1993] CLJ 212.
[22] See the fourth edition of Megarry and Wade, *The Law of Real Property* (1975) at p 673.
[23] *National Carriers Ltd v Panalpina (Northern) Ltd* [1981] 1 All ER 161 (HL) and also *Hussein v Mehlman* [1992] 2 EGLR 87.
[24] K. Gray, *Elements of Land Law* (2nd edn, 1993), p 676, (3rd edn published 2001).

Restrictive covenants

A restrictive covenant provides perhaps one of the most acute examples of the transformation of a personal right into a proprietary one. In the context of real property, a covenant is an agreement in a deed whereby one person (the covenantor) promises the other (the covenantee) that he will either perform or not perform certain activity in respect of a defined area of land. In this respect, covenants can be positive (where, for example, the covenantor is to perform a certain act) or they can be negative (that is, where the covenantor refrains from doing something on the land). Covenants have their roots in the law of contract and are a useful means by which land can be utilised efficiently. For example, an owner of adjacent land may enter into an agreement with his neighbour to the effect that his neigbour is to maintain a fence. The maintenance of the fence is obviously important in maintaining the value of land to which it is supplied. Another example is that of an adjacent owner of land who enters into an agreement with his neighbour to the effect that he will not erect any further buildings on his land. Such a covenant, which is negative in nature, can serve the function of maintaining the value of land by preserving the land from excessive buildings in the form of factories. Seen in this way, covenants provide a useful means by which land use can be privately controlled by individuals.

Whilst covenants have their roots in contract so that the original parties are clearly bound by the covenant, the purpose for which such covenants are entered into is not served if such covenants do not bind third parties. Whilst A may enter into an agreement with B so that B, the covenantor, agrees to supply water from his land to A's land, the continued value of A's land is dependent on whether B continues to supply the water even after A parts with the land and transfers it to C. Likewise, if A covenants with B to the effect that A will not erect any further building on his land, B has the security of knowing that he will be living in a pleasant un-built-up area. This may be advantageous to B and will enhance the value of B's land. However, if the covenant is not enforceable against A's successors in title then B does not have any advantage which enhances the value of his land. The common law rule has been that the benefit of a positive covenant can run with the land.[25]

---

[25] See *P & A Swift Investments* v *Combined English Stores Group Plc* [1989] AC 632. Under the common law rule the benefit of the covenant will pass if certain criteria are satisfied. First, the covenant must 'touch and concern' the land. This requires the covenant to affect the land as regards its occupation and use; the covenant must not be collateral or confer a mere personal benefit on the covenantee. Second, the covenantee must have a legal estate to be benefited. Third, the assignee must have a legal estate in the land benefited. Finally, there must have been an intention that the benefit should run with the land owned by the covenantee at the date of the covenant. A further statutory method of transferring the benefit is under s 136 of the Law of Property Act 1925 by way of an assignment of a chose in action. This requires writing and notice to the covenantor. For a general discussion of s 136 in relation to choses in action, see Chapter 9.

However, the burden of a covenant does not run with the land at common law.[26] The rationale of the rule lies in the fact that third parties cannot be made liable on a contract to which they are not privy. Furthermore, there appear to be both social and economic grounds for the rule. It will be remembered that in the nineteenth century, with the growth of industry and commerce, land would only become profitable for business if business persons could develop on the land. Covenants which had the effect of restricting the types of use to which land could be put were clearly not conducive to the social and economic climate which emphasised the exchange value of land as opposed to its use value.[27]

Although in the nineteenth century it was important to keep land unfettered from burdens so as to maintain its optimal value for industry, there was also a growing recognition toward the end of the century that the pace of industrial and urban growth would seriously undermine land use in the country.[28] In the landmark decision in *Tulk v Moxhay*,[29] Lord Cottenham LC held that a successor of a negative covenant who had notice of the covenant was thereby bound in conscience to honour it. On the facts of the case, the covenantor had agreed with the covenantee that he would maintain a garden at Leicester Square uncovered with any buildings. Although the sale of the covenantor's land to his successor contained no provision in the conveyance relating to the garden, it bound the successor of the covenantor on the grounds of notice.[30] The effect of the ruling in *Tulk v Moxhay* was to recognise a new equitable interest in land capable of binding third parties, despite having its origins in contract and starting out as a personal right.

The decision to enforce the negative covenant in *Tulk v Moxhay* by Lord Cottenham was based not on any labelling process. It was not enforced because the covenant was thought to have created a property right; rather the decision to enforce was based on equitable grounds, the conclusion of which characterised the right into a proprietary right rather than a mere personal one. In the words of Lord Cottenham, the matter was not 'whether the covenant runs with the land, but whether a party shall be permitted to use

---

[26] *Austerberry v Corporation of Oldham* (1885) 29 Ch D 750.

[27] This desire to keep land unfettered from burdens imposed on previous owners of land is well illustrated in *Keppell v Bailey* (1834) 2 My & K 517, 39 ER 1042, where Lord Brougham refused to allow that 'incidents of a novel kind can be devised and attached to land at the fancy and caprice of any owner' (at 535 and 1049 respectively).

[28] See W.R. Cornish and G. de N. Clarke, *Law and Society in England 1750–1950* (1989) at p 150.

[29] (1884) 2 Ph 774, 41 ER 1143.

[30] Restrictive covenants made after 1925 are now governed by the principles of registration that apply to equitable interests in land. In unregistered land they constitute a Class D(ii) land charge: see Land Charges Act 1972, s 2(5)(ii). In the case of a registered title they constitute a minor interest protected by entry of a notice: see Land Registration Act 1925, s 50(1).

land in a manner inconsistent with the contract entered into by his vendor, and notice of which he purchased. Of course the price would be affected by the covenant, and nothing could be more inequitable than that the original purchaser should be able to sell the property the next day for a greater price, in consideration of the assignee being allowed to escape from the liability which he had himself undertaken.'[31] The intervention of equity in according proprietary status to negative covenants undoubtedly cannot be divorced from the social and economic demands of preserving land from rapid urban growth. In this way equity acted in a manner to meet the social and economic demands of society. One writer commenting on, *inter alia*, the decision in *Tulk* v *Moxhay* wrote: '... Equity has been the vehicle of equity: it has been a means of entry for new social demands into legal cognizance, and an acceptable method of meeting them.'[32]

Lease/licence distinction

A person who enters upon another's land without permission commits a trespass. However, where the owner of the land grants permission, no such trespass is committed; the person with such permission is said to have been given a licence.[33] A licence confers a personal right in the licensee; it does not grant a proprietary interest in the land belonging to the licensor. Examples of licences include permission given to a lodger to reside in a house, a cinemagoer and a football supporter at a stadium. In contrast, a lease, as seen above, confers a tenant a proprietary interest in land for the duration of the lease. It gives the tenant exclusive possession of the land so that the tenant can exclude everyone, including the freehold owner, from the land. Although the freehold owner can sell the freehold title, such sale is subject to the rights of the tenant, which are said to be rights *in rem*. A lease binds third parties whereas a licence does not.[34]

Despite the clear differences between a lease and a licence, the courts are often asked to decide whether on a given set of facts a lease or a licence has been created. In many cases this is a straightforward task; as seen in the last chapter, a lease for more than three years will have to comply with certain formalities. Where a lodger who does not have any exclusive possession of his room – as for example, a cleaner may have access to the room – there is no doubt that a licence has been granted. However, there are many non-exclusive occupation agreements drawn up by potential landlords that have as their purpose a deliberate attempt to avoid creating a tenancy. These are

---

[31] (1848) 2 Ph 774 at 777, 41 ER 1143 at 1144.
[32] I.W. Duncanson, 'Equity and Obligations' (1976) 39 MLR 268 at p 270.
[33] *Thomas* v *Sorrell* (1673) Vaugh 330 at 351.
[34] *Ashburn Anstalt* v *Arnold* [1989] Ch 1.

often referred to as 'sham agreements' and their sole purpose is to avoid the statutory protection afforded to a tenant.[35] In the seminal case of *Street* v *Mountford*,[36] the House of Lords held that the key question in determining whether a lease or a licence had been created was whether exclusive possession for a term had been granted. Lord Templeman held that exclusive possession existed whenever the tenant was in a position to exclude all others from the premises.[37] This being so, what does a court do when it is faced with an agreement where a person is, as a matter of substance, granted exclusive possession, but the agreement is drafted in such terms as to grant a mere licence? A fundamental principle of contract law is freedom of contract. Parties to an agreement should be free to contract as they wish and upon such terms as they can agree. The courts should not interfere with such agreements simply on the basis that they dislike them. On the other hand, drafting an agreement – which as a matter of substance grants a tenancy – as a licence in order to defeat statutory provision allows a horse and cart to be driven through such legislation. The property law principle would hold that if exclusive possession is granted then a tenancy should be construed.

The caselaw in relation to the problem of sham licence agreements has followed the property law principle. The intention of the parties, which at one time was used to resolve the issue,[38] is no longer conclusive of the finding of a licence agreement. In *Street* v *Mountford* Lord Templeman held that 'although the Rent Acts must not be allowed to alter or influence the construction of an agreement, the court should, in my opinion, be astute to detect and frustrate sham devices and artificial transactions whose only object is to disguise the grant of a tenancy to evade the Rent Acts.'[39] A recent extension of this property law approach is evident in the House of Lords decision in *Bruton* v *London & Quadrant Housing Trust*;[40] however, the decision is not without controversy. In so far as concerns the lease/licence distinction issue, the decision of the House of Lords is sound. On the facts, a local authority granted to London & Quadrant Housing Trust, a housing trust, a licence to use council property as short-term accommodation for homeless people pending the commencement of development work. The trust entered into an agreement with Bruton to allow him exclusive possession of a flat; however, the agreement was referred to as a licence. Bruton brought an action against the Trust in order to enforce the implied covenants of repair contained in the Landlord and Tenant Act 1985, s 11(1). The success of this

---

[35] Such as the Rent Act 1977.
[36] [1985] 2 All ER 289.
[37] *Ibid*, at 300.
[38] *Somma* v *Hazelhurst* [1978] 1 WLR 1014.
[39] [1985] 2 All ER 289 at 299; see also *Antoniades* v *Villiers and Another* [1988] 3 WLR 1205.
[40] [2000] 1 AC 406.

action depended on whether Bruton was granted a tenancy or a licence. The House of Lords held that, given that Bruton had exclusive possession of the flat, he had been granted a tenancy. According to Lord Hoffmann, it was irrelevant that the agreement was referred to as a licence. The problematic aspect of this case, however, is the fact that the Trust had no power to grant a tenancy since they only had a licence in the land.[41] The House of Lords, however, decided that it was irrelevant that the Trust had no title since it was the character of the agreement, rather than the character of the landlord or his title, which determined whether a lease or a licence had been granted. Lord Hoffmann's judgment in this case almost seems to suggest that it is possible to create a relationship of landlord and tenant without the landlord having any estate in land.[42]

Occupational licences

In the latter part of the twentieth century the concept of a licence became very popular as a means for setting up the living arrangements of modern families. The movement of the licence into the sphere of family residential arrangements also brought with it a host of problems for the courts. The primary problem related to whether a licence, and here predominantly a contractual licence, constituted a personal interest in land or whether it was proprietary. Although towards the close of the twentieth century the courts had clarified the position that a contractual licence does not confer a proprietary right in land, it remains the position that something which starts out as a contractual licence can, with the aid of equitable intervention, be elevated to the status of a proprietary right in land. This intervention is based on social factors that demand a solution and the recognition that rules applicable to one context are not necessarily adequate in determining legal rights in another socially different context. In relation to the application of orthodox contract principles to licences in the occupation context, one commentator writes:

---

[41] In *London Borough of Camden v Shortlife Community Housing et al* [1993] 3 WLR 150 it was held that there could be no tenancy if the grantor had no power to grant a tenancy – for example, if he merely had a licence himself.

[42] The approach of Lord Hoffmann in respect of this matter is extremely difficult to justify on grounds of principle and authority. In *Milmo v Carreras* [1946] KB 306, Lord Greene MR commented (at 310): 'I myself find it impossible to conceive of a relationship of landlord and tenant that has not got the essential element of tenure in it, and that implies that the tenant holds of his landlord, and he can only do that if the landlord has a reversion. You cannot have a purely contractual tenure'. There is much to be said for the judgment of Millet LJ in the Court of Appeal [1998] QB 834, where it was held that Quadrant Housing Trust were incapable of granting a tenancy to Bruton simply because they had no estate in the land. On the question of whether it is possible to have leases without estates, see S. Bright, 'Leases, Exclusive Possession, and Estates' (2000) 111 MLR at pp 7–11.

'in all these cases a remedy is being sought by a promisee who is unable to pro-
ceed in common law contract. Unlike a plaintiff before 1832, who could have
no remedy if there was no form of action, the twentieth century plaintiff is
defeated by the absence of a category. The result, however, is the same: a con-
ceptualist's heaven. What is required is, first the possibility of a solution to a
social problem which appears to be similar to that associated with contract, but
is in fact different; secondly, since the justification of a remedy which deviates
from the normal legal rules is the exceptional nature of the circumstances, a discretion to balance and vary the weights of interests...'.[43]

At the close of the nineteenth century the law relating to licences did not on
the whole present too many problems for the courts. A bare licence – that is,
a licence granted for no consideration – presented hardly any problems. Such
a licence – for example, a permission to enter upon another's land – could be
revoked at any time[44] provided the licensor gave the licensee reasonable
notice.[45] A contractual licence, on the other hand, granted for consideration
was treated a little differently. Examples of such contractual licences in the
early law include permission to see a picture at a cinema and permission to
enter a sports ground to watch a sporting event. In so far as revocation is
concerned the early rule was that a contractual licence could be revoked at
any time despite the fact that the revocation amounted to a breach of contract.[46] This early rule was modified as a result of the intervention of equity,
and in particular, the availability of injunctive relief. The Judicature Acts of
1873 and 1875 had established the power of the courts to administer
common law and equity in one court. Thus, where the licensor had done
nothing wrong as concerned the licence, the courts began to see the licence in
the context of the contract to which it pertained. Where the contract allowed
the licensee a permission to stay on the licensor's land for a defined period of
time, it was plainly obvious that there was an implied obligation on the part
of the licensor not to revoke the licence for that defined period of time.[47] If
the licence was revoked, the court could grant the remedies of an injunction
and specific performance. In so far as third parties were concerned, the rule
was that the contractual licence did not bind third parties even though such
parties may have had notice of the licence.[48] This rule recognised the personal nature of a licence and the doctrine of privity of contract.

---

[43] I.W. Duncanson, 'Equity and Obligations' (1976) 39 MLR 268 at pp 271–272.

[44] *Wood v Leadbitter* (1845) 13 M & W 838 at 844.

[45] *Aldin v Latimer, Clarke, Muirhead & Co* [1894] 2 Ch 437.

[46] *Wood v Leadbitter* (1845) 13 M & W 838: here the plaintiff had purchased a ticket admitting
him to the Doncaster races. When the plaintiff had been forcibly thrown out of the ground
where the races were to take place, he sued for damages for assault and false imprisonment. The
action in assault and false imprisonment failed on the grounds that the plaintiff simply had no
right to be on the defendant's ground once permission to enter had been revoked. The plaintiff
was, however, entitled to sue for damages for breach of contract.

[47] *Millennium Productions Ltd v Winter Garden Theatre (London) Ltd* [1946] 1 All ER 678.

[48] *King v David Allen & Sons Billposting Ltd* [1916] 2 AC 54, and more recently, *Ashburn
Anstalt v Arnold* [1989] Ch 1.

The application of the law relating to contractual licences does not present much difficulty to cases such as watching a movie at a cinema or watching the races at a racecourse. However, as mentioned above, the contractual licence began as a useful means by which families and other cohabitees set up their domestic living arrangements in modern society. In such cases of occupational licences it soon became obvious that the strict application of the law relating to licences, which was essentially contract law based, would cause much hardship to plaintiffs. A more appropriate approach would be a property based one where the rights of the occupational licensee were seen as more akin to property rights.

The following examples may provide an illustration of the problems faced by the courts and property law in general. A son may ask his mother to come and live with him and his wife on the understanding that she will have a roof over her head for the rest of her life. This may be a convenient living arrangement for a couple who have careers. The mother may help look after the children and arrange other aspects of the household. A further example is the case where a young couple wish to purchase a house of their own, but lack the financial ability to do so. One way to resolve the problem may be for the parents to purchase a house in their own names and allow the young couple to reside there until such time as all the mortgage monies are repaid by the couple, followed by a conveyance of the property to them. In these examples it is clear that only a licence is conferred (for example, on the mother and the couple). These persons have no proprietary rights in the land. Whilst they may have some relief during the continuance of the licence between the original parties in the form of an injunction and specific performance, they face a real problem if the land subject to the licence is sold. The land may be deliberately sold to destroy any rights the licensees may have in the land, for example, where there is a breakdown in the relationship between the licensor and licensee. Since a contractual licence does not bind third parties the licensee would lose the right to remain on the land. Although a licensee may be able to sue for damages, in an age of residential security, such a position appears rather controversial. The controversy arises because of the long-term expectation that the licensee has been given. In one sense it amounts to a form of security relied on by the licensee, just like an owner of land.

Unless a licence in the context of occupational arrangements can be elevated to the status of a property right, the law surely fails to meet the needs of modern social circumstances which require 'a common equitable solution'.[49] This process of arriving at a common equitable solution is, however, not an easy task since it involves consideration of other matters, especially the impact of the introduction of novel property rights within the

---

[49] I.W. Duncanson, *op cit*, at p 271.

existing conveyancing framework. This process of arriving at a common equitable solution to the problem of occupational licences began in 1952 by Lord Denning.[50] It is fair to say that the Denning contribution to this area of the law has generally been received with much criticism and caution. This is, however, not surprising since Lord Denning's contribution often failed to adhere to established legal doctrine and failed to follow the decisions of the higher courts. For the orthodox and traditionalist legal mind the Denning jurisprudence was hard to understand. The arguments have been that the Denning approach is not based on doctrine, is inconsistent with the established decisions of the higher courts and also inconsistent with statute.[51] However, recognising the fact that the licence was operating in a socially different context, Lord Denning not only contributed to the process of recognising the interests of certain occupational licences as proprietary, but also illustrated in the process that rules developed in one social context cannot without question be applied to another.

The year 1952 is important because it was in that year that the decision in *Errington v Errington & Woods*[52] was delivered by the Court of Appeal. Here, a father bought a house with the aid of mortgage finance and allowed his son and daughter-in-law to live in the house. The understanding was that if the son and daughter-in-law paid off all the mortgage monies the house would be theirs. Before all the instalments had been paid the father died leaving a will in which he devised all his property to his wife. The relationship between the son and daughter-in-law broke down with the consequence that the son went to live with his widowed mother while the daughter-in-law continued to live in the house purchased by the father; she continued to pay the mortgage monies. The widow brought an action to recover the house from the daughter-in-law on the grounds that her husband had granted a revocable licence, to occupy the house. Now that she was the owner of the house she had a right to terminate the licence, and in any event, not being privy to the licence, she was not bound by it. Denning LJ had no problem in defeating the revocability argument on the grounds that the licence agreement between the father and the daughter-in-law amounted to a unilateral contract, which could not be revoked once the performance of the obligation began.[53] Equity could grant the daughter-in-law an injunction to prevent breach of the contract. As regards the argument that the widow was a third party, and therefore not privy to the licence agreement, Denning LJ faced a real problem. The

---

[50] *Errington v Errington & Woods* [1952] 1 KB 290.

[51] See Megarry and Wade, *The Law of Real Property* (6th edn, 2000) at p 1054. The approach is inconsistent with statute because the recognition of licences as equitable interests in land is contrary to s 4(1) of the Law of Property Act 1925 which prohibits the creation of novel types of equitable interests in land.

[52] [1952] 1 KB 290.

[53] *Ibid*, at 295.

traditional rule would certainly find in favour of the widow and cause tremendous hardship and injustice to the daughter-in-law. Denning LJ, however, proceeded on the grounds that the daughter-in-law, as a contractual licensee, was able to enforce her rights against a third party who took the land with notice of the licence. This approach suggested that the daughter-in-law had an equitable proprietary right in the property. The conclusion of this case, albeit subject to tremendous criticism, suggested that a contractual licence constituted an equitable property interest in land.

A second important case is that of *Binions* v *Evans*[54] where trustees of an estate agreed with one of the estate's employee's widow, Mrs Evans, that she could reside in a cottage on the estate rent-free for the rest of her life. The widow was, however, to keep the cottage in a state of repair and the agreement was put into writing. This agreement constituted a licence to occupy the cottage for the remainder of the licensee's life. The trustees sold the estate to Mr and Mrs Binions subject to the rights of Mrs Evans in the cottage. The Binions paid a reduced price for the estate in view of the rights that Mrs Evans had in the cottage. After the title to the estate was conveyed to the Binions, they brought an action to recover the cottage from Mrs Evans, who was now almost 80 years of age. Lord Denning, in the Court of Appeal, held that the Binions were bound by Mrs Evans' interest in the cottage on the grounds of a constructive trust.[55] The constructive trust arose simply because it would be inequitable for the Binions to deny Mrs Evans her rights in the cottage which they clearly knew from day one and as a result of which they had the advantage of paying a reduced price for the estate. Megaw and Stephenson LJJ, however, inclined to take the view that Mrs Evans had been granted a life interest in the cottage. Although the decision in *Binions* v *Evans* did not concern a third party, the significance of the constructive trust is that it conferred an equitable interest in land which could thereafter be subject to the normal rules of enforceability against third parties.[56] *Binions* v

---

[54] [1972] Ch 359.

[55] The type of constructive trust used here was the 'new model' constructive trust which Lord Denning explained in *Hussey* v *Palmer* [1972] 1 WLR 1286 as arising whenever justice and good conscience required it. Lord Denning explained (at 1290) that 'it is a liberal process, founded upon large principles of equity, to be applied in cases where the legal owner cannot conscientiously keep the property for himself alone, but ought to allow another to have the property or the benefit of it or a share of it'.

[56] G. Battersby, however, explains that 'it is a moot point whether the purchaser's successor would also be bound. Arguably, the constructive trust in this context is being used in remedial fashion to impose personal liability on the purchaser whose conscience is affected': 'Informally Created Interests in Land' in S. Bright and J. Dewar (eds), *Land Law: Themes and Perspectives* (1998) at p 502, n 79. Other writers, however, treat the constructive trust as creating an equitable interest in the licensee which would bind third parties on the normal rules of enforceability of equitable interests; authorities like *Re Sharpe* (see next note) would support this view – see Megarry and Wade, *The Law of Real Property* (6th edn, 2000) at p 1056.

Evans was taken by other cases as authority for the proposition that a licence could bind third parties if coupled with a constructive trust.[57]

Although the Court of Appeal has now clearly explained that a contractual licence does not bind third parties, a contractual licence may, if supported by equitable principles and doctrines, bind third parties.[58] The two equitable doctrines that have played a significant role in this area of the law are, first, the constructive trust, and, second, proprietary estoppel. In relation to the former, the decision in *Binions* v *Evans* illustrates the proper application of the constructive trust in order to bind the purchasers of land to the right of the licensee. In this case their conscience had been affected by the notice of the licensee's presence and the reduced payment for the land subject to the licence. In *Ashburn Anstalt* v *Arnold*,[59] the Court of Appeal explained that there could be no simple assertion that an occupational licence gave rise to a constructive trust. The purchaser's notice of the licence was insufficient to impose a constructive trust.[60] The crucial factor is whether the conscience of the purchaser has been affected so as to justify the imposition of the constructive trust.[61]

The second equitable doctrine, which has contributed to the recognition of occupational licences as proprietary interests in land, is proprietary estoppel. Like the constructive trust, the doctrine of proprietary estoppel is founded on unconscionable behaviour.[62] The doctrine operates where one party (O) knowingly encourages another party (P) to believe that he or she will enjoy some right or benefit over O's land.[63] P then acts to his detriment in reliance upon his belief that he will enjoy some right or benefit over O's land. In such a case it becomes unconscionable for O to withdraw the assurance, so that P has equity in his favour.[64] The equity in favour of P entitles P to seek equitable relief from

---

[57] In *Re Sharpe* [1982] 1 WLR 219 a nephew purchased a house with the aid of a loan from his aunt on the understanding that the aunt could live in the house for the rest of her life. The nephew subsequently went bankrupt and his trustees in bankruptcy contracted to sell the house to a purchaser. It was held that the aunt had an irrevocable licence in the land until the loan was repaid and this was binding upon the trustees in bankruptcy by way of constructive trust. Lord Browne-Wilkinson did, however, comment (at 226) that the law in this area was 'very confused and difficult to fit in with established equitable principles'.

[58] *Ashburn Anstalt* v *Arnold* [1989] Ch 1.

[59] *Ibid.*

[60] *Ibid*, at 25.

[61] In *IDC Group Ltd* v *Clark* [1992] EGLR187 Browne-Wilkinson VC held that a constructive trust would only be imposed on a purchaser with notice of the licensee in circumstances where there 'were very special circumstances showing that the transferee of the property undertook a new liability to give effect to provisions for the benefit of third parties'. On this basis the decision in *Re Sharpe* (see note 57) is inappropriate on the grounds that the trustees' conscience had not been affected and neither did they have any reply from the aunt as to her interest in the nephew's house.

[62] See, generally, K. Gray, *Elements of Land Law* (2nd edn, 1993) at pp 312–368, (3rd edn published 2001).

[63] Encouragement includes acquiescence.

[64] *Taylor Fashions Ltd* v *Liverpool Victoria Trustees Co Ltd* [1982] 1 QB 133.

the court; the court has a wide discretion as to the manner in which the equity can be satisfied. The court will examine all the relevant circumstances and seek to give to P that which he believed he would get in O's land. The discretion of the court is powerful and, where appropriate, it can order the whole legal title to be conveyed to P if that is what P was led to believe he would get.[65]

There are a number of cases illustrating the application of the doctrine of proprietary estoppel to licences. In *Inwards* v *Baker*,[66] a father encouraged his son to build a bungalow on his land and live there. The son built the bungalow; however, no formal interest in the land belonging to his father had been granted to the son. The father died in 1951 and the land was given to trustees for the benefit of other persons. In 1963 the trustees commenced possession proceedings against the son. Although his father had granted the son a mere licence, the Court of Appeal held that the son had a right to live in the bungalow as long as he wanted. Although in this case the court exercised its discretion in a negative way – that is, simply refusing the trustees from interfering with the son's irrevocable licence – in other cases the discretion has been exercised in a positive way. In *Pascoe* v *Turner*[67] the plaintiff purchased a house and resided there along with the defendant. When the relationship broke down the plaintiff began to reside elsewhere, but told the defendant that she could continue to live in the house and that the house and everything in it was hers. The defendant, in reliance of this assurance, expended money on the house. Later the plaintiff served the defendant with a notice to quit the licence. The Court of Appeal held that the defendant had established equity in her favour and this was best satisfied with an order for conveyance of the house in her favour.

Although proprietary estoppel in the context of occupational licences may operate so as to raise an equity in favour of the licensee, the question remains controversial as to whether the equity created by this type of estoppel confers a proprietary interest in the land. There are many schools of thought on this question. Megarry and Wade point to the fact that 'although an equity arising by estoppel is probably best regarded as a species of equitable proprietary right, it is questionable whether an estoppel licence can do so. There was no case prior to 1926 in which a licence made irrevocable by estoppel was held to bind a third party.'[68] However, this statement must be read in context since it is doubtful that licences operated in the same context then as they do today. A handful of post 1926 authorities suggest that the equity raised by estoppel is capable of binding third parties.[69] In *ER Ives Investment Ltd* v *High*[70] Lord

---

[65] As, for example, in *Pascoe* v *Turner* [1979] 1 WLR 431.

[66] [1965] 2 QB 29.

[67] [1979] 1 WLR 431.

[68] *Op cit*, at p 733.

[69] See also G. Battersby, 'Informally Created Interests in Land' in S. Bright and J. Dewar (eds), *op cit*, at pp 501–504.

[70] [1967] 2 QB 379.

Denning MR held that the an estoppel interest was capable of binding a purchaser with actual notice. Similarly, in *Voyce* v *Voyce*[71] Dillon LJ said *obiter* that the equity created by estoppel was sufficient to grant an equitable property right in the estoppel claimant.[72] This equitable property right was binding on third parties so that in the present case a donee of the legal title was ordered to convey the legal title to the estoppel claimant. In relation to the occupational licence cases, *Inwards* v *Baker*[73] illustrates that the estoppel licence was binding on the personal representatives of the licensor.

Even though there appears to be no direct authority on the issue as to whether an estoppel licence is capable of binding a purchaser for value with notice, there appear to be arguments suggesting that it should bind third parties. Take the case of *Pascoe* v *Turner*,[74] where the estoppel claimant was awarded the conveyance of the house in her favour: clearly the exercise of the court's discretion here was to order the plaintiff to convey the title to the house to the defendant who had satisfied the court that an equity by virtue of estoppel arose in her favour. However, what would have been the position if the court had not yet exercised discretion simply because there had been no litigation, but the plaintiff sold to a purchaser who may have had notice of the defendant's existence on the land? To hold that the interest of the defendant does not bind the third party seems rather odd because, had the court exercised its discretion to grant relief, the defendant surely would be vested with a legal title binding the whole world. Simply because no litigation has occurred to grant relief, the defendant is left with nothing. In other words, an estoppel claimant wins all or loses everything depending on whether the equity has been crystallised with the award of a remedy. This does appear to be rather inconsistent and incoherent.[75]

One of the fundamental concerns about treating licences as property rights in land relates to the conveyancing problems that are caused thereby. The English conveyancing system has a fairly defined approach to the types of

---

[71] (1991) 62 P & CR 290.

[72] *Ibid*, at 294.

[73] [1965] 2 QB 29.

[74] [1979] 1 WLR 431.

[75] K. Gray argues that, in order for doctrinal coherence, a conscience-based solution should be sought. Rather than treating the equity created by estoppel as a general equitable property right subject to the general equitable rules relating to enforceability against third parties, one should look to the conscience of the third party on notice. If the third party has notice of the equity, this alone would be insufficient; rather, the question would be whether the third party 'has burdened his title with an independent conscientious obligation towards the estoppel claimant': *Elements of Land Law* (2nd edn, 1993) at p 367, (3rd edn published 2001). Whilst there may be many merits in this *in personam* jurisdiction, it still does not explain cases such as *Pascoe* v *Turner* [1979] 1 WLR 431, where the claimant who seeks litigation can take the entire title to the land if that is what the estoppel encouraged, yet in the absence of litigation lose everything to an innocent third party who has not burdened his title with the equity in favour of the estoppel claimant.

proprietary interests in land that are subject to the principles of registration. The 1925 property legislation attempted to define the types of equitable interests that were capable of existing in land and how they were to be protected in the case of unregistered and registered titles to land. Novel types of equitable rights were not allowed to be created. The registration of equitable interests provided a means by which certainty to title could be introduced, thereby facilitating transfer of title. The problem with the licences supported by the finding of a constructive trust and licences by estoppel is that they have no home in the 1925 system of registration of equitable interests. As such they are disliked as being contrary to the objectives of the 1925 legislation. This may be so; however, there is some doubt as to why social and economic conditions of one period of time, which set the scene for a statutory framework of rights, should be a panacea for all rights in future periods of time. In unregistered land, licences by estoppel are not registrable charges and so they are dependent on the doctrine of notice. In registered land an estoppel licence may well be treated as being in actual occupation pursuant to section 70(1)(g) of the Land Registration Act 1925.[76]

PROPERTY AND PERSONAL RIGHTS IN THE COMMERCIAL CONTEXT

The distinction between proprietary rights and personal rights is significant in a commercial context. The significance lies in the event of insolvency proceedings. Where a person is vested with a proprietary right he has the advantage in that he can claim his assets in the hands of the insolvent. Such assets cannot be used to meet the claims of creditors of the insolvent. A proprietary right therefore entitles the holder of the right priority over secured and unsecured creditors in insolvency proceedings. A person vested with a mere personal right ranks as an unsecured creditor and generally must fight for the debtor's estate that exists after proprietary and secured creditor claims have been satisfied. It is much more desirable for a person in insolvency proceedings to be vested with a proprietary right rather than a mere personal right. The question, however, arises as to when and the extent to which a person in insolvency proceedings can be regarded as being vested with a property right. This is an extremely important question both for creditors and those persons who lay down large amounts of money in commercial ventures. From the point of view of creditors, the greater recognition of property rights in insolvency has the effect of making the debtor's estate worthless in meeting their personal claims to money. From the point of view of investors, the recognition of a proprietary right attached to their investment provides security in the event of the commercial failure of a project.

---

[76] *National Provincial Bank Ltd v Hastings Car Mart Ltd* [1964] Ch 665.

From the latter part of the twentieth century the scope for a greater recognition of property rights in commercial transactions has been influenced by equity jurisdiction. The equitable intervention in commercial transactions has had the effect of allowing certain persons to gain priority over other creditors in insolvency proceedings.[77] The principal tool employed in order to gain priority in the event of the insolvency of another is the trust. For example, the trust has provided a powerful means by which legal title to goods can be transferred to one party in a commercial transaction in order to fulfill contractual obligations, but with equitable title being retained until such time as payment under the contract has been made. The advantage of this is that, in the event of the insolvency of the party receiving the legal title to goods, these goods do not form part of that party's estate for distribution amongst other creditors. It will be seen later that it is not just goods to which the trust doctrine has been employed; it extends to money and the proceeds of sale. The use of the trust device in this respect has been controversial since no reasonable investigation of title would disclose to secured and unsecured creditors that company assets were held upon trust for another. Although since towards the end of the twentieth century there has been a growing recognition of the powerful way in which property rights can be adjusted in insolvency proceedings with the use of equitable doctrines such as the trust,[78] there are many instances in commercial law where personal rights founded upon contract can still be elevated to proprietary rights.

Throughout the course of the last 130 years both academics and judges have questioned the proper role of equity in commercial law. Sometimes equity is said to have infiltrated commercial law.[79] In one nineteenth century case, Bramwell LJ commented: '[N]ow I do not desire to find fault with the various intricacies and doctrines connected with trusts, but I should be very sorry to see them introduced into commercial transactions, and an agent in a commercial case turned into a trustee with all the troubles that attend that relation.'[80] More recently, in *Westdeutsche Landesbank Girozentrale* v *Islington Borough Council*, Lord Browne-Wilkinson commented in respect of the application of the equitable doctrine of resulting trusts to interest rate swap transactions, 'the consequential commercial uncertainty which any extension of proprietary interests in personal property is bound to

---

[77] See R. Goode, 'Ownership and Obligation in Commercial Transactions' (1987) 103 LQR 433; J. Ulph, 'Equitable Proprietary Rights in Insolvency: The Ebbing Tide' (1996) JBL 482; W. Goodhart and G. Jones, 'The Infiltration of Equitable Doctrine into English Commercial Law' (1980) 43 MLR 489; and G.A. Kennedy, 'Equity in a Commercial Context' in Finn (ed), *Equity in a Commercial Context* (1987) at pp 1–18.

[78] See P. Birks, 'Proprietary Rights as Remedies' in P. Birks (ed), *The Frontiers of Liability* (1994) Vol 2, at p 218.

[79] Goodhart and Jones, *op cit*, at p 489.

[80] *New Zealand & Australian Land Co* v *Watson* (1881) 7 QBD 374 at 382.

produce.'[81] Although in a commercial, and primarily contractual, context equity is often looked upon with suspicion, it would be absurd to suggest that equity has no role to play in such a context. Law and equity work hand in hand regardless of the context in which they operate. Equity tempers the rigour of legal doctrine when that rigour proves to be inappropriate in any factual situation. In this respect there is much to be said for the words of Ulph who, in the context of considering whether equitable rights are more difficult to establish in the commercial sphere, writes, '... the true picture is complex and the court's response may depend on the type of claim that is being made rather than the context in which it arises.'[82]

Prepayment for goods

In a commercial transaction such as a sale of goods, a purchaser may be asked to make payment for the goods before they are dispatched to him. In the normal course of events the contract is completed by the delivery of the goods to the purchaser. However, problems may arise when the purchaser under the contract has made payment, but the vendor becomes insolvent without having made delivery of the goods to the purchaser. From a contractual point of view, the purchaser has a contractual remedy in the form of damages for failure of the vendor to perform his obligations under the contract. This contractual remedy arises on the basis that the purchaser is vested with a personal right enforceable against the vendor. However, a personal right may be insignificant in the context of the vendor's insolvency because the claims of the secured and preferential creditors may exhaust the vendor's estate to such an extent that the personal claim by the purchaser cannot be satisfied. A more serious problem here is the fact that other creditors of the vendor receive a windfall in that they receive not only the prepayment of money but also the goods as 'assets' to meet their claims.

Where prepayment for goods has been made, it is more appropriate for the purchaser to be vested with a proprietary right in either the monies advanced until such time as the goods are delivered to him or the goods themselves. In either case, given the fact that property remains vested in the purchaser in respect of the money or goods, these assets cannot be used to meet the claims of other creditors. In so far as property in the goods is concerned, the matter depends on the type of goods in question. Where the goods are specific goods – that is, goods identified and appropriated to the contract – property passes when the contract is made.[83] In such a case there

---

[81] [1996] 2 All ER 961 at 992.
[82] J. Ulph, 'Equitable Proprietary Rights in Insolvency: The Ebbing Tide' (1996) JBL 482 at p 482.
[83] Sale of Goods Act 1979, s 18, rule 1; see Chapter 9.

is no problem in the event of the insolvency of the vendor because the purchaser can follow his property into the hands of the company's liquidator. The problem is more acute in the context of goods which form part of a bulk and are not ascertained. No property can pass in such goods until such time as the goods have been unconditionally appropriated to the contract.[84] In such a case the purchaser has a mere personal claim against the vendor. It is said that a proprietary claim to such goods would 'appear to embarrass to a most serious degree the ordinary operations of buying and selling, and the banking operations that attend to them.'[85] However, as observed in Chapter 9, there may be some lifeline for purchasers of unascertained goods: the Sale of Goods (Amendment) Act 1995 allows the purchasers of bulk goods to acquire undivided shares in the bulk.[86]

Whilst it may be difficult to establish proprietary rights to the goods which form the subject-matter of a prepayment sale, in some circumstances a proprietary claim may exist in the monies paid under the contract so as to give the purchaser a proprietary claim in the event of the vendor's insolvency. In *Re Kayford*[87] an accountant of a mail order company advised the company to open a separate account called a 'Customers' Trust Deposit Account' where monies advanced by customers could be deposited until such time as their goods had been dispatched to them. This advice was given at a time when Kayford Ltd, a mail order company, was experiencing financial problems. The intention was to protect the interests of their customers, who had prepaid for goods but were awaiting delivery, which had been slowed down by the supply problems caused by the financial state of the company. Despite the advice, Kayford Ltd deposited the customers' money in a dormant deposit account which had a small credit balance belonging to it. It was only later that the name of the dormant account was changed. Megarry J had no problem in this case in holding that Kayford Ltd held the money in the account on trust for the customers. As such the customers had equitable rights to the money and the money did not belong to the general pool of assets available for meeting the claims of creditors. The fact that there was a trust in favour of the customers was clear from the steps taken by Kayford Ltd. It had shown an intention to hold the money for the customers until such time as they received their goods. In this case there was no question of preferential treatment of creditors because the customers had not become creditors; they were simply benefi-

---

[84] *Ibid*, s 18, rule 5.
[85] *Re Wait* [1927] 1 Ch 606 at 628–629.
[86] See Chapter 9, where this legislation was considered in more detail.
[87] [1975] 1 All ER 604.

ciaries under the trust.[88] The decision in *Re Kayford* has been justified from a consumer point of view. Unlike trade creditors, consumer creditors are not in the same position to insure against bad debts; this policy argument goes some way in explaining the approach of Megarry J.[89]

Loan transactions

Where one person lends money to another, a personal relationship is created between the lender and borrower. The lender has a personal right to be repaid by the borrower and his right is a right *in personam*. A loan creates a contractual debt; however, debts need not be contractual – for example, a legatee under a will has a right to be paid his legacy by the personal representatives of the deceased. In respect of a contractual debt, the rights and duties of the lender and borrower are spelt out by the contract. Despite being based on contract, a contractual debt is a rather peculiar creature because it also finds a home in the law of property. Given that a debt is capable of assignment as a *chose in action*, it comprises a personal property interest in law. It is property because of the mere fact that it is capable of assignment to third parties.[90] The proprietary essence of the debt lies in the fact that the contractual right to be paid, that is the right *in personam*, can be transferred to third parties. However, as between debtor and creditor the right is essentially personal. If A has loaned money to B, A has a personal right to be repaid by B. If B becomes insolvent, A has a personal right to be paid by the liquidator or trustee in bankruptcy of B. The chances of being paid depend on whether the value of B's estate is capable of meeting the demands of unsecured creditors.

Although a loan gives the lender a personal right to be paid by the borrower, in some circumstances the lender may have a proprietary claim to the monies loaned so as to remove those monies from the general pool of assets belonging to the borrower. This will arise when a loan is impressed with a trust relationship. For example, A may lend money to B for a specified purpose and require B to put the money in a separate account until such time as

---

[88] Placing the company's own money on trust with a desire of preferring a particular group of creditors would be voidable as a preference if done within six months of winding up: see Insolvency Act 1986, s 239. Megarry J took the view that, because the customers became beneficiaries, there could be no scope for the argument that a fraudulent preference had been given to any creditor under the similar provisions in the Companies Act 1948, ss 302 and 320. However, Goodhart and Jones disagree on the grounds that the customers never new about the trust arrangement and, furthermore, Kayford was under no trust obligations when the money was paid into their own account: see W. Goodhart and G. Jones, 'The Infiltration of Equitable Doctrine into English Commercial Law' (1980) 43 MLR 489 at pp 496–497.

[89] J. Ulph, 'Equitable Proprietary Rights in Insolvency: The Ebbing Tide' (1996) JBL 482 at p 492.

[90] See Chapter 8.

the specified purpose can be carried out. The question is whether this type of arrangement creates a loan, or does B hold money upon trust for A? The question is obviously acute in the context of the insolvency or bankruptcy of B. If the money is still in the hands of B, the creditors of B will wish to see the money used to discharge the debts owed by B to secured and other creditors. On the other hand, A will wish to argue that the money is held on trust for A because the purpose for which the money was advanced has now failed. Equally, however, there is nothing to prevent any persons who had an interest in the specified purpose to argue that they have a claim to the money; after all, they seem to be the most obvious beneficiaries of the loan.

The House of Lords in *Barclays Bank Ltd* v *Quistclose Investments Ltd*[91] considered the extent to which a loan and trust could co-exist. On the facts of the case, Rolls Razor Ltd, who owed a large amount of money to Barclays Bank, borrowed some £209,719 from Quistclose in order to pay dividends which it had declared on its shares. The money was paid into a separate account at Barclays Bank on the understanding that it was only to be used for the specified purpose of paying the dividends. Barclays Bank had full knowledge of the arrangement between Rolls Razor Ltd and Quistclose. Before the dividends had been paid, Rolls Razor Ltd went into liquidation and the question arose whether Barclays Bank could use the money in the separate account to off-set the overdraft that Rolls Razor Ltd had with it, or whether the money belonged to Quistclose on the basis that it was held on trust by Rolls Razor Ltd for them. The House of Lords unanimously held that a loan and trust relations could exist. Lord Wilberforce, delivering the unanimous decision of the court, held that the money in the separate account was impressed with a trust in favour of Quistclose as soon as the failure of the primary purpose of the trust.[92] Furthermore, since Barclays Bank had notice of the trust arrangement they were clearly bound by the trust in favour of Quistclose.

The decision of the House of Lords in *Barclays Bank Ltd* v *Quistclose Investments Ltd* has been generally accepted as appropriate by other cases and also academic writings.[93] In *Carreras Rothmans Ltd* v *Freeman Mathews Treasure Ltd*[94] where monies were advanced by one company to another for a specified purpose and to be kept in a separate account, the court explained that '... equity fastens on the conscience of the person who receives from

---

[91] [1970] AC 567.

[92] *Ibid*, at 581–582.

[93] What is, however, unresolved is the basis upon which a Quistclose trust is enforced in favour of the original lender. Trust lawyers have generally debated whether the Quistclose trust, when enforced in favour of the original lender, is enforced on the basis of an express or implied trust. For an excellent account and review of some of the leading debates on this point, see G. Moffat, *Trust Law: Text and Materials* (3rd edn, 1999) at pp 595–600.

[94] [1985] Ch 207; see also *Re EVTR* [1987] BCLC 646 where a Quistclose trust was accepted when money had been advanced for the specific purpose of buying machinery.

another property transferred for a specific purpose only and not, therefore, for the recipient's own purpose, so that such person shall not be permitted to treat the property as his own or to use it for other than the purpose stated.'[95] Goodhart and Jones comment that '*Quistclose* is a just and commendable decision. No creditor had been misled into making a further loan by the existence of the separate dividend account; and there was no doubt that the bank knew of the agreement between the parties.'[96] Other commentators have pointed to the commercial advantages of the Quistclose trust: in particular, the fact that the borrower can continue trading and avoid insolvency.[97] Continuity of trading is obviously important from an insolvency point of view because it avoids the creation of fresh liabilities to creditors. In this respect Ulph writes:

> 'Quistclose trusts are frequently beneficial in the sense of providing an injection of capital which may rescue the company in financial difficulties. Moreover, these trusts are short term expediencies which cease to exist once the primary purpose is fulfilled and the provider of the funds is then in the position of an ordinary creditor, standing in line with others. The risk of a large and previously undisclosed class of claimants forcing themselves up in the insolvency queue by asserting proprietary claims under Quistclose trusts is therefore not significant as yet.'[98]

Retention of title

Attempts to retain equitable proprietary rights in money transfers in the context of prepayment for goods and loan transactions have generally escaped judicial and academic criticism. So, while rights which essentially look personal in their nature have been elevated to the status of property, this has been done in recognition of the context in which they have arisen. The decision in *Re Kayford* must be appreciated in the consumer context in which it arose and the sympathetic approach of the courts towards protecting the rights of consumers with relatively less bargaining power. It cannot be argued that in that case there were deliberate attempts to achieve preferential status in insolvency matters. With *Quistclose* there was nothing improper with the way in which the lender set up the arrangement, and from a commercial point of view the employment of the trust will invariably be beneficial from an insolvency point of view. What is, however, more controversial is the

---

[95] [1985] Ch 207 at 222.

[96] W. Goodhart and G. Jones, 'The Infiltration of Equitable Doctrine into English Commercial Law' (1980) 43 MLR 489 at p 494.

[97] G. Moffat, *Trust Law: Text and Materials* (3rd edn, 1999) at p 594.

[98] J. Ulph, 'Equitable Proprietary Rights in Insolvency: The Ebbing Tide' (1996) JBL 482 at pp 495–496.

extent to which a supplier of goods may acquire equitable rights in goods supplied to a purchaser. The need to retain a property interest in the goods supplied may be crucial if the purchaser of the goods has not yet paid for them – for example, when they are supplied on credit. If the purchaser becomes insolvent before payment to the supplier, the supplier will only have a contractual claim *in personam* against the liquidators of the purchaser. In other words, the supplier will be a mere unsecured creditor. In the meantime, the goods supplied will become available for meeting the claims of other creditors such as those with a floating charge. In this context it becomes crucial for a supplier of goods, just like a person lending money to another, to protect his interests in the event of the insolvency of the purchaser. The question, however, is how and to what extent he can do this?

Although a supplier of goods will have a personal claim against a purchaser for supplying goods on credit, a proprietary claim, if available, is much more appropriate. Possible proprietary claims could be made to the goods supplied under the contract, items manufactured with the goods supplied or the proceeds of sale of items manufactured and sold by the purchaser. The extent to which these claims can be made and the corresponding law in this area of law has been described as 'a maze if not a minefield'.[99] It is generally fair to say that, unlike prepayment for goods and loan transactions of the Quistclose nature, judicial and academic attitude to such claims in this context have been much more cautious. It is in this context that there exists a real danger of adjusting the claims of certain creditors on insolvency without any real justification on grounds of policy.

It is trite law that a seller of goods can retain ownership in the goods supplied until such time as the purchaser makes payment.[100] A clause in a sale of goods contract which seeks to do this is often called a retention of title clause or a reservation of title clause, and sometimes a *Romalpa Clause*, taking this last name from the leading case *Aluminium Industrie Vaassen BV v Romalpa Aluminium Ltd*[101] (*Romalpa* hereafter). A retention of title clause in its simplest form reserves ownership in the supplier until payment is made under the contract. If the purchaser of goods supplied becomes   insolvent, the supplier will have a proprietary claim to the goods in possession of the purchaser. This is sufficient for him to remove those goods from the general pool of assets available for distribution amongst the creditors of the insolvent purchaser. In practice, however, retention of title clauses are not drafted in a simple way; they tend to be rather complex and seek to exert proprietary claims over not only the original goods supplied but a whole host of other

---

[99] Review Committee on Insolvency Law and Practice (Cmnd 8558, 1982), paras 1587–1651.
[100] See Sale of Goods Act 1979, s 19.
[101] [1976] 1 WLR 676.

things. These things include ownership of items manufactured with the use of the supplier's goods, ownership of the proceeds of sale of the   original goods sold by the purchaser, and, ownership of the sale of items manufactured with the use of the supplier's goods. In this sense such clauses can be very extensive and, if effective, give suppliers of goods substantial benefit in the insolvency of a purchaser of goods. The question then is: how far are such clauses effective in law in turning what are essentially personal claims in insolvency into proprietary ones?[102]

In the landmark decision in *Romalpa*,[103] aluminium foil was supplied by the vendors (AIV) to the defendant manufacturing company (Romalpa). The contract of sale incorporated a reservation of title clause covering matters such as reserving title in the foil supplied, goods manufactured with the use of the foil and the proceeds of any sub-sales of the foil or goods manufactured with it. The clause also contained provisions relating to the storage of the foil, basically requiring the defendant to store it in such a manner that it was the property of AIV. The defendant manufacturing company subsequently got into financial difficulty with the consequence of a receiver being appointed. At the time of the insolvency Romalpa owed AIV some £122,000. It had in its possession unused foil and some £35,000 representing the proceeds of sale of unmixed foil to sub-buyers; AIV claimed to be entitled to the unused foil and the £35,000 in the separate bank account. The Court of Appeal allowed AIV to claim both the unused foil and the proceeds of sale. In respect of the unused foil, this was not problematic, but rather a simple application of legal doctrine: AIV had retained ownership in the foil and had a proprietary base which entitled them to follow the foil into the hands of the receiver.

In respect of the £35,000 representing the proceeds of sale, the Court of Appeal allowed AIV to recover these, however not without subsequent judicial and academic reservation.[104] The only basis upon which AIV could claim the proceeds as theirs was if they could point to a property interest in the proceeds. It is clear that Romalpa had legal title to the proceeds; the only property AIV could point to had to be an equitable proprietary interest in the proceeds of sale. If AIV could point to an initial fiduciary relationship and an equitable proprietary interest, it could trace the proceeds in equity under the principles in *Re Diplock*.[105] Examples of fiduciary relationships include the rights of a beneficiary under a trust and the rights of other fiduciaries such as

---

[102] Amongst the vast literature on this question, see G. McCormack, *Retention of Title* (2nd edn, 1995); S. Worthington, *Proprietary Interests in Commercial Transactions* (1996) and R. Goode, *Proprietary Rights and Insolvency in Sales Transactions* (2nd edn, 1989).

[103] A decision described as having a greater impact on commercial law than any other decision decided in the twentieth century: see R. Goode, *ibid*, at p 84.

[104] R. Goode, 'The Right to Trace and Its Impact in Commercial Transactions' (1976) 92 LQR 360.

[105] [1948] Ch 465.

a principal under an agency relationship. In the present case there appeared to be no fiduciary relationship and no equitable property interest sufficient to allow AIV to trace the proceeds of sale into the hands of the receivers. The Court of Appeal, however, held that Romalpa were agents for AIV and, as well as being bailees of the foil, there were sufficient grounds for AIV to trace the proceeds in equity.[106]

The net effect of the decision of the Court of Appeal in *Romalpa* was quite extensive and controversial. In the first place, it illustrated the potential for one set of creditors to obtain undisclosed priority in insolvency proceedings. A retention of title clause is generally not subject to the registration principle under the Companies Act 1985,[107] which warns potential creditors of the existence of charges over the assets of the company. In the second place, the finding of a fiduciary relationship in commercial contracts is not necessarily a straightforward process, as seems to be suggested by the decision in *Romalpa*. It is therefore not surprising that in the years following the decision in *Romalpa* the courts adopted a more restrictive approach as regards the extent to which retention of title clauses would be effective: in particular, a process in which retention of title clauses were to be clearly distinguished from charges that would require registration for their validity in insolvency matters. Moreover, the recent, and perhaps single most important decision relating to equity – *Westdeutsche Landesbank Girozentrale v Islington Borough Council*[108] – casts large doubts over the liberal approach adopted to tracing in *Romalpa*. In *Westdeutsche* the plaintiff had entered into an interest rate swap transaction with a local authority which was *ultra vires*. In relation to the question whether the plaintiff had an equitable proprietary interest in monies paid under the transaction, Lord Browne-Wilkinson spelt out the core principles of trust, included therein the fact that the right to trace in equity required both a fiduciary relationship and an equitable interest existing independently of the legal title.[109]

So what, then, is the present position with regard to the employment of retention of title clauses in supply contracts? In so far as concerns a simple retention of title clause covering goods which have not been used in a manufacturing process, it is clear that the supplier has a right to claim such goods in the hands of a company receiver or liquidator. Such a simple clause is not

---

[106] Roskill LJ explained that 'if an agent lawfully sells his principal's goods, he stands in a fiduciary relationship to his principal for those goods and their proceeds. A bailee is in like position in relation to his bailors' goods.' [1976] 1 WLR 676 at 690.

[107] See s 395 of the Companies Act 1985. This section requires the registration of certain charges – for example, a floating charge – with the Registrar of Companies.

[108] [1996] AC 669.

[109] His Lordship held (at 714): 'Your Lordships should not be taken as casting any doubt on the principles of tracing as established in *Re Diplock*'.

subject to registration because no property passes to the buying company. In *Clough Mill Ltd* v *Martin*[110] the Court of Appeal held that, where no title passed to the buyer, the supplier could claim any unused goods supplied (in the present case yarn) without recourse to registration of a charge. If property passed to the buyer, the only way in which the supplier could be regarded as attaining any property rights was if the buyer conferred a charge over his property. Where goods supplied by the supplier are mixed with other goods so as to produce another product, the supplier will be unable to rely on a retention of title clause in order to claim the new product as his. In *Re Bond Worth Ltd*,[111] where yarn had been spun with other fibres to produce carpet, Slade J rejected the argument by the vendor that he had priority over the carpet on the basis of a retention clause in the contract of sale. Not only had ownership in the yarn been lost by the mixing of it with other fibres, but also there was no fiduciary relationship between the supplier and purchaser so as to grant an equitable proprietary interest in the supplier. The supplier did, however, have a charge created by the purchaser but this was void for non-registration. The same approach was taken by the Court of Appeal in *Borden (UK) Ltd* v *Scottish Timber Products Ltd*.[112]

In so far as proceeds of sale are concerned, there is a general consensus of opinion that claims to such proceeds will rarely be successful. The primary reason for this lies in the difficulty in finding a fiduciary relationship within the sale of goods contract so as to allow the supplier to trace in equity. In *Romalpa*, Roskill LJ was of the opinion that a fiduciary relationship existed between the supplier and the purchaser on the basis of the contract. The goods had been delivered in such a way that the purchaser was, albeit vested with a power to sell and use the foil, accountable to the supplier. Roskill LJ likened this to an agency and bailment relationship. However, not all bailment relationships give rise to a fiduciary relationship. Although there is no doubt that contractual and fiduciary relationships may co-exist, not every contractual relationship can be said to be fiduciary. Indeed, the general position appears to be that a fiduciary relationship 'dehors the contract for reasons of trust and confidence reposed, ascendancy and dependence...'.[113] In supply contracts that include the granting of credit and the ability of the purchaser to use the goods supplied in any manner he thinks fit, it is extremely difficult to conceive of the purchaser as a fiduciary acting in the interests of the supplier. Indeed, the provision of credit is indicative of the fact that the purchaser acts on his own account and not for the supplier. In

---

[110] [1985] 1 WLR 111.

[111] [1980] Ch 228.

[112] [1981] Ch 25.

[113] P. Finn, 'Fiduciary Law' in E. McKendrick (ed), *Commercial Aspects of Trust and Fiduciary Obligation* (1992) at p 14.

this sense the relationship is essentially one of normal debtor and creditor. In *Re Andrabell Ltd*[114] and *Hendy Lennox (Industrial Engines) Ltd* v *Grahame Puttick Ltd*[115] claims to the proceeds of sale were denied because in neither case had the court been satisfied that a fiduciary relationship had been created between supplier and purchaser.

---

[114] [1984] 3 All ER 407.
[115] [1984] 2 All ER 152.

INDEX